Cram101 Textbook Outlines to accompany:

Western Civilization : Volume B: 1300 to 1815

Jackson Spielvogel, 1st Edition

A Content Technologies Inc. publication (c) 2012.

Cram101 Textbook Outlines and Cram101.com are Cram101 Inc. publications and services. All notes, highlights, reviews, and practice tests are written and prepared by Content Technologies and Cram101, all rights reserved.

WHY STOP HERE... THERE'S MORE ONLINE

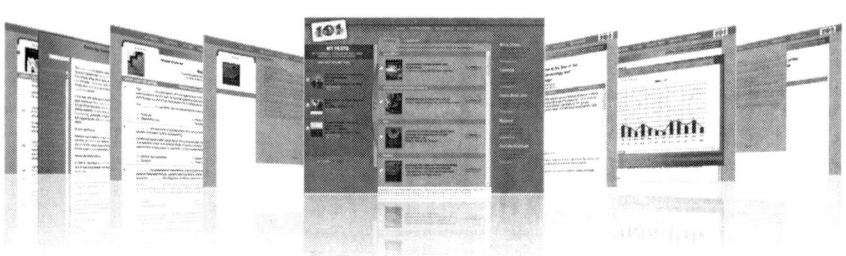

With technology and experience, we've developed tools that make studying easier and efficient. Like this Cram101 textbook notebook, Cram101.com offers you the highlights from every chapter of your actual textbook. However, unlike this notebook, Cram101.com gives you practice tests for each of the chapters. You also get access to in-depth reference material for writing essays and papers.

By purchasing this book, you get 50% off the normal subscription free!. Just enter the promotional code **'DK73DW17337'** on the Cram101.com registration screen.

CRAM101.COM FEATURES:

Outlines & Highlights
Just like the ones in this notebook, but with links to additional information.

Integrated Note Taking
Add your class notes to the Cram101 notes, print them and maximize your study time.

Problem Solving
Step-by-step walk throughs for math, stats and other disciplines.

Practice Exams
Five different test taking formats for every chapter.

Easy Access
Study any of your books, on any computer, anywhere.

Unlimited Textbooks
All the features above for virtually all your textbooks, just add them to your account at no additional cost.

TRY THE FIRST CHAPTER FREE!

Be sure to use the promo code above when registering on Cram101.com to get 50% off your membership fees.

STUDYING MADE EASY

This Cram101 notebook is designed to make studying easier and increase your comprehension of the textbook material. Instead of starting with a blank notebook and trying to write down everything discussed in class lectures, you can use this Cram101 textbook notebook and annotate your notes along with the lecture.

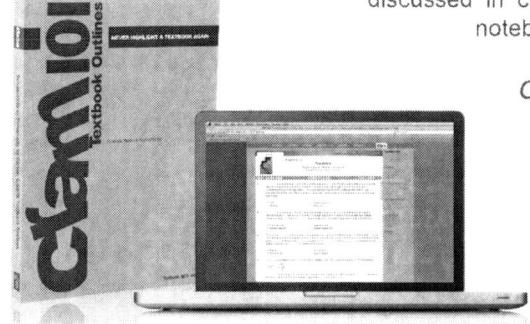

Our goal is to give you the best tools for success.

For a supreme understanding of the course, pair your notebook with our online tools. Should you decide you prefer Cram101.com as your study tool,

we'd like to offer you a trade...

Our Trade In program is a simple way for us to keep our promise and provide you the best studying tools, regardless of where you purchased your Cram101 textbook notebook. As long as your notebook is in *Like New Condition**, you can send it back to us and we will immediately give you a Cram101.com account free for 120 days!

Let The *Trade In* Begin!

THREE SIMPLE STEPS TO TRADE:

1. Go to www.cram101.com/tradein and fill out the packing slip information.
2. Submit and print the packing slip and mail it in with your Cram101 textbook notebook.
3. Activate your account after you receive your email confirmation.

* Books must be returned in *Like New Condition*, meaning there is no damage to the book including, but not limited to; ripped or torn pages, markings or writing on pages, or folded / creased pages. Upon receiving the book, Cram101 will inspect it and reserves the right to terminate your free Cram101.com account and return your textbook notebook at the owners expense.

Learning System

Cram101 Textbook Outlines is a learning system. The notes in this book are the highlights of your textbook, you will never have to highlight a book again.

How to use this book. Take this book to class, it is your notebook for the lecture. The notes and highlights on the left hand side of the pages follow the outline and order of the textbook. All you have to do is follow along while your instructor presents the lecture. Circle the items emphasized in class and add other important information on the right side. With Cram101 Textbook Outlines you'll spend less time writing and more time listening. Learning becomes more efficient.

Cram101.com Online

Increase your studying efficiency by using Cram101.com's practice tests and online reference material. It is the perfect complement to Cram101 Textbook Outlines. Use self-teaching matching tests or simulate in-class testing with comprehensive multiple choice tests, or simply use Cram's true and false tests for quick review. Cram101.com even allows you to enter your in-class notes for an integrated studying format combining the textbook notes with your class notes.

Visit **www.Cram101.com**, click Sign Up at the top of the screen, and enter **DK73DW17337** in the promo code box on the registration screen. Your access to www.Cram101.com is discounted by 50% because you have purchased this book. Sign up and stop highlighting textbooks forever.

Copyright © 2011 by Cram101, Inc. All rights reserved. "Cram101"® and "Never Highlight a Book Again!"® are registered trademarks of Cram101, Inc. ISBN(s): 9781614906056. PUBX-3.201166

Western Civilization : Volume B: 1300 to 1815
Jackson Spielvogel, 1st

CONTENTS

1. THE LATER MIDDLE AGES: CRISIS AND DISINTEGRATION IN THE FOURTEENTH CENTURY 2
2. RECOVERY AND REBIRTH: THE AGE OF THE RENAISSANCE 46
3. REFORMATION AND RELIGIOUS WARFARE IN THE SIXTEENTH CENTURY 94
4. EUROPE AND THE WORLD: NEW ENCOUNTERS, 1500-1800 156
5. STATE BUILDING AND THE SEARCH FOR ORDER IN THE SEVENTEENTH CENTURY 202
6. TOWARD A NEW HEAVEN AND A NEW EARTH 264
7. THE EIGHTEENTH CENTURY: AN AGE OF ENLIGHTENMENT 282
8. THE EIGHTEENTH CENTURY: EUROPEAN STATES, INTERNATIONAL WARS, AND CHANGE 324
9. A REVOLUTION IN POLITICS: THE ERA OF THE FRENCH REVOLUTION AND NAPOLEON 366

Clam101

Chapter 1. THE LATER MIDDLE AGES: CRISIS AND DISINTEGRATION IN THE FOURTEENTH CENTURY

Black Death	The Black Death was one of the most devastating pandemics in human history, peaking in Europe between 1348 and 1350. It is widely thought to have been an outbreak of plague caused by the bacterium Yersinia pestis, an argument supported by recent forensic research, although this view has been challenged by a number of scholars. Thought to have started in China, it travelled along the Silk Road and had reached the Crimea by 1346. From there, probably carried by Oriental rat fleas residing on the black rats that were regular passengers on merchant ships, it spread throughout the Mediterranean and Europe. The Black Death is estimated to have killed 30% - 60% of Europe's population, reducing the world's population from an estimated 450 million to between 350 and 375 million in 1400. This has been seen as having created a series of religious, social and economic upheavals, which had profound effects on the course of European history.
Henry	Henry is an English male given name and a surname, from the Old French Henry derived itself from the Germanic name Haimric, which was derived from the word elements haim, meaning "home" and ric, meaning "power, ruler". Harry, its English short form, was considered the "spoken form" of Henry in medieval England. Most English kings named Henry were called Harry.
Middle Ages	The Middle Ages is a historical period following the Iron Age, beginning in the 5th century and lasting to the 15th century, and preceded the Early Modern Era. In Europe, the period saw the large-scale European Migration and fall of the Western Roman Empire. In South Asia, the middle kingdoms of India were the classical period of the region.
18th century	The 18th century lasted from 1701 to 1800 in the Gregorian calendar. However, Western historians have occasionally defined the 18th century otherwise for the purposes of their work. For example, the "short" 18th century may be defined as 1715-1789, denoting the period of time between the death of Louis XIV of France and the start of the French Revolution with an emphasis on directly interconnected events.
America	America is a Wild West-themed real-time strategy. It is set during the era after the American civil war. The player can choose to play Native Americans (Sioux tribe), Mexicans, Outlaws or Settlers.

Chapter 1. THE LATER MIDDLE AGES: CRISIS AND DISINTEGRATION IN THE FOURTEENTH CENTURY

Chapter 1. THE LATER MIDDLE AGES: CRISIS AND DISINTEGRATION IN THE FOURTEENTH CENTURY

Central Asia	Central Asia is a core region of the Asian continent from the Caspian Sea in the west, China in the east, Afghanistan in the south, and Russia in the north. It is also sometimes referred to as Middle Asia, and, colloquially, "the 'stans" (as the five countries generally considered to be within the region all have names ending with that suffix) and is within the scope of the wider Eurasian continent. Various definitions of its exact composition exist, and no one definition is universally accepted.
Columbian Exchange	The Columbian Exchange was a dramatically widespread exchange of animals, plants, culture, human populations (including slaves), communicable diseases, and ideas between the Eastern and Western hemispheres (Old World and New World). It was one of the most significant events concerning ecology, agriculture, and culture in all of human history. Christopher Columbus' first voyage to the Americas in 1492 launched the era of large-scale contact between the Old and the New Worlds that resulted in this ecological revolution, hence the name "Columbian" Exchange.
High Middle Ages	The High Middle Ages is a historical period following the Early Middle Ages. Chronologically, this Middle Ages period occurs around the 11th, 12th, and 13th centuries (c. 1000-1200). The High Middle Ages is followed by the Late Middle Ages, which by convention end around 1500.
Little Ice Age	The Little Ice Age was a period of cooling that occurred after the Medieval Warm Period. While not a true ice age, the term was introduced into scientific literature by François E. Matthes in 1939. It is conventionally defined as a period extending from the 16th to the 19th centuries, though climatologists and historians working with local records no longer expect to agree on either the start or end dates of this period, which varied according to local conditions. NASA defines the term as a cold period between 1550 AD and 1850 AD and notes three particularly cold intervals: one beginning about 1650, another about 1770, and the last in 1850, each separated by intervals of slight warming.
Silk Road	The Silk Road is an extensive interconnected network of trade routes across the Asian continent connecting East, South, and Western Asia with the Mediterranean world, as well as North and Northeast Africa and Europe.

Chapter 1. THE LATER MIDDLE AGES: CRISIS AND DISINTEGRATION IN THE FOURTEENTH CENTURY

Chapter 1. THE LATER MIDDLE AGES: CRISIS AND DISINTEGRATION IN THE FOURTEENTH CENTURY

	In recent years, both the maritime and overland Silk Routes are again being used, often closely following the ancient routes.
	The name
	The Silk Road gets its name from the lucrative Chinese silk trade, a major reason for the connection of trade routes into an extensive trans-continental network.
Genoa	Genoa is a city and an important seaport in northern Italy, the capital of the Province of Genoa and of the region of Liguria.
	The city has a population of about 608,000 and the urban area has a population of about 900,000. Genoa's Metropolitan Area has a population of about 1,400,000. It is also called la Superba ("the Superb one") due to its glorious past. The city's rich art, music, gastronomy, architecture and history, made it 2004's EU Capital of Culture.
Tournai	Tournai is a Walloon city and municipality of Belgium located 85 kilometres southwest of Brussels, on the river Scheldt, in the province of Hainaut.
	Along with Tongeren, Tournai is the oldest city in Belgium and it has played an important role in the country's cultural history.
	Geography
	Tournai is located in the lowlands of Belgium, at the southern limit of the Flemish plain, in the basin of the river Scheldt .

Chapter 1. THE LATER MIDDLE AGES: CRISIS AND DISINTEGRATION IN THE FOURTEENTH CENTURY

Chapter 1. THE LATER MIDDLE AGES: CRISIS AND DISINTEGRATION IN THE FOURTEENTH CENTURY

Gigue	The gigue is a lively baroque dance originating from the British jig. It was imported into France in the mid-17th century and usually appears at the end of a suite. The gigue was probably never a court dance, but it was danced by nobility on social occasions and several court composers wrote gigues.
Flagellant	Flagellants are practitioners of an extreme form of mortification of their own flesh by whipping it with various instruments. History Flagellantism was a 13th and 14th centuries movement, consisting of radicals in the Catholic Church. It began as a militant pilgrimage and was later condemned by the Catholic Church as heretical.
Chinas	The Chinas are a people mentioned in ancient Indian literature from the first millennium BC, such as the Mahabharata, Laws of Manu, as well the Puranic literature. They are believed to have been Chinese. Etymology The name Cina is commonly believed to have been derived from either the Qin (Tsin or Chin) dynasty which rule in China from 221 BC or the earlier Qin state which later became the Qin dynasty.
Jacob	Jacob is a German/Italian/American movie from 1994, based on the novel Giacobbe by Francesco Maria Nappi, which is in turn based on the Bible story about Jacob. Plot Jacob defrauds his twin Brother Esau and hlollogas to flee. In Haran he gets to know his cousin Rachel, and falls in love with her.

Chapter 1. THE LATER MIDDLE AGES: CRISIS AND DISINTEGRATION IN THE FOURTEENTH CENTURY

CLAM 101

Chapter 1. THE LATER MIDDLE AGES: CRISIS AND DISINTEGRATION IN THE FOURTEENTH CENTURY

England	"England" is a song written by Justin Hawkins from The Darkness(music) ' Chas Bayfield (lyrics) and released by him under the name British Whale and used as the unofficial World Cup single for the England National Team in 2006
Jacquerie	The Jacquerie was a popular revolt in late medieval Europe by peasants that took place in northern France in the summer of 1358, during the Hundred Years' War. The revolt, which was violently suppressed after a few weeks of violence, centered in the Oise valley north of Paris. This rebellion became known as the Jacquerie because the nobles derided peasants as "Jacques" or "Jacques Bonhomme" for their padded surplice called "jacque".
John Ball	John Ball was an English Lollard priest who took a prominent part in the Peasants' Revolt of 1381. Biography Little is known of Ball's early years. He lived in St. Albans, Hertfordshire and subsequently at Colchester during the Black Death.
Berlin	Berlin is the capital city of Germany and is one of the 16 states of Germany. It has a population of 3.4 million people, and is Germany's largest city. It is the second most populous city proper and the eighth most populous urban area in the European Union.
Chronicle	Generally a chronicle is a historical account of facts and events ranged in chronological order, as in a time line. Typically, equal weight is given for historically important events and local events, the purpose being the recording of events that occurred, seen from the perspective of the chronicler. This is in contrast to a narrative or history, which sets selected events in a meaningful interpretive context and excludes those the author does not see as important.
Prussia	Prussia was a German kingdom and historic state originating out of the Duchy of Prussia and the Margraviate of Brandenburg. For centuries, the House of Hohenzollern ruled Prussia, successfully expanding its size by way of an unusually well-organized and effective army. Prussia shaped the history of Germany, with its capital in Berlin after 1451. After 1871, Prussia was increasingly merged into Germany, losing its distinctive identity.

Chapter 1. THE LATER MIDDLE AGES: CRISIS AND DISINTEGRATION IN THE FOURTEENTH CENTURY

Chapter 1. THE LATER MIDDLE AGES: CRISIS AND DISINTEGRATION IN THE FOURTEENTH CENTURY

Republic	Republic is a Hungarian rock band formed in Budapest in 1989. Their style is a unique mix of Western rock music and traditional Hungarian folk music. The band is popular in its native country and among Hungarian speaking minorities elsewhere. Members The two founding members are László Bódi and Lászlo Attila Nagy.
Capetian dynasty	The Capetian dynasty (/k?'pi??(?n/) is the largest and oldest European royal house, consisting of the descendants of Hugh Capet of France in the male line. In contemporary times, both King Juan Carlos of Spain and Grand Duke Henri of Luxembourg are members of this family, both through the Bourbon branch of the dynasty. The meaning of "Capet" (a nickname rather than a surname of the modern sort) is unknown.
Gascony	Gascony is an area of southwest France that was part of the "Province of Guyenne and Gascony" prior to the French Revolution. The region is vaguely defined and the distinction between Guyenne and Gascony is unclear; sometimes they are considered to overlap, and sometimes Gascony is considered a part of Guyenne. Most definitions put Gascony east and south of Bordeaux.
Longbow	A longbow is a type of bow that is tall (roughly equal to the height of the person who uses it); this will allow its user a fairly long draw, at least to the jaw (the average length of arrowshafts recovered from the 1545 sinking of the Mary Rose is 75 cm/30 in). A longbow is not significantly recurved. Its limbs are relatively narrow so that they are circular or D-shaped in cross section.
American Revolution	The American Revolution was the political upheaval during the last half of the 18th century in which thirteen colonies in North America joined together to break free from the British Empire, combining to become the United States of America. They first rejected the authority of the Parliament of Great Britain to govern them from overseas without representation, and then expelled all royal officials. By 1774 each colony had established a Provincial Congress, or an equivalent governmental institution, to form individual self-governing states. The British responded by sending combat troops to re-impose direct rule.

Chapter 1. THE LATER MIDDLE AGES: CRISIS AND DISINTEGRATION IN THE FOURTEENTH CENTURY

Chapter 1. THE LATER MIDDLE AGES: CRISIS AND DISINTEGRATION IN THE FOURTEENTH CENTURY

Classicism	Classicism, in the arts, refers generally to a high regard for classical antiquity, as setting standards for taste which the classicists seek to emulate. The art of classicism typically seeks to be formal and restrained: of the Discobolus Sir Kenneth Clark observed, "if we object to his restraint and compression we are simply objecting to the classicism of classic art. A violent emphasis or a sudden acceleration of rhythmic movement would have destroyed those qualities of balance and completeness through which it retained until the present century its position of authority in the restricted repertoire of visual images." Classicism, as Clark noted, implies a canon of widely accepted ideal forms, whether in the Western canon that he was examining in The Nude (1956), or the Chinese classics.
Joan of Arc	Saint Joan of Arc is considered a national heroine of France and a Catholic saint. A peasant girl born in eastern France who claimed Divine guidance, she led the French army to several important victories during the Hundred Years' War which paved the way for the coronation of Charles VII. She was captured by the Burgundians, sold to the English, tried by an ecclesiastical court, and burned at the stake when she was nineteen years old. She was beatified in 1909 and canonized in 1920. She is, along with St. Denis, St. Martin of Tours, St. Louis IX, and St. Theresa of Lisieux, one of the patron saints of France.
Messenger	Messenger of the fullness of the Gospel is a Mormon fundamentalist publication, originally printed in Birmingham, England starting in 1991, which was in print in that country until 2001, and continues as a web-based publication. It went under the original title of "Truth Seeker" magazine, until it was found that there was an existing periodical that shared that name. Although originally printed quarterly, it was printed bi-monthly when it moved to an American-produced edition in 2003.
Common	The Common is a part of the Christian liturgy that consists of texts common to an entire category of saints, such as Apostles or Martyrs. The term is used in contrast to the ordinary, which is that part of the liturgy that is reasonably constant, or at least selected without regard to date, and to the proper, which is the part of the liturgy that varies according to the date, either representing an observance within the Liturgical Year, or of a particular saint or significant event.

Chapter 1. THE LATER MIDDLE AGES: CRISIS AND DISINTEGRATION IN THE FOURTEENTH CENTURY

Chapter 1. THE LATER MIDDLE AGES: CRISIS AND DISINTEGRATION IN THE FOURTEENTH CENTURY

	Commons contain collects, psalms, readings from Scripture, prefaces, and other portions of services that are common to a category of saints.
House	A house is a home, building or structure that is a dwelling or place for habitation by human beings. The term house includes many kinds of dwellings ranging from rudimentary huts of nomadic tribes to free standing individual structures. In some contexts, "house" may mean the same as dwelling, residence, home, abode, lodging, accommodation, or housing, among other meanings.
Rose	A rose is a perennial plant of the genus Rosa, within the family Rosaceae. There are over 100 species. They form a group of erect shrubs, and climbing or trailing plants, with stems that are often armed with sharp prickles.
Wars of the Roses	The Wars of the Roses were a series of dynastic civil wars for the throne of England fought between supporters of two rival branches of the royal House of Plantagenet: the houses of Lancaster and York (the "red" and the "white" rose, respectively). They were fought in several sporadic episodes between 1455 and 1485, although there was related fighting both before and after this period. The final victory went to a relatively remote Lancastrian claimant, Henry Tudor, who defeated the last Yorkist king Richard III and married Edward IV's daughter Elizabeth of York to unite the two houses.
Baron	Baron is a title of nobility. The word baron comes from Old French baron, itself from Old High German and Latin (liber) baro meaning "(free) man, (free) warrior"; it merged with cognate Old English beorn meaning "nobleman". Barons in the United Kingdom and the Commonwealth In the British peer system, barons rank below viscounts, and form the lowest rank in the peerage.

Chapter 1. THE LATER MIDDLE AGES: CRISIS AND DISINTEGRATION IN THE FOURTEENTH CENTURY

CLAM101

Chapter 1. THE LATER MIDDLE AGES: CRISIS AND DISINTEGRATION IN THE FOURTEENTH CENTURY

Catholic	The word catholic comes from the Greek phrase καθ?λου (kath'holou), meaning "on the whole," "according to the whole" or "in general", and is a combination of the Greek words κατ? meaning "about" and ?λος meaning "whole". The word in English can mean either "including a wide variety of things; all-embracing" or "of the Roman Catholic faith." as "relating to the historic doctrine and practice of the Western Church." It was first used to describe the Christian Church in the early 2nd century to emphasize its universal scope. In the context of Christian ecclesiology, it has a rich history and several usages.
Catholic Church	The Catholic Church, is the world's largest Christian church. Headed by the Pope, it sees its mission as spreading the gospel of Christ, administering its sacraments and exercising charity. The Catholic Church is one of the oldest religious institutions in the world and has played a prominent role in the history of Western civilisation.
Christian	A Christian is a person who adheres to Christianity, an Abrahamic, monotheistic religion based on the life and teachings of Jesus of Nazareth as recorded in the Canonical gospels and the letters of the New Testament. Central to the Christian faith is love or Agape. Christians also believe Jesus is the Messiah prophesied in the Hebrew Bible, the Son of God, and the savior of mankind from their sins.
Christian humanism	Christian humanism is the belief that human freedom and individualism are intrinsic (natural) parts of, or are at least compatible with, Christian doctrine and practice. It is a philosophical union of Christian and humanist principles. Origins

Chapter 1. THE LATER MIDDLE AGES: CRISIS AND DISINTEGRATION IN THE FOURTEENTH CENTURY

CLAM 101

Chapter 1. THE LATER MIDDLE AGES: CRISIS AND DISINTEGRATION IN THE FOURTEENTH CENTURY

	Christian humanism may have begun as early as the 2nd century, with the writings of St. Justin Martyr, an early theologian-apologist of the early Christian Church.
Church	A church building is a building or structure whose primary purpose is to facilitate the meeting of a church. Originally, Jewish Christians met in synagogues, such as the Cenacle, and in one another's homes, known as house churches. As Christianity grew and became more accepted by governments, notably with the Edict of Milan, rooms and, eventually, entire buildings were set aside for the explicit purpose of Christian worship, such as the Church of the Holy Sepulchre.
German	German is a South Slavic mythological being, recorded in the folklore of eastern Serbia and northern Bulgaria. He is a male spirit associated with bringing rain and hail. His influence on these precipitations can be positive, resulting with the amount of rain beneficial for agriculture, or negative, with a drought, downpours, or hail.
Germany	The Germany Pavilion is part of the World Showcase within Epcot at the Walt Disney World Resort. History The original design of the pavilion called for a boat ride along the Rhine river. It was to have focused on German folklore, in a similar manner to the Mexico and Norway rides.
Lutheranism	Lutheranism is a major branch of Western Christianity that identifies with the theology of Martin Luther, a German reformer. Luther's efforts to reform the theology and practice of the church launched the Protestant Reformation. Beginning with the 95 Theses, Luther's writings disseminated internationally, spreading the ideas of the Reformation beyond the ability of governmental and churchly authorities to control it.
Saxony	The Saxony is a breed of domestic duck originating in the Saxony region of Germany. History

Chapter 1. THE LATER MIDDLE AGES: CRISIS AND DISINTEGRATION IN THE FOURTEENTH CENTURY

Clam101

Chapter 1. THE LATER MIDDLE AGES: CRISIS AND DISINTEGRATION IN THE FOURTEENTH CENTURY

	It was initially bred by Albert Franz of Chemnitz in the 1930s, but almost all of his original stock was lost during World War II. He cross bred Rouen, German Pekin, and Blue Pomeranian ducks. Resuming his efforts, Franz's work resulted in the recognition of the Saxony by 1957. In 1984, David Holderread (who later developed his own breed, the Golden Cascade), imported some Saxony ducks to the US, and it was recognized by the American Poultry Association in 2000 by admittance in to the Standard of Perfection.
Estates of the realm	The Estates of the realm were the broad social orders of the hierarchically conceived society, recognized in the Middle Ages and Early Modern period in Christian Europe; they are sometimes distinguished as the three estates: the clergy, the nobility, and commoners. "Medieval political speculation is imbued to the marrow with the idea of a structure of society based upon distinct orders," Johan Huizinga observes. The virtually synonymous terms estate and order designated a great variety of social realities, not at all limited to a class, Huizinga concluded, but applied to every social function, every trade, every recognizable grouping.
Humanism	Humanism is an approach in study, philosophy, or practice that focuses on human values and concerns. The term can mean several things, for example: 1. A cultural movement of the Italian Renaissance based on the study of classical works. 2. An approach to education that uses literary means or a focus on the humanities to inform students. 3. A variety of perspectives in philosophy and social science which affirm some notion of 'human nature' (by contrast with anti-humanism). 4. A secular ideology which espouses reason, ethics, and justice, whilst specifically rejecting supernatural and religious dogma as a basis of morality and decision-making. The last interpretation may be attributed to Secular Humanism as a specific humanistic life stance. Modern meanings of the word have therefore come to be associated with a rejection of appeals to the supernatural or to some higher authority.
Anjou	Anjou is a former county (c. 880), duchy (1360) and province centred on the city of Angers in the lower Loire Valley of western France. It corresponds largely to the present-day département of Maine-et-Loire. Its traditional Latin name is Andegavia.

Chapter 1. THE LATER MIDDLE AGES: CRISIS AND DISINTEGRATION IN THE FOURTEENTH CENTURY

Chapter 1. THE LATER MIDDLE AGES: CRISIS AND DISINTEGRATION IN THE FOURTEENTH CENTURY

Austria	Austria officially the Republic of Austria, is a landlocked country of roughly 8.3 million people in Central Europe. It is bordered by the Czech Republic and Germany to the north, Slovakia and Hungary to the east, Slovenia and Italy to the south, and Switzerland and Liechtenstein to the west. The territory of Austria covers 83,855 square kilometres (32,377 sq mi) and has a temperate and alpine climate.
Condottieri	Condottieri were the mercenary soldier leaders (or warlords) of the professional, military free companies contracted by the Italian city-states and the Papacy, from the late Middle Ages and throughout the Renaissance. In Renaissance Italian, condottiero meant "contractor", and was synonymous with the modern English title Mercenary Captain, which, historiographically, does not connote the hired soldier's nationality. In contemporary Italian, "condottiero" acquired the broader meaning of "military leader" (e.g., not restricted to mercenaries).
Duchy	A duchy is a territory, fief, or domain ruled by a duke or duchess. Some duchies were sovereign in areas that would become unified realms only during the Modern era. In contrast, others were subordinate districts of those kingdoms that unified either partially or completely during the Medieval era (such as England, France, and Spain).
The Fellowship	The Fellowship, is a U.S.-based religious and political organization founded in 1935 by Abraham Vereide. The stated purpose of the Fellowship is to provide a fellowship forum for decision makers to share in Bible studies, prayer meetings, worship experiences and to experience spiritual affirmation and support. The organization has been described as one of the most politically well-connected ministries in the United States.
Republic of Venice	The Republic of Venice or Venetian Republic was a state originating from the city of Venice in Northeastern Italy. It existed for over a millennium, from the late 7th century until 1797. It was formally known as the Most Serene Republic of Venice and is often referred to as La Serenissima, in reference to its title as a one of the "Most Serene Republics". It preferred to trade rather than participate in unnecessary war activities.

Chapter 1. THE LATER MIDDLE AGES: CRISIS AND DISINTEGRATION IN THE FOURTEENTH CENTURY

Chapter 1. THE LATER MIDDLE AGES: CRISIS AND DISINTEGRATION IN THE FOURTEENTH CENTURY

Signoria	A Signoria was an abstract noun meaning (roughly) 'government; governing authority; de facto sovereignty; lordship in many of the Italian city states during the medieval and renaissance periods.
	The perennial "power vacuum" of medieval Italy
	In the sixth century AD, the Emperor Justinian reconquered Italy from the Ostrogoths. The invasion of a new wave of Germanic tribes, the Lombards, doomed this attempt to resurrect the Western Roman Empire, but the repercussions of Justinian's failure resounded further still.
Pope	The Pope (from Latin: papa; from Greek: π?ππας (pappas), a child's word for father) is the Bishop of Rome, a position that makes him the leader of the worldwide Catholic Church . The current office-holder is Pope Benedict XVI, who was elected in a papal conclave on 19 April 2005.
	The office of the pope is known as the Papacy.
Neoclassicism	Neoclassicism is the name given to quite distinct movements in the decorative and visual arts, literature, theatre, music, and architecture that draw upon Western classical art and culture (usually that of Ancient Greece or Ancient Rome). These movements were dominant in northern Europe during the mid-18th to the end of the 19th century.
	Overview
	What any "neo-classicism" depends on most fundamentally is a consensus about a body of work that has achieved canonic status (illustration, below).
Netherlands	More than one name is used to refer to the Netherlands, both in English and in other languages. Some of these names refer to different, but overlapping geographical, linguistic and political areas of the country. This is a common source of confusion for outsiders.

Chapter 1. THE LATER MIDDLE AGES: CRISIS AND DISINTEGRATION IN THE FOURTEENTH CENTURY

Chapter 1. THE LATER MIDDLE AGES: CRISIS AND DISINTEGRATION IN THE FOURTEENTH CENTURY

Papal bull	A Papal bull is a particular type of letters patent or charter issued by a pope. It is named after the bulla that was appended to the end in order to authenticate it. Papal bulls were originally issued by the pope for many kinds of communication of a public nature, but after the fifteenth century, only for the most formal or solemn of occasions.
Southern Netherlands	Southern Netherlands were a part of the Low Countries controlled by Spain, Austria and annexed by France (1794-1815). This region comprised most of modern Belgium (except for three Lower-Rhenish territories: the Prince-Bishopric of Liège, the Imperial Abbey of Stavelot-Malmedy and the County of Bouillon) and Luxembourg (including the homonymous present Belgian province), and in addition some parts of the Netherlands (namely the Duchy of Limburg now split in a Dutch and Belgian part) as well as, until 1678, most of the present Nord-Pas-de-Calais region in northern France. Unlike French Burgundy and the republican Northern Netherlands, these allodial states kept access to the Burgundian Circle of the Holy Roman Empire until its end.
Bull	The worship of the Sacred Bull throughout the ancient world is most familiar to the Western world in the biblical episode of the idol of the Golden Calf made by people left behind by Moses during visit to mountain peak and worshipped by the Hebrews in the wilderness of Sinai (Exodus). Marduk is the "bull of Utu". Shiva's steed is Nandi, the Bull.
State	The term state is used in various senses by Catholic theologians and spiritual writers. It may be taken to signify a profession or calling in life, as where St. Paul says, in I Corinthians 7:20: "Let every man abide in the same calling in which he was called". States are classified in the Catholic Church as the clerical state, the religious state, and the secular state; and among religious states, again, we have those of the contemplative, the active, and the mixed orders.
Catherine of Siena	Saint Catherine of Siena T.O.S.D (25 March 1347 in Siena - 29 April 1380 in Rome) was a tertiary of the Dominican Order, and a Scholastic philosopher and theologian. She also worked to bring the Papacy back to Rome from its displacement in France, and to establish peace among the Italian city-states. She was proclaimed a Doctor of the Church in 1970. She is one of the two patron saints of Italy, together with Francis of Assisi.

Chapter 1. THE LATER MIDDLE AGES: CRISIS AND DISINTEGRATION IN THE FOURTEENTH CENTURY

Chapter 1. THE LATER MIDDLE AGES: CRISIS AND DISINTEGRATION IN THE FOURTEENTH CENTURY

Papal States	The Papal States, State(s) of the Church, or Pontifical States were among the major historical states of Italy from roughly the 6th century until the Italian peninsula was unified in 1861 by the Kingdom of Piedmont-Sardinia (after which the Papal States, in less territorially extensive form, continued to exist until 1870).
	The Papal States comprised territories under direct sovereign rule of the papacy, and at its height it covered most of the modern Italian regions of Romagna, Marche, Umbria and Lazio. This governing power is commonly called the temporal power of the Pope, as opposed to his ecclesiastical primacy.
Alexander	Saint Alexander was a martyr and companion of St. Pothinus. Alexander was a physician in Vienne, Gaul, when he converted to Christianity. Arrested during the persecutions conducted under Emperor Marcus Aurelius.
Conciliarism	Conciliarism, was a reform movement in the 14th, 15th and 16th century Roman Catholic Church which held that final authority in spiritual matters resided with the Roman Church as a corporation of Christians, embodied by a general church council, not with the pope. The movement emerged in response to the Avignon papacy; the popes were removed from Rome and subjected to pressures from the kings of France-- and the ensuing schism that inspired the summoning of the Council of Pisa (1409), the Council of Constance (1414-1418) and the Council of Basel (1431-1449). The eventual victor in the conflict was the institution of the Papacy, confirmed by the condemnation of conciliarism at the Fifth Lateran Council, 1512-17. The final gesture however, the doctrine of Papal Infallibility, was not promulgated until the First Vatican Council of 1870.
Conciliarism	Conciliarism, was a reform movement in the 14th, 15th and 16th century Roman Catholic Church which held that final authority in spiritual matters resided with the Roman Church as a corporation of Christians, embodied by a general church council, not with the pope. The movement emerged in response to the Avignon papacy; the popes were removed from Rome and subjected to pressures from the kings of France-- and the ensuing schism that inspired the summoning of the Council of Pisa (1409), the Council of Constance (1414-1418) and the Council of Basel (1431-1449). The eventual victor in the conflict was the institution of the Papacy, confirmed by the condemnation of conciliarism at the Fifth Lateran Council, 1512-17. The final gesture however, the doctrine of Papal Infallibility, was not promulgated until the First Vatican Council of 1870.

Chapter 1. THE LATER MIDDLE AGES: CRISIS AND DISINTEGRATION IN THE FOURTEENTH CENTURY

Chapter 1. THE LATER MIDDLE AGES: CRISIS AND DISINTEGRATION IN THE FOURTEENTH CENTURY

Brethren of the Common Life	The Brethren of the Common Life was a Roman Catholic pietist religious community founded in the 14th century by Gerard Groote, formerly a successful and worldly educator who had had a religious experience and preached a life of simple devotion to Jesus Christ. Without taking up irrevocable vows, the Brethren banded together in communities, giving up their worldly goods to live chaste and strictly regulated lives in common houses, devoting every waking hour to attending divine service, reading and preaching of sermons, labouring productively and taking meals in common that were accompanied by the reading aloud of Scripture: "judged from the ascetic discipline and intention of this life, it had few features which distinguished it from life in a monastery", observes Hans Baron. The Brethren and the Devotio Moderna The Brethren's confraternity is the best known fruits of the Devotio Moderna, the Modern Devotion.
Faith	"Faith" was a #1 song, written and performed by George Michael, released as a single on Columbia Records, from his 1987 Faith album. According to Billboard magazine, it was the top-selling single of the year in the United States in 1988. Track listing 7": UK / Epic EMU 2 1. "Faith" - 3:14 2. "Hand To Mouth" - 4:36 12": UK / Epic EMU T2 1. "Faith" - 3:14 2. "Faith" (Instrumental) - 3:08 3. "Hand to Mouth" - 4:36

Chapter 1. THE LATER MIDDLE AGES: CRISIS AND DISINTEGRATION IN THE FOURTEENTH CENTURY

Chapter 1. THE LATER MIDDLE AGES: CRISIS AND DISINTEGRATION IN THE FOURTEENTH CENTURY

U.S. CD single

1. "Faith" - 3:16
2. "Faith" (dance remix radio edit) - 4:54
3. "Faith" (album version) - 3:16
4. "Hand to Mouth" - 5:49

Mixes

1. Album version - 3:16
2. 7" version - 3:14
3. Instrumental - 3:08
4. Dance remix radio edit - 5:22

History

Having disbanded Wham! the previous year, there was a keen expectation for Michael's solo career and "Faith" would go on to become one of his most popular and enduring songs, as well as being the most simplistic in its production.

Devotio Moderna	Devotio Moderna, was a religious movement of the Late Middle Ages. It arose at the same time as Christian Humanism, a meshing of Renaissance Humanism and Christianity, and is related to German mysticism and other movements which promoted an intense personal relationship with God. By the late 15th century the advent of the printing press increased the reach of the movement; The Imitation of Christ was printed in several languages by the end of the century.
Purgatory	Purgatory is the condition or process of purification or temporary punishment in which, it is believed, the souls of those who die in a state of grace are made ready for Heaven. This is an idea that has ancient roots and is well-attested in early Christian literature, while the conception of purgatory as a geographically situated place is largely the creation of medieval Christian piety and imagination.

Chapter 1. THE LATER MIDDLE AGES: CRISIS AND DISINTEGRATION IN THE FOURTEENTH CENTURY

Chapter 1. THE LATER MIDDLE AGES: CRISIS AND DISINTEGRATION IN THE FOURTEENTH CENTURY

	The notion of purgatory is associated particularly with the Latin Rite of the Catholic Church (in the Eastern sui juris churches or rites it is a doctrine, though often without using the name "Purgatory"); Anglicans of the Anglo-Catholic tradition generally also hold to the belief.
Salvation	In religion, salvation is the concept that, as part of divine providence, a God, or gods, or power saves people from either or all of the following: 1. from biological death, by providing for them an eternal life or long-lasting afterlife (cf. afterlife). 2. from spiritual death, by providing divine law, illumination, and judgment. 3. Acceptance into heaven. The world's religions hold varying positions on the way to attain salvation and on what it means. The theological study of salvation is called soteriology.
Spiritualities	The Spiritualities, and consisted almost entirely of tithes, glebe lands, and house. History Spiritualities is a term, often used in the Middle Ages, that refers to the income sources of a diocese or other ecclesiastical establishment that came from tithes. It also referred to income that came from other religious sources, such as offerings from church services or ecclesiastical fines.
Charity	In Christian theology charity, means an unlimited loving-kindness toward all others.

Chapter 1. THE LATER MIDDLE AGES: CRISIS AND DISINTEGRATION IN THE FOURTEENTH CENTURY

Chapter 1. THE LATER MIDDLE AGES: CRISIS AND DISINTEGRATION IN THE FOURTEENTH CENTURY

	The term should not be confused with the more restricted modern use of the word charity to mean benevolent giving.
	Caritas: altruistic love
	In Christian theology charity, or love (agape), is the greatest of the three theological virtues:
	Deus caritas est - "God is love".
	Love, in this sense of an unlimited loving-kindness towards all others, is held to be the ultimate perfection of the human spirit, because it is said to both glorify and reflect the nature of God.
Divine Comedy	The Divine Comedy is an epic poem written by Dante Alighieri between 1308 and his death in 1321. It is widely considered the preeminent work of Italian literature, and is seen as one of the greatest works of world literature. The poem's imaginative and allegorical vision of the afterlife is a culmination of the medieval world-view as it had developed in the Western Church. It helped establish the Tuscan dialect in which it is written as the standardized Italian.
Canterbury	1°05′13″E? / ?51.275°N 1.087°E
	Canterbury is an English city which lies at the heart of the City of Canterbury, a district of Kent in South East England. It lies on the River Stour.
	Originally a Brythonic settlement, it was renamed Durovernum Cantiacorum by the Roman conquerors in the 1st century AD. After it became the chief Jutish settlement, it gained its English name Canterbury, itself derived from the Old English Cantwareburh ("Kent people's stronghold").
Baroque	Baroque is an artistic style prevalent from the late 16th century to the early 18th century in Europe.

Chapter 1. THE LATER MIDDLE AGES: CRISIS AND DISINTEGRATION IN THE FOURTEENTH CENTURY

Chapter 1. THE LATER MIDDLE AGES: CRISIS AND DISINTEGRATION IN THE FOURTEENTH CENTURY

The popularity and success of the Baroque style was encouraged by the Roman Catholic Church, which had decided at the time of the Council of Trent, in response to the Protestant Reformation, that the arts should communicate religious themes in direct and emotional involvement. The aristocracy also saw the dramatic style of Baroque architecture and art as a means of impressing visitors and expressing triumphant power and control.

Realism

Realism was a general movement in 19th-century theatre that developed a set of dramatic and theatrical conventions with the aim of bringing a greater fidelity to real life to texts and performances.

Realism began earlier in the 19th century in Russia than elsewhere in Europe and took a more uncompromising form. Beginning with the plays of Ivan Turgenev (who used "domestic detail to reveal inner turmoil"), Aleksandr Ostrovsky, Aleksey Pisemsky (whose A Bitter Fate (1859) anticipated Naturalism), and Leo Tolstoy (whose The Power of Darkness (1886) is "one of the most effective of naturalistic plays"), a tradition of psychological realism in Russia culminated with the establishment of the Moscow Art Theatre by Constantin Stanislavski and Vladimir Nemirovich-Danchenko.

Chapel

A chapel is a building used by Christians, members of other religions, and sometimes interfaith communities, as a place of fellowship and worship. A church, college, hospital, palace, prison or funeral home, located on board a military or commercial ship, or it may be an entirely free-standing building, sometimes with its own grounds. Many military installations have chapels for the use of military personnel, normally under the leadership of a military chaplain.

Brothel

A brothel, cathouse, whorehouse, sporting house, gentleman's club, house of ill fame, house of prostitution, bawdy house etc., is an establishment dedicated to prostitution, providing the prostitutes a place to meet and to have sexual intercourse with clients.

History

Chapter 1. THE LATER MIDDLE AGES: CRISIS AND DISINTEGRATION IN THE FOURTEENTH CENTURY

Chapter 1. THE LATER MIDDLE AGES: CRISIS AND DISINTEGRATION IN THE FOURTEENTH CENTURY

	The earliest recorded mention of prostitution as an occupation, appears in Sumerian records from before 4000 BC, and describes a temple-bordello operated by Sumerian priests in the city of Uruk. The 'kakum' or temple, was dedicated to the goddess Isthar and housed three grades of women.
Children	"Children" is a single by electronica composer Robert Miles from his album Dreamland. "Children" is Miles' most successful single, being certified Gold and Platinum in several countries and it reaching #1 in more than 12 countries. Miles created several remixes himself with an additional remix by Tilt.
Martin Luther	Martin Luther was a German priest and professor of theology who initiated the Protestant Reformation. He strongly disputed the claim that freedom from God's punishment of sin could be purchased with money. He confronted indulgence salesman Johann Tetzel with his Ninety-Five Theses in 1517. His refusal to retract all of his writings at the demand of Pope Leo X in 1520 and the Holy Roman Emperor Charles V at the Dict of Worms in 1521 resulted in his excommunication by the pope and condemnation as an outlaw by the emperor.
Fronde	The Fronde was a civil war in France, occurring in the midst of the Franco-Spanish War, which had begun in 1635. The word fronde means sling, which Parisian mobs used to smash the windows of supporters of Cardinal Mazarin. The Fronde was divided into two campaigns, the Fronde of the parlements and the Fronde of the nobles. The timing of the outbreak of the Fronde des parlements, directly after the Peace of Westphalia (1648) that ended the Thirty Years War, was significant.
Medical school	A medical school is a tertiary educational institution--or part of such an institution--that teaches medicine. In addition to a medical degree program, some medical schools offer programs leading to a Master's Degree, Doctor of Philosophy (PhD), Bachelor/Doctor of Medicine (MBBS, BMed, MDCM, MD, MBChB, etc)., Doctor of Osteopathic Medicine (DO-USA), or other post-secondary education. Many medical schools also offer a Physician Assistant/Associate program.

Chapter 1. THE LATER MIDDLE AGES: CRISIS AND DISINTEGRATION IN THE FOURTEENTH CENTURY

Chapter 1. THE LATER MIDDLE AGES: CRISIS AND DISINTEGRATION IN THE FOURTEENTH CENTURY

Scientific revolution	The Scientific Revolution was a period when new ideas in physics, astronomy, biology, human anatomy, chemistry, and other sciences led to a rejection of doctrines that had prevailed starting in Ancient Greece and continuing through the Middle Ages, and laid the foundation of modern science. According to most accounts, the scientific revolution began in Europe towards the end of the Renaissance era and continued through the late 18th century, the latter period known as The Enlightenment. It was sparked by the publication (1543) of two works that changed the course of science: Nicolaus Copernicus's De revolutionibus orbium coelestium (On the Revolutions of the Heavenly Spheres) and Andreas Vesalius's De humani corporis fabrica (On the Fabric of the Human body).

Chapter 1. THE LATER MIDDLE AGES: CRISIS AND DISINTEGRATION IN THE FOURTEENTH CENTURY

Chapter 2. RECOVERY AND REBIRTH: THE AGE OF THE RENAISSANCE

Chapel	A chapel is a building used by Christians, members of other religions, and sometimes interfaith communities, as a place of fellowship and worship. A church, college, hospital, palace, prison or funeral home, located on board a military or commercial ship, or it may be an entirely free-standing building, sometimes with its own grounds. Many military installations have chapels for the use of military personnel, normally under the leadership of a military chaplain.
Michelangelo	Michelangelo di Lodovico Buonarroti Simoni (6 March 1475 - 18 February 1564), commonly known as Michelangelo, was an Italian Renaissance painter, sculptor, architect, poet, and engineer. Despite making few forays beyond the arts, his versatility in the disciplines he took up was of such a high order that he is often considered a contender for the title of the archetypal Renaissance man, along with his rival and fellow Italian, Leonardo da Vinci. Michelangelo's output in every field during his long life was prodigious; when the sheer volume of correspondence, sketches, and reminiscences that survive is also taken into account, he is the best-documented artist of the 16th century.
Rembrandt	Rembrandt Harmenszoon van Rijn was a Dutch painter and etcher. He is generally considered one of the greatest painters and printmakers in European art history and the most important in Dutch history. His contributions to art came in a period that historians call the Dutch Golden Age.
Black Death	The Black Death was one of the most devastating pandemics in human history, peaking in Europe between 1348 and 1350. It is widely thought to have been an outbreak of plague caused by the bacterium Yersinia pestis, an argument supported by recent forensic research, although this view has been challenged by a number of scholars. Thought to have started in China, it travelled along the Silk Road and had reached the Crimea by 1346. From there, probably carried by Oriental rat fleas residing on the black rats that were regular passengers on merchant ships, it spread throughout the Mediterranean and Europe. The Black Death is estimated to have killed 30% - 60% of Europe's population, reducing the world's population from an estimated 450 million to between 350 and 375 million in 1400. This has been seen as having created a series of religious, social and economic upheavals, which had profound effects on the course of European history.

Chapter 2. RECOVERY AND REBIRTH: THE AGE OF THE RENAISSANCE

Chapter 2. RECOVERY AND REBIRTH: THE AGE OF THE RENAISSANCE

Catholic	The word catholic comes from the Greek phrase καθ?λου (kath'holou), meaning "on the whole," "according to the whole" or "in general", and is a combination of the Greek words κατ? meaning "about" and ?λος meaning "whole". The word in English can mean either "including a wide variety of things; all-embracing" or "of the Roman Catholic faith." as "relating to the historic doctrine and practice of the Western Church."
	It was first used to describe the Christian Church in the early 2nd century to emphasize its universal scope. In the context of Christian ecclesiology, it has a rich history and several usages.
Catholic Church	The Catholic Church, is the world's largest Christian church. Headed by the Pope, it sees its mission as spreading the gospel of Christ, administering its sacraments and exercising charity.
	The Catholic Church is one of the oldest religious institutions in the world and has played a prominent role in the history of Western civilisation.
Church	A church building is a building or structure whose primary purpose is to facilitate the meeting of a church. Originally, Jewish Christians met in synagogues, such as the Cenacle, and in one another's homes, known as house churches. As Christianity grew and became more accepted by governments, notably with the Edict of Milan, rooms and, eventually, entire buildings were set aside for the explicit purpose of Christian worship, such as the Church of the Holy Sepulchre.
Humanism	Humanism is an approach in study, philosophy, or practice that focuses on human values and concerns. The term can mean several things, for example: 1. A cultural movement of the Italian Renaissance based on the study of classical works. 2. An approach to education that uses literary means or a focus on the humanities to inform students. 3. A variety of perspectives in philosophy and social science which affirm some notion of 'human nature' (by contrast with anti-humanism). 4. A secular ideology which espouses reason, ethics, and justice, whilst specifically rejecting supernatural and religious dogma as a basis of morality and decision-making.

Chapter 2. RECOVERY AND REBIRTH: THE AGE OF THE RENAISSANCE

Chapter 2. RECOVERY AND REBIRTH: THE AGE OF THE RENAISSANCE

	The last interpretation may be attributed to Secular Humanism as a specific humanistic life stance. Modern meanings of the word have therefore come to be associated with a rejection of appeals to the supernatural or to some higher authority.
Italy	The Italy Pavilion is a part of the World Showcase within Epcot at the Walt Disney World Resort. Layout The Italian Pavilion features a plaza surrounded by a collection of buildings evocative of Venetian, Florentine, and Roman architecture. Venetian architecture is represented by a re-creation of St Mark's Campanile (bell tower) and a replica of the Doge's Palace.
Jacob	Jacob is a German/Italian/American movie from 1994, based on the novel Giacobbe by Francesco Maria Nappi, which is in turn based on the Bible story about Jacob. Plot Jacob defrauds his twin Brother Esau and hlollogas to flee. In Haran he gets to know his cousin Rachel, and falls in love with her.
Renaissance	The Renaissance is a cultural movement that spanned roughly the 14th to the 17th century, beginning in Florence in the Late Middle Ages and later spreading to the rest of Europe. The term is also used more loosely to refer to the historic era, but since the changes of the Renaissance were not uniform across Europe, this is a general use of the term. As a cultural movement, it encompassed a resurgence of learning based on classical sources, the development of linear perspective in painting, and gradual but widespread educational reform.
Bruges	Bruges is the capital and largest city of the province of West Flanders in the Flemish Region of Belgium. It is located in the northwest of the country.

Chapter 2. RECOVERY AND REBIRTH: THE AGE OF THE RENAISSANCE

Chapter 2. RECOVERY AND REBIRTH: THE AGE OF THE RENAISSANCE

	The historic city centre is a prominent World Heritage Site of UNESCO. It is oval-shaped and about 430 hectares in size.
French Renaissance	French Renaissance is a recent term used to describe a cultural and artistic movement in France from the late 15th century to the early 17th century. It is associated with the pan-European Renaissance that many cultural historians believe originated in northern Italy in the fourteenth century. The French Renaissance traditionally extends from (roughly) the French invasion of Italy in 1494 during the reign of Charles VIII until the death of Henry IV in 1610. This chronology not withstanding, certain artistic, technological or literary developments associated with the Italian Renaissance arrived in France earlier (for example, by way of the Burgundy court or the Papal court in Avignon); however, the Black Death of the 14th century and the Hundred Years' War kept France economically and politically weak until the late 15th century and this prevented the full use of these influences.
Norway	The Norway pavilion is part of the World Showcase within Epcot at the Walt Disney World Resort. Layout The 58,000-square-foot (5,400 m^2) Norway pavilion is designed to look like a Norwegian village. The village includes a detailed Stave church, and the exterior of its main table-service restaurant, Restaurant Akershus, resembles its namesake in Oslo.
Columbian Exchange	The Columbian Exchange was a dramatically widespread exchange of animals, plants, culture, human populations (including slaves), communicable diseases, and ideas between the Eastern and Western hemispheres (Old World and New World). It was one of the most significant events concerning ecology, agriculture, and culture in all of human history. Christopher Columbus' first voyage to the Americas in 1492 launched the era of large-scale contact between the Old and the New Worlds that resulted in this ecological revolution, hence the name "Columbian" Exchange.

Chapter 2. RECOVERY AND REBIRTH: THE AGE OF THE RENAISSANCE

Chapter 2. RECOVERY AND REBIRTH: THE AGE OF THE RENAISSANCE

Italian Renaissance	The Italian Renaissance began the opening phase of the Renaissance, a period of great cultural change and achievement in Europe that spanned the period from the end of the 13th century to about 1600, marking the transition between Medieval and Early Modern Europe. The term renaissance is in essence a modern one that came into currency in the 19th century, in the work of historians such as Jacob Burckhardt. Although the origins of a movement that was confined largely to the literate culture of intellectual endeavor and patronage can be traced to the earlier part of the 14th century, many aspects of Italian culture and society remained largely Medieval; the Renaissance did not come into full swing until the end of the century.
The Fellowship	The Fellowship, is a U.S.-based religious and political organization founded in 1935 by Abraham Vereide. The stated purpose of the Fellowship is to provide a fellowship forum for decision makers to share in Bible studies, prayer meetings, worship experiences and to experience spiritual affirmation and support. The organization has been described as one of the most politically well-connected ministries in the United States.
Patrician	The term patrician, including both their natural and adopted members. In the late Roman Empire, the class was broadened to include high council officials, and after the fall of the Western Empire it remained a high honorary title in the Byzantine Empire. Medieval patrician classes were once again formally defined groups of elite burgher families in many medieval Italian republics, such as Venice and Genoa, and subsequently "patrician" became a vaguer term used for aristocrats and elite bourgeoisie in many countries.
Estates of the realm	The Estates of the realm were the broad social orders of the hierarchically conceived society, recognized in the Middle Ages and Early Modern period in Christian Europe; they are sometimes distinguished as the three estates: the clergy, the nobility, and commoners. "Medieval political speculation is imbued to the marrow with the idea of a structure of society based upon distinct orders," Johan Huizinga observes. The virtually synonymous terms estate and order designated a great variety of social realities, not at all limited to a class, Huizinga concluded, but applied to every social function, every trade, every recognizable grouping.

Chapter 2. RECOVERY AND REBIRTH: THE AGE OF THE RENAISSANCE

Chapter 2. RECOVERY AND REBIRTH: THE AGE OF THE RENAISSANCE

Working class	Working class is a term used in the social sciences and in ordinary conversation to describe those employed in lower tier jobs (as measured by skill, education and lower incomes), often extending to those in unemployment or otherwise possessing below-average incomes. Working classes are mainly found in industrialized economies and in urban areas of non-industrialized economies. As with many terms describing social class, working class is defined and used in many different ways.
18th century	The 18th century lasted from 1701 to 1800 in the Gregorian calendar. However, Western historians have occasionally defined the 18th century otherwise for the purposes of their work. For example, the "short" 18th century may be defined as 1715-1789, denoting the period of time between the death of Louis XIV of France and the start of the French Revolution with an emphasis on directly interconnected events.
Africa	Africa is the world's second-largest and second most-populous continent, after Asia. At about 30.2 million km² (11.7 million sq mi) including adjacent islands, it covers 6% of the Earth's total surface area and 20.4% of the total land area. With 1.0 billion people in 61 territories, it accounts for about 14.72% of the world's human population.
Children	"Children" is a single by electronica composer Robert Miles from his album Dreamland. "Children" is Miles' most successful single, being certified Gold and Platinum in several countries and it reaching #1 in more than 12 countries. Miles created several remixes himself with an additional remix by Tilt.
Faith	"Faith" was a #1 song, written and performed by George Michael, released as a single on Columbia Records, from his 1987 Faith album. According to Billboard magazine, it was the top-selling single of the year in the United States in 1988. Track listing

Chapter 2. RECOVERY AND REBIRTH: THE AGE OF THE RENAISSANCE

Chapter 2. RECOVERY AND REBIRTH: THE AGE OF THE RENAISSANCE

7": UK / Epic EMU 2

1. "Faith" - 3:14
2. "Hand To Mouth" - 4:36

12": UK / Epic EMU T2

1. "Faith" - 3:14
2. "Faith" (Instrumental) - 3:08
3. "Hand to Mouth" - 4:36

U.S. CD single

1. "Faith" - 3:16
2. "Faith" (dance remix radio edit) - 4:54
3. "Faith" (album version) - 3:16
4. "Hand to Mouth" - 5:49

Mixes

1. Album version - 3:16
2. 7" version - 3:14
3. Instrumental - 3:08
4. Dance remix radio edit - 5:22

History

Having disbanded Wham! the previous year, there was a keen expectation for Michael's solo career and "Faith" would go on to become one of his most popular and enduring songs, as well as being the most simplistic in its production.

Protestantism | Protestantism is one of the three major divisions (Catholicism, Orthodoxy, and Protestantism) within Christianity. It is a movement that began in northern Europe in the early 16th century as a reaction against medieval Roman Catholic doctrines and practices.

Chapter 2. RECOVERY AND REBIRTH: THE AGE OF THE RENAISSANCE

Chapter 2. RECOVERY AND REBIRTH: THE AGE OF THE RENAISSANCE

	The doctrines of the various Protestant denominations and non-denominations vary, but most non-denominational doctrines include justification by grace through faith and not through works, known as Sola Fide, the priesthood of all believers, and the Bible as the ultimate authority in matters of faith and order, known as Sola Scriptura, which is Latin for 'by scripture alone'.
World	WORLD Magazine is a biweekly Christian news magazine, published in the United States of America by God's World Publications, a non-profit 501(c)(3) organization based in Asheville, North Carolina. WORLD differs from most other news magazines in that its declared perspective is one of conservative evangelical Protestantism. Its mission statement is "To report, interpret, and illustrate the news in a timely, accurate, enjoyable, and arresting fashion from a perspective committed to the Bible as the inerrant Word of God." Each issue features both U.S. and international news, cultural analysis, editorials and commentary, as well as book, music and movie reviews.
Maria	The gens Maria was a plebeian family at Rome. Its most celebrated member was Gaius Marius, one of the greatest generals of antiquity, and seven times consul. Origin of the gens The nomen Marius appears to be derived from the Oscan praenomen Marius, in which case the family is probably of Sabine or Sabellic origin.
Austria	Austria officially the Republic of Austria, is a landlocked country of roughly 8.3 million people in Central Europe. It is bordered by the Czech Republic and Germany to the north, Slovakia and Hungary to the east, Slovenia and Italy to the south, and Switzerland and Liechtenstein to the west. The territory of Austria covers 83,855 square kilometres (32,377 sq mi) and has a temperate and alpine climate.

Chapter 2. RECOVERY AND REBIRTH: THE AGE OF THE RENAISSANCE

Chapter 2. RECOVERY AND REBIRTH: THE AGE OF THE RENAISSANCE

Condottieri	Condottieri were the mercenary soldier leaders (or warlords) of the professional, military free companies contracted by the Italian city-states and the Papacy, from the late Middle Ages and throughout the Renaissance. In Renaissance Italian, condottiero meant "contractor", and was synonymous with the modern English title Mercenary Captain, which, historiographically, does not connote the hired soldier's nationality. In contemporary Italian, "condottiero" acquired the broader meaning of "military leader" (e.g., not restricted to mercenaries).
Duchy	A duchy is a territory, fief, or domain ruled by a duke or duchess. Some duchies were sovereign in areas that would become unified realms only during the Modern era. In contrast, others were subordinate districts of those kingdoms that unified either partially or completely during the Medieval era (such as England, France, and Spain).
Republic	Republic is a Hungarian rock band formed in Budapest in 1989. Their style is a unique mix of Western rock music and traditional Hungarian folk music. The band is popular in its native country and among Hungarian speaking minorities elsewhere. Members The two founding members are László Bódi and László Attila Nagy.
Republic of Venice	The Republic of Venice or Venetian Republic was a state originating from the city of Venice in Northeastern Italy. It existed for over a millennium, from the late 7th century until 1797. It was formally known as the Most Serene Republic of Venice and is often referred to as La Serenissima, in reference to its title as a one of the "Most Serene Republics". It preferred to trade rather than participate in unnecessary war activities.
State	The term state is used in various senses by Catholic theologians and spiritual writers.

Chapter 2. RECOVERY AND REBIRTH: THE AGE OF THE RENAISSANCE

Chapter 2. RECOVERY AND REBIRTH: THE AGE OF THE RENAISSANCE

	It may be taken to signify a profession or calling in life, as where St. Paul says, in I Corinthians 7:20: "Let every man abide in the same calling in which he was called". States are classified in the Catholic Church as the clerical state, the religious state, and the secular state; and among religious states, again, we have those of the contemplative, the active, and the mixed orders.
Papal States	The Papal States, State(s) of the Church, or Pontifical States were among the major historical states of Italy from roughly the 6th century until the Italian peninsula was unified in 1861 by the Kingdom of Piedmont-Sardinia (after which the Papal States, in less territorially extensive form, continued to exist until 1870).
	The Papal States comprised territories under direct sovereign rule of the papacy, and at its height it covered most of the modern Italian regions of Romagna, Marche, Umbria and Lazio. This governing power is commonly called the temporal power of the Pope, as opposed to his ecclesiastical primacy.
Mantua	A Mantua is an article of women's clothing worn in the late 17th century and 18th century. Originally a loose gown, the later mantua was an overgown or robe typically worn over stays, stomacher and a co-ordinating petticoat.
	Evolution of the mantua
	The earliest mantuas emerged in the late 17th century as a comfortable alternative to the boned bodices and separate skirts then widely worn.
Francis	Francis is a French and English first name and a surname of Latin origin.
	Francis is a name that has many derivatives in most European languages. The female version of the name in English is Frances, and (less commonly) Francine.

Chapter 2. RECOVERY AND REBIRTH: THE AGE OF THE RENAISSANCE

Chapter 2. RECOVERY AND REBIRTH: THE AGE OF THE RENAISSANCE

House of Habsburg	The House of Habsburg, also found as Hapsburg, and also known as House of Austria was one of the most important aristocratic royal houses of Europe and is best known for being an origin of all of the formally elected Holy Roman Emperors between 1438 and 1740, as well as rulers of the Austrian Empire and Spanish Empire and several other countries. Originally from Switzerland, the dynasty first reigned in Austria, which they ruled for over six centuries. A series of dynastic marriages enabled the family to vastly expand its domains, to include Burgundy, Spain, Bohemia, Hungary, and other territories into the inheritance.
Alexander	Saint Alexander was a martyr and companion of St. Pothinus. Alexander was a physician in Vienne, Gaul, when he converted to Christianity. Arrested during the persecutions conducted under Emperor Marcus Aurelius.
Cesare	Cesare, the Italian version of the given name Caesar, may refer to: - Giuseppe Cesare Abba (1838-1910), Italian patriot and writer - Cesare Battisti (disambiguation) - Cesare Borgia (1475 1507), Italian general and statesman - Joe Cesare Colombo, Italian industrial designer - Cesare Emiliani (1922-1995), Italian-American scientist - Cesare Negri, the late Renaissance dancing-master - Cesare Pavese (1908-1950), Italian poet and novelist - Cesare Bonizzi, Franciscan monk and heavy metal singer - Cesare, Marquis of Beccaria (1738-1794), an Italian philosopher and politician - Cesare, a manga series by Souryo Fuyumi
Martin Luther	Martin Luther was a German priest and professor of theology who initiated the Protestant Reformation. He strongly disputed the claim that freedom from God's punishment of sin could be purchased with money. He confronted indulgence salesman Johann Tetzel with his Ninety-Five Theses in 1517. His refusal to retract all of his writings at the demand of Pope Leo X in 1520 and the Holy Roman Emperor Charles V at the Diet of Worms in 1521 resulted in his excommunication by the pope and condemnation as an outlaw by the emperor.
Secularism	Secularism is the concept that government or other entities should exist separately from religion and/or religious beliefs.

Chapter 2. RECOVERY AND REBIRTH: THE AGE OF THE RENAISSANCE

Chapter 2. RECOVERY AND REBIRTH: THE AGE OF THE RENAISSANCE

	In one sense, secularism may assert the right to be free from religious rule and teachings, and the right to freedom from governmental imposition of religion upon the people within a state that is neutral on matters of belief. In another sense, it refers to the view that human activities and decisions, especially political ones, should be based on evidence and fact unbiased by religious influence.
Christian	A Christian is a person who adheres to Christianity, an Abrahamic, monotheistic religion based on the life and teachings of Jesus of Nazareth as recorded in the Canonical gospels and the letters of the New Testament.
	Central to the Christian faith is love or Agape. Christians also believe Jesus is the Messiah prophesied in the Hebrew Bible, the Son of God, and the savior of mankind from their sins.
Desiderius	Desiderius was the last king of the Lombard Kingdom of northern Italy (died c. 786). He is chiefly known for his connection to Charlemagne, who married his daughter and conquered his realm.
	Rise to power
	Desiderius Romae was originally a royal officer, the dux Langobardorum et comes stabuli, "constable and duke of the Lombards," an office apparently similar to the contemporaneous Frankish office of dux Francorum.
Desiderius Erasmus	Desiderius Erasmus Roterodamus (October 28, 1466 - July 12, 1536), sometimes known as Desiderius Erasmus of Rotterdam, was a Dutch Renaissance humanist and a Catholic priest and theologian. His scholarly name Desiderius Erasmus Roterodamus comprises the following three elements: the Latin noun desiderium ; the Greek adjective ?ρ?σμιος (erásmios) meaning "desired", and, in the form Erasmus, also the name of a St. Erasmus of Formiae; and the Latinized adjectival form for the city of Rotterdam (Roterodamus = "of Rotterdam").

Chapter 2. RECOVERY AND REBIRTH: THE AGE OF THE RENAISSANCE

Chapter 2. RECOVERY AND REBIRTH: THE AGE OF THE RENAISSANCE

	Erasmus was a classical scholar who wrote in a "pure" Latin style and enjoyed the sobriquet "Prince of the Humanists." He has been called "the crowning glory of the Christian humanists." Using humanist techniques for working on texts, he prepared important new Latin and Greek editions of the New Testament.
Cicero	Marcus Tullius Cicero, was a Roman philosopher, statesman, lawyer, political theorist, and Roman constitutionalist. He came from a wealthy municipal family of the equestrian order, and is widely considered one of Rome's greatest orators and prose stylists.
	He introduced the Romans to the chief schools of Greek philosophy and created a Latin philosophical vocabulary (with neologisms such as humanitas, qualitas, quantitas, and essentia) distinguishing himself as a linguist, translator, and philosopher.
Greece	Greece also known as Hellas and officially the Hellenic Republic (Ελληνικ? Δημοκρατ?α, Elliniki´ Dimokratía, IPA:), is a country in southeastern Europe. Situated on the southern end of the Balkan Peninsula, Greece has land borders with Albania, the Republic of Macedonia and Bulgaria to the north, and Turkey to the east. The Aegean Sea lies to the east of mainland Greece, the Ionian Sea to the west, and the Mediterranean Sea to the south.
Giordano Bruno	Giordano Bruno born Filippo Bruno, was an Italian Dominican friar, philosopher, mathematician and astronomer, who is best known as a proponent of the infinity of the universe. His cosmological theories went beyond the Copernican model in identifying the Sun as just one of an infinite number of independently moving heavenly bodies: he is the first European to have conceptualized the universe as a continuum where the stars we see at night are identical in nature to the Sun. He was burned at the stake by civil authorities in 1600 after the Roman Inquisition found him guilty of heresy and turned him over to the state, which at that time considered heresy illegal.
Divinity	Divinity is the study of Christian and other theology and ministry at a school, divinity school, university, or seminary. The term is sometimes a synonym for theology as an academic, speculative pursuit, and sometimes is used for the study of applied theology and ministry to make a distinction between that and academic theology. It most often refers to Christian study which is linked with the professional degrees for ordained ministry or related work, though it is also used in an academic setting by other faith traditions.

Chapter 2. RECOVERY AND REBIRTH: THE AGE OF THE RENAISSANCE

Chapter 2. RECOVERY AND REBIRTH: THE AGE OF THE RENAISSANCE

Euripides	Euripides was the last of the three great tragedians of classical Athens (the other two being Aeschylus and Sophocles). Ancient scholars thought that Euripides had written ninety-five plays, although four of those were probably written by Critias. Eighteen or nineteen of Euripides' plays have survived complete.
Neoplatonism	Neoplatonism is the modern term for a school of religious and mystical philosophy that took shape in the 3rd century AD, founded by Plotinus and based on the teachings of Plato and earlier Platonists. Neoplatonists would have considered themselves simply Platonists, and the modern distinction is due to the perception that their philosophy contained sufficiently unique interpretations of Plato to make it substantially different from what Plato wrote and believed. Neoplatonism attempted to reconcile Christian doctrine with the classical philosophies of Greek and Roman society.
Pantheism	Pantheism is the view that the Universe (Nature) and God are identical. Pantheists thus do not believe in a personal, anthropomorphic or creator god. As such, pantheism denotes the idea that "God" is best seen as a way of relating to the Universe.
Plato	Plato, was a Classical Greek philosopher, mathematician, student of Socrates, writer of philosophical dialogues, and founder of the Academy in Athens, the first institution of higher learning in the Western world. Along with his mentor, Socrates, and his student, Aristotle, Plato helped to lay the foundations of Western philosophy and science.
Sophocles	Sophocles is one of three ancient Greek tragedians whose plays have survived. His first plays were written later than those of Aeschylus, and earlier than those of Euripides. According to the Suda, a 10th century encyclopedia, Sophocles wrote 123 plays during the course of his life, but only seven have survived in a complete form: Ajax, Antigone, Trachinian Women, Oedipus the King, Electra, Philoctetes and Oedipus at Colonus.
Dark Ages	"Dark Ages" is a historical periodization emphasizing the cultural and economic deterioration that supposedly occurred in Europe following the decline of the Roman Empire. The label employs traditional light-versus-darkness imagery to contrast the "darkness" of the period with earlier and later periods of "light". Originally, the term characterized the bulk of the Middle Ages (c. 5th - 15th century) as a period of intellectual darkness between the extinguishing of the light of Rome and the Renaissance or rebirth from the 14th century onwards.

Chapter 2. RECOVERY AND REBIRTH: THE AGE OF THE RENAISSANCE

Chapter 2. RECOVERY AND REBIRTH: THE AGE OF THE RENAISSANCE

Histories	Histories is a book by Tacitus, written c. 100-110, which covers the Year of Four Emperors following the downfall of Nero, the rise of Vespasian, and the rule of the Flavian Dynasty (69-96) up to the death of Domitian. Subject matter In one of the first chapters of the Agricola Tacitus said that he wished to speak about the years of Domitian, of Nerva, and of Trajan. In the Historiae the project has been modified: in the introduction, Tacitus says that he will deal with the age of Nerva and Trajan at a later time.
Nakaz	Nakaz, of Catherine the Great was a statement of legal principles authored by Catherine II of Russia, and permeated with the ideas of the French Enlightenment. It was compiled as a guide for the All-Russian Legislative Commission convened in 1767 for the purpose of replacing the mid-17th-century Muscovite code of laws with a modern law code. Catherine believed that to strengthen law and institutions was above all else to strengthen the monarchy.
Bible	The Bible is the various collections of sacred scripture of the various branches of Judaism and Christianity. The Bible, in its various editions, is the best-selling book in history. There is no single Bible, and both the individual books (Biblical canon), their contents and their order vary between denominations.
Brancacci Chapel	The Brancacci Chapel is a chapel in the Church of Santa Maria del Carmine in Florence, central Italy. It is sometimes called the "Sistine Chapel of the early Renaissance" for its painting cycle, among the most famous and influential of the period. Construction of the chapel was commissioned by Pietro Brancacci and begun in 1386. Public access is currently gained via the neighbouring convent, designed by Brunelleschi.
Masaccio	Masaccio born Tommaso di Ser Giovanni di Simone, was the first great painter of the Quattrocento period of the Italian Renaissance. According to Vasari, Masaccio was the best painter of his generation because of his skill at recreating lifelike figures and movements as well as a convincing sense of three-dimensionality.

Chapter 2. RECOVERY AND REBIRTH: THE AGE OF THE RENAISSANCE

Chapter 2. RECOVERY AND REBIRTH: THE AGE OF THE RENAISSANCE

	Despite his brief career, he had a profound influence on other artists. He was one of the first to use Linear perspective in his painting, employing techniques such as vanishing point in art for the first time. He also moved away from the International Gothic style and elaborate ornamentation of artists like Gentile da Fabriano to a more naturalistic mode that employed perspective and chiaroscuro for greater realism.
Neoclassicism	Neoclassicism is the name given to quite distinct movements in the decorative and visual arts, literature, theatre, music, and architecture that draw upon Western classical art and culture (usually that of Ancient Greece or Ancient Rome). These movements were dominant in northern Europe during the mid-18th to the end of the 19th century. Overview What any "neo-classicism" depends on most fundamentally is a consensus about a body of work that has achieved canonic status (illustration, below).
Realism	Realism was a general movement in 19th-century theatre that developed a set of dramatic and theatrical conventions with the aim of bringing a greater fidelity to real life to texts and performances. Realism began earlier in the 19th century in Russia than elsewhere in Europe and took a more uncompromising form. Beginning with the plays of Ivan Turgenev (who used "domestic detail to reveal inner turmoil"), Aleksandr Ostrovsky, Aleksey Pisemsky (whose A Bitter Fate (1859) anticipated Naturalism), and Leo Tolstoy (whose The Power of Darkness (1886) is "one of the most effective of naturalistic plays"), a tradition of psychological realism in Russia culminated with the establishment of the Moscow Art Theatre by Constantin Stanislavski and Vladimir Nemirovich-Danchenko.
Baroque	Baroque is an artistic style prevalent from the late 16th century to the early 18th century in Europe.

Chapter 2. RECOVERY AND REBIRTH: THE AGE OF THE RENAISSANCE

Chapter 2. RECOVERY AND REBIRTH: THE AGE OF THE RENAISSANCE

The popularity and success of the Baroque style was encouraged by the Roman Catholic Church, which had decided at the time of the Council of Trent, in response to the Protestant Reformation, that the arts should communicate religious themes in direct and emotional involvement. The aristocracy also saw the dramatic style of Baroque architecture and art as a means of impressing visitors and expressing triumphant power and control.

Donatello

Donato di Niccolò di Betto Bardi (circa 1386 - December 13, 1466), also known as Donatello, was an early Renaissance Italian artist and sculptor from Florence. He is, in part, known for his work in bas-relief, a form of shallow relief sculpture that, in Donatello's case, incorporated significant 15th century developments in perspectival illusionism.

Early life

Donatello was the son of Niccolò di Betto Bardi, who was a member of the Florentine Wool Combers Guild, and was born in Florence, most likely in the year 1386. Donatello was educated in the house of the Martelli family.

Renaissance architecture

Renaissance architecture is the architecture of the period between the early 15th and early 17th centuries in different regions of Europe, demonstrating a conscious revival and development of certain elements of ancient Greek and Roman thought and material culture. Stylistically, Renaissance architecture followed Gothic architecture and was succeeded by Baroque architecture. Developed first in Florence, with Filippo Brunelleschi as one of its innovators, the Renaissance style quickly spread to other Italian cities.

House

A house is a home, building or structure that is a dwelling or place for habitation by human beings. The term house includes many kinds of dwellings ranging from rudimentary huts of nomadic tribes to free standing individual structures. In some contexts, "house" may mean the same as dwelling, residence, home, abode, lodging, accommodation, or housing, among other meanings.

Chapter 2. RECOVERY AND REBIRTH: THE AGE OF THE RENAISSANCE

Chapter 2. RECOVERY AND REBIRTH: THE AGE OF THE RENAISSANCE

High Renaissance

The expression High Renaissance, in art history, is a periodizing convention used to denote the apogee of the visual arts in the Italian Renaissance. The High Renaissance period is usually taken to begin in the 1490s, with Leonardo's fresco of the Last Supper in Milan and the death of Lorenzo de' Medici in Florence, and to have ended in 1527 with the sacking of Rome by the troops of Charles V.

Overview

The High Renaissance is generally taken to refer to a period of exceptional artistic production in the Italian states, principally Rome, capital of the Papal States, under Pope Julius II. Assertions about where and when the period begins and ends vary, but in general the best-known exponents of Italian Renaissance painting are painters of the High Renaissance, including Leonardo da Vinci, Michelangelo and early Raphael. Extending the general rubric of Renaissance culture, the visual arts of the High Renaissance were marked by a renewed emphasis upon the classical tradition, the expansion of networks of patronage, and a gradual attenuation of figural forms into the style later termed Mannerism.

Last Supper

According to Christian belief, The Last Supper is the final meal that Jesus Christ shared with his Twelve Apostles in Jerusalem before his crucifixion. The Last Supper provides the scriptural basis for the ceremony known as "the Eucharist", "communion" or "the Lord's Supper."

Paul's First Epistle to the Corinthians is the earliest surviving mention of the Last Supper. It is later described in more detail in the Synoptic Gospels, and in the Gospel of John (which, however, omits the institution of the Eucharistic use of the bread and wine).

Athens

Athens is the capital and largest city of Greece. Athens dominates the Attica periphery and it is one of the world's oldest cities, as its recorded history spans around 3,400 years.

The Greek capital has a population of 745,514 (in 2001) within its administrative limits and a land area of 39 km^2 (15 sq mi).

Chapter 2. RECOVERY AND REBIRTH: THE AGE OF THE RENAISSANCE

Chapter 2. RECOVERY AND REBIRTH: THE AGE OF THE RENAISSANCE

Basilica	The Latin word basilica, was originally used to describe a Roman public building, usually located in the forum of a Roman town. Public basilicas began to appear in Hellenistic cities in the 2nd century BC.
	The term was also applied to buildings used for religious purposes. The remains of a large subterranean Neopythagorean basilica dating from the 1st century AD were found near the Porta Maggiore in Rome in 1915. The stuccoes on the interior vaulting have survived, though their exact interpretation remains a matter for debate.
Platonic Academy	The Platonic Academy was a 15th century discussion group in Florence. It was founded after Gemistus Pletho reintroduced Plato's thoughts to Western Europe during the 1438 - 1439 Council of Florence. It was sponsored by Cosimo de' Medici and led by Marsilio Ficino.
Madrigal	A madrigal is a type of secular vocal music composition, written during the Renaissance and early Baroque eras. Throughout most of its history it was polyphonic and unaccompanied by instruments, with the number of voices varying from two to eight, but most frequently three to six. The earliest examples of the genre date from Italy in the 1520s, and while the center of madrigal production remained in Italy, madrigals were also written in England and Germany, especially late in the 16th and early in the 17th centuries.
Renaissance music	Renaissance music is European music written during the Renaissance. Defining the beginning of the musical era is difficult, given the gradually adopted "Renaissance" characteristics: musicologists have placed its beginnings from as early as 1300 to as late as the 1470s.
	Overview
	The increasing reliance on the interval of the third as a consonance is one of the most pronounced features of early Renaissance European art music .
Anjou	Anjou is a former county (c. 880), duchy (1360) and province centred on the city of Angers in the lower Loire Valley of western France. It corresponds largely to the present-day département of Maine-et-Loire. Its traditional Latin name is Andegavia.

Chapter 2. RECOVERY AND REBIRTH: THE AGE OF THE RENAISSANCE

Chapter 2. RECOVERY AND REBIRTH: THE AGE OF THE RENAISSANCE

Maine	Le Maine is one of the traditional provinces of France (not to be confused with La Maine, the river). It corresponds to the old county of Maine, with its center, the city of Le Mans. Location Bordering the county of Anjou in the south and the Duchy of Normandy in the north, Maine was a small matter of contention between the rulers of these more powerful principalities.
American Revolution	The American Revolution was the political upheaval during the last half of the 18th century in which thirteen colonies in North America joined together to break free from the British Empire, combining to become the United States of America. They first rejected the authority of the Parliament of Great Britain to govern them from overseas without representation, and then expelled all royal officials. By 1774 each colony had established a Provincial Congress, or an equivalent governmental institution, to form individual self-governing states. The British responded by sending combat troops to re-impose direct rule.
Chinas	The Chinas are a people mentioned in ancient Indian literature from the first millennium BC, such as the Mahabharata, Laws of Manu, as well the Puranic literature. They are believed to have been Chinese. Etymology The name Cina is commonly believed to have been derived from either the Qin (Tsin or Chin) dynasty which rule in China from 221 BC or the earlier Qin state which later became the Qin dynasty.
Court	The court of a monarch, or at some periods an important nobleman, is a term for the extended household and all those who regularly attended on the ruler or central figure. In the largest courts many thousands of individuals comprised the court, many officials or servants in the permanent employ of the ruler, and others attending in hope of political or financial gain, or merely for the society and entertainments offered. As well as being the centre of political life, courts were usually the drivers of fashion, and often where literary, musical and artistic trends first developed.

Chapter 2. RECOVERY AND REBIRTH: THE AGE OF THE RENAISSANCE

Chapter 2. RECOVERY AND REBIRTH: THE AGE OF THE RENAISSANCE

England	"England" is a song written by Justin Hawkins from The Darkness(music) ' Chas Bayfield (lyrics) and released by him under the name British Whale and used as the unofficial World Cup single for the England National Team in 2006
Henry	Henry is an English male given name and a surname, from the Old French Henry derived itself from the Germanic name Haimric, which was derived from the word elements haim, meaning "home" and ric, meaning "power, ruler". Harry, its English short form, was considered the "spoken form" of Henry in medieval England. Most English kings named Henry were called Harry.
Star Chamber	The Star Chamber was an English court of law that sat at the royal Palace of Westminster until 1641. It was made up of Privy Counsellors, as well as common-law judges and supplemented the activities of the common-law and equity courts in both civil and criminal matters. The court was set up to ensure the fair enforcement of laws against prominent people, those so powerful that ordinary courts could never convict them of their crimes. Court sessions were held in secret, with no indictments, no right of appeal, no juries, and no witnesses.
Inquisition	The term Inquisition can apply to any one of several institutions which fought against heretics (or other offenders against canon law) within the justice-system of the Roman Catholic Church. Although similar institutions existed within Calvinist and other Protestant churches, the term "Inquisition" is usually applied to that of the Catholic Church. It may also refer to: - an ecclesiastical tribunal - the institution of the Roman Catholic Church for combating heresy - a number of historical expurgation movements against heresy (orchestrated by some groups/individuals within the Catholic Church or within a Catholic state) - the trial of an individual accused of heresy. Inquisition tribunals and institutions Before the 12th century, the Roman Catholic Church already suppressed heresy, usually through a system of ecclesiastical proscription or imprisonment, but without using torture and seldom resorting to executions.

Chapter 2. RECOVERY AND REBIRTH: THE AGE OF THE RENAISSANCE

Chapter 2. RECOVERY AND REBIRTH: THE AGE OF THE RENAISSANCE

Bohemia	Bohemia is a historical region in central Europe, occupying the western two-thirds of the traditional Czech Lands. It is located in the contemporary Czech Republic with its capital in Prague. In a broader meaning, it often refers to the entire Czech territory, including Moravia and Czech Silesia, especially in historical contexts, such as the Kingdom of Bohemia.
Catholicism	Catholicism is a broad term for the body of the Catholic faith, its theologies and doctrines, its liturgical, ethical, spiritual, and behavioral characteristics, as well as a religious people as a whole.
	For many the term usually refers to Christians and churches belonging to the Roman Catholic Church in full communion with the Holy See. For others it refers to the churches of the first millennium, including, besides the Roman Catholic Church, the Eastern Orthodox Church, the Oriental Orthodox Church, and the Assyrian Church of the East.
Czechs	Czechs are a western Slavic people of Central Europe, living predominantly in the Czech Republic. Small populations of Czechs also live in Slovakia, Austria, the United States, the United Kingdom, Chile, Argentina, Canada, Germany, Russia and other countries. They speak the Czech language, which is closely related to the Slovak and Upper Sorbian language.
Granada	Granada is a 2009 German-style board game developed by Dirk Henn and published by Queen Games. It is based on and heavily inspired by Henn's earlier game, the Spiel des Jahres-winning Alhambra. Due to its similar theme, it is published as a "standalone game in the Alhambra family".
Holy Roman Empire	The Holy Roman Empire (Holy Roman Empire; German: Heiliges Römisches Reich (HRR), Latin: Imperium Romanum Sacrum (IRS), Italian: Sacro Romano Impero (SRI)) was a realm that existed for about a millennium in Central Europe, ruled by a Holy Roman Emperor. Its character changed during the Middle Ages and the Early Modern period, when the power of the emperor gradually weakened in favour of the princes. In its last centuries, its character became quite close to a union of territories.

Chapter 2. RECOVERY AND REBIRTH: THE AGE OF THE RENAISSANCE

Chapter 2. RECOVERY AND REBIRTH: THE AGE OF THE RENAISSANCE

Huguenot	The Huguenots were members of the Protestant Reformed Church of France from the sixteenth to the seventeenth centuries. Since the seventeenth century, Huguenots have been commonly designated "French Protestants," the title being suggested by their German co-religionists or "Calvinists." Protestants in France were inspired by the writings of John Calvin in the 1530s and the name Huguenots was already in use by the 1560s. By the end of the 17th century, roughly 200,000 Huguenots had been driven from France during a series of religious persecutions.
Hungary	Hungary officially the Republic of Hungary , is a landlocked country in Central Europe. It is situated in the Pannonian Basin and it is bordered by Slovakia to the north, Ukraine and Romania to the east, Serbia and Croatia to the south, Slovenia to the southwest and Austria to the west. The capital and largest city is Budapest.
Hussite	The Hussites were a Christian movement following the teachings of Czech reformer Jan Hus (c. 1369-1415), who became one of the forerunners of the Protestant Reformation. This predominantly religious movement was propelled by social issues and strengthened Czech national awareness. After the Council of Constance lured Jan Hus in with a letter of indemnity, and then the state put him to death on 6 July 1415, the Hussites fought a series of wars (1420-1434) for their religious and political cause.
Hussite Wars	The Hussite Wars, also called the Bohemian Wars involved the military actions against and amongst the followers of Jan Hus in Bohemia in the period 1419 to circa 1434. The Hussite Wars were arguably the first European war in which hand-held gunpowder weapons such as hand cannons (aka pistols) made a decisive contribution. The Hussite warriors were basically infantry, and their many defeats of larger armies with heavily armoured knights helped effect the infantry revolution. In the end, it was an inconclusive war.
Luxembourg	Luxembourg, officially the Grand Duchy of Luxembourg, is a landlocked country in western Europe, bordered by Belgium, France, and Germany. Luxembourg has a population of over half a million people in an area of approximately 2,586 square kilometres (999 sq mi). A representative democracy with a constitutional monarch, it is ruled by a grand duke.
Bulgaria	Bulgaria is a country in Southeast Europe. Bulgaria borders five other countries: Romania to the north (mostly along the Danube), Serbia and the Republic of Macedonia to the west, and Greece and Turkey to the south.

Chapter 2. RECOVERY AND REBIRTH: THE AGE OF THE RENAISSANCE

Chapter 2. RECOVERY AND REBIRTH: THE AGE OF THE RENAISSANCE

Heresy	Heresy is a controversial or novel change to a system of beliefs, especially a religion, that conflicts with established dogma. It is distinct from apostasy, which is the formal denunciation of one's religion, principles or cause, and blasphemy, which is irreverence toward religion. The founder or leader of a heretical movement is called a heresiarch, while individuals who espouse heresy or commit heresy, are known as heretics.
Lollardy	Lollardy was the political and religious movement of the Lollards from the mid-14th century to the English Reformation. The term Lollards refers to the followers of John Wycliffe, a prominent theologian who was dismissed from the University of Oxford in 1381 for criticism of the Church, especially his doctrine on the Eucharist. Its demands were primarily for reform of Western Christianity.
Orthodox Christianity	The term Orthodox Christianity may refer to - Eastern Orthodoxy: the Ancient communion of Eastern Christian Churches, historically of eastern Europe and parts of Asia, that recognize the Council of Chalcedon and the other of the first seven Ecumenical Councils. - Oriental Orthodoxy: the Miaphysite Eastern Christian churches adhering to the first three Ecumenical Councils and the 449 Council of Ephesus, and rejecting the Council of Chalcedon and the later councils that Eastern Orthodoxy classifies as ecumenical.
Reform	Reform is an evangelical organization within Anglicanism, active in the Church of England and the Church of Ireland. Reform describes itself as a "network of churches and individuals within the Church of England, committed to the reform of ourselves, our congregation and our world by the gospel". Several large Anglican churches in England are members of Reform, such as Jesmond Parish Church (in Newcastle upon Tyne), St Ebbe's, Oxford, and St Helen's Bishopsgate (located in the City of London).

Chapter 2. RECOVERY AND REBIRTH: THE AGE OF THE RENAISSANCE

Chapter 3. REFORMATION AND RELIGIOUS WARFARE IN THE SIXTEENTH CENTURY

Diet of Worms	The Diet of Worms 1521 was a diet that took place in the city of Worms in what is now Germany, and is most memorable for the Edict of Worms (Wormser Edikt), which addressed Martin Luther and the effects of the Protestant Reformation. It was conducted from 28 January to 25 May 1521, with Emperor Charles V presiding. Other Imperial diets at Worms were convened in the years 829, 926, 1076, 1122, 1495, and 1545. Unqualified mentions of a Diet of Worms usually refer to the 1521 assembly.
Martin Luther	Martin Luther was a German priest and professor of theology who initiated the Protestant Reformation. He strongly disputed the claim that freedom from God's punishment of sin could be purchased with money. He confronted indulgence salesman Johann Tetzel with his Ninety-Five Theses in 1517. His refusal to retract all of his writings at the demand of Pope Leo X in 1520 and the Holy Roman Emperor Charles V at the Diet of Worms in 1521 resulted in his excommunication by the pope and condemnation as an outlaw by the emperor.
Martin Luther	Martin Luther was a German priest and professor of theology who initiated the Protestant Reformation. He strongly disputed the claim that freedom from God's punishment of sin could be purchased with money. He confronted indulgence salesman Johann Tetzel with his Ninety-Five Theses in 1517. His refusal to retract all of his writings at the demand of Pope Leo X in 1520 and the Holy Roman Emperor Charles V at the Diet of Worms in 1521 resulted in his excommunication by the pope and condemnation as an outlaw by the emperor.
Brethren of the Common Life	The Brethren of the Common Life was a Roman Catholic pietist religious community founded in the 14th century by Gerard Groote, formerly a successful and worldly educator who had had a religious experience and preached a life of simple devotion to Jesus Christ. Without taking up irrevocable vows, the Brethren banded together in communities, giving up their worldly goods to live chaste and strictly regulated lives in common houses, devoting every waking hour to attending divine service, reading and preaching of sermons, labouring productively and taking meals in common that were accompanied by the reading aloud of Scripture: "judged from the ascetic discipline and intention of this life, it had few features which distinguished it from life in a monastery", observes Hans Baron. The Brethren and the Devotio Moderna

Chapter 3. REFORMATION AND RELIGIOUS WARFARE IN THE SIXTEENTH CENTURY

Chapter 3. REFORMATION AND RELIGIOUS WARFARE IN THE SIXTEENTH CENTURY

	The Brethren's confraternity is the best known fruits of the Devotio Moderna, the Modern Devotion.
Christian	A Christian is a person who adheres to Christianity, an Abrahamic, monotheistic religion based on the life and teachings of Jesus of Nazareth as recorded in the Canonical gospels and the letters of the New Testament.
	Central to the Christian faith is love or Agape. Christians also believe Jesus is the Messiah prophesied in the Hebrew Bible, the Son of God, and the savior of mankind from their sins.
Christian Church	The Christian Church is a Mainline Protestant denomination in North America. It is often referred to as The Christian Church, The Disciples of Christ, or more simply as The Disciples. The Christian Church was a charter participant in the formation of both the World Council of Churches and the Federal Council of Churches (now the National Council of Churches), and it continues to be engaged in ecumenical conversations.
	The Disciples' local churches are congregationally governed.
Christian humanism	Christian humanism is the belief that human freedom and individualism are intrinsic (natural) parts of, or are at least compatible with, Christian doctrine and practice. It is a philosophical union of Christian and humanist principles.
	Origins
	Christian humanism may have begun as early as the 2nd century, with the writings of St. Justin Martyr, an early theologian-apologist of the early Christian Church.

Chapter 3. REFORMATION AND RELIGIOUS WARFARE IN THE SIXTEENTH CENTURY

Chapter 3. REFORMATION AND RELIGIOUS WARFARE IN THE SIXTEENTH CENTURY

Common	The Common is a part of the Christian liturgy that consists of texts common to an entire category of saints, such as Apostles or Martyrs. The term is used in contrast to the ordinary, which is that part of the liturgy that is reasonably constant, or at least selected without regard to date, and to the proper, which is the part of the liturgy that varies according to the date, either representing an observance within the Liturgical Year, or of a particular saint or significant event. Commons contain collects, psalms, readings from Scripture, prefaces, and other portions of services that are common to a category of saints.
Desiderius	Desiderius was the last king of the Lombard Kingdom of northern Italy (died c. 786). He is chiefly known for his connection to Charlemagne, who married his daughter and conquered his realm. Rise to power Desiderius Romae was originally a royal officer, the dux Langobardorum et comes stabuli, "constable and duke of the Lombards," an office apparently similar to the contemporaneous Frankish office of dux Francorum.
Desiderius Erasmus	Desiderius Erasmus Roterodamus (October 28, 1466 - July 12, 1536), sometimes known as Desiderius Erasmus of Rotterdam, was a Dutch Renaissance humanist and a Catholic priest and theologian. His scholarly name Desiderius Erasmus Roterodamus comprises the following three elements: the Latin noun desiderium ; the Greek adjective ?ρ?σμιος (erásmios) meaning "desired", and, in the form Erasmus, also the name of a St. Erasmus of Formiae; and the Latinized adjectival form for the city of Rotterdam (Roterodamus = "of Rotterdam"). Erasmus was a classical scholar who wrote in a "pure" Latin style and enjoyed the sobriquet "Prince of the Humanists." He has been called "the crowning glory of the Christian humanists." Using humanist techniques for working on texts, he prepared important new Latin and Greek editions of the New Testament.

Chapter 3. REFORMATION AND RELIGIOUS WARFARE IN THE SIXTEENTH CENTURY

Chapter 3. REFORMATION AND RELIGIOUS WARFARE IN THE SIXTEENTH CENTURY

Handbook	The Handbook is a two-volume book of instructions and policies for leaders of The Church of Jesus Christ of Latter-day Saints (LDS Church). The books are prepared by the First Presidency and Quorum of the Twelve Apostles of the church. Along with the Church's standard works (i.e., its scriptural canon), the Handbook stands as the preeminent policy and practice guide for the leaders of the LDS Church.
Northern Renaissance	The Northern Renaissance is the term used to describe the Renaissance in northern Europe, or more broadly in Europe outside Italy. Before 1450 Italian Renaissance humanism had little influence outside Italy. From the late 15th century the ideas spread around Europe.
Renaissance	The Renaissance is a cultural movement that spanned roughly the 14th to the 17th century, beginning in Florence in the Late Middle Ages and later spreading to the rest of Europe. The term is also used more loosely to refer to the historic era, but since the changes of the Renaissance were not uniform across Europe, this is a general use of the term. As a cultural movement, it encompassed a resurgence of learning based on classical sources, the development of linear perspective in painting, and gradual but widespread educational reform.
Renaissance humanism	Renaissance humanism was an activity of cultural and educational reform engaged by scholars, writers, and civic leaders who are today known as humanists. It developed during the fourteenth and the beginning of the fifteenth centuries, and was a response to the challenge of Mediæval scholastic education, emphasising practical, pre-professional and -scientific studies. Scholasticism focused on preparing men to be doctors, lawyers or professional theologians, and was taught from approved textbooks in logic, natural philosophy, medicine, law and theology.
Church	A church building is a building or structure whose primary purpose is to facilitate the meeting of a church. Originally, Jewish Christians met in synagogues, such as the Cenacle, and in one another's homes, known as house churches. As Christianity grew and became more accepted by governments, notably with the Edict of Milan, rooms and, eventually, entire buildings were set aside for the explicit purpose of Christian worship, such as the Church of the Holy Sepulchre.

Chapter 3. REFORMATION AND RELIGIOUS WARFARE IN THE SIXTEENTH CENTURY

Chapter 3. REFORMATION AND RELIGIOUS WARFARE IN THE SIXTEENTH CENTURY

Humanism	Humanism is an approach in study, philosophy, or practice that focuses on human values and concerns. The term can mean several things, for example: 1. A cultural movement of the Italian Renaissance based on the study of classical works. 2. An approach to education that uses literary means or a focus on the humanities to inform students. 3. A variety of perspectives in philosophy and social science which affirm some notion of 'human nature' (by contrast with anti-humanism). 4. A secular ideology which espouses reason, ethics, and justice, whilst specifically rejecting supernatural and religious dogma as a basis of morality and decision-making. The last interpretation may be attributed to Secular Humanism as a specific humanistic life stance. Modern meanings of the word have therefore come to be associated with a rejection of appeals to the supernatural or to some higher authority.
England	"England" is a song written by Justin Hawkins from The Darkness(music) ' Chas Bayfield (lyrics) and released by him under the name British Whale and used as the unofficial World Cup single for the England National Team in 2006
Folly	Folly was a common allegorical figure in medieval morality plays and in allegorical artwork through the Renaissance. The depiction is generally of a young man, often similar in appearance to a jester or the tarot card, The Fool. In contrast to the many obvious classical allusions in such works, the depictions owe little to the Greek goddess Atë.
Henry	Henry is an English male given name and a surname, from the Old French Henry derived itself from the Germanic name Haimric, which was derived from the word elements haim, meaning "home" and ric, meaning "power, ruler". Harry, its English short form, was considered the "spoken form" of Henry in medieval England. Most English kings named Henry were called Harry.
Thomas More	Sir Thomas More, was an English lawyer, social philosopher, author, statesman and noted Renaissance humanist. He was an important counsellor to Henry VIII of England and for three years toward the end of his life he was Lord Chancellor. He is recognised as a saint within the Catholic Church and in the Anglican Communion.

Chapter 3. REFORMATION AND RELIGIOUS WARFARE IN THE SIXTEENTH CENTURY

Chapter 3. REFORMATION AND RELIGIOUS WARFARE IN THE SIXTEENTH CENTURY

Praise	Praise is the name of Knott's Berry Farm's annual Christian music festival held in Buena Park, California, USA. Each year, on New Year's Eve, the park invites a number of popular Christian bands and comedians to perform. The event is always named "Praise" and the year it will be at midnight (e.g. "Praise 2006"). At midnight, they also launch fireworks.
Vulgate	The Vulgate is a late 4th-century Latin version of the Bible, and largely the result of the labors of St. Jerome, who was commissioned by Pope Damasus I in 382 to make a revision of the old Latin translations. By the 13th century this revision had come to be called the versio vulgata, that is, the "commonly used translation", and ultimately it became the definitive and officially promulgated Latin version of the Bible in the Roman Catholic Church. Composition The Vulgate is a compound work whose constituent books varied across different regions and periods.
Franciscan	Most Franciscans are members of Roman Catholic religious orders founded by Saint Francis of Assisi. Besides Roman Catholic communities, there are also Old Catholic, Anglican, and ecumenical Franciscan communities. The most prominent group is the Order of Friars Minor, commonly called simply the "Franciscans." They seek to follow most directly the manner of life that Saint Francis led.
Indulgence	In Catholic theology, an indulgence is the full or partial remission of temporal punishment due for sins which have already been forgiven. The indulgence is granted by the Catholic Church after the sinner has confessed and received absolution. The belief is that indulgences draw on the Treasure House of Merit accumulated by Christ's superabundantly meritorious sacrifice on the cross and the virtues and penances of the saints.
Saxony	The Saxony is a breed of domestic duck originating in the Saxony region of Germany. History

Chapter 3. REFORMATION AND RELIGIOUS WARFARE IN THE SIXTEENTH CENTURY

Chapter 3. REFORMATION AND RELIGIOUS WARFARE IN THE SIXTEENTH CENTURY

It was initially bred by Albert Franz of Chemnitz in the 1930s, but almost all of his original stock was lost during World War II. He cross bred Rouen, German Pekin, and Blue Pomeranian ducks. Resuming his efforts, Franz's work resulted in the recognition of the Saxony by 1957. In 1984, David Holderread (who later developed his own breed, the Golden Cascade), imported some Saxony ducks to the US, and it was recognized by the American Poultry Association in 2000 by admittance in to the Standard of Perfection.

Conciliarism

Conciliarism, was a reform movement in the 14th, 15th and 16th century Roman Catholic Church which held that final authority in spiritual matters resided with the Roman Church as a corporation of Christians, embodied by a general church council, not with the pope. The movement emerged in response to the Avignon papacy; the popes were removed from Rome and subjected to pressures from the kings of France-- and the ensuing schism that inspired the summoning of the Council of Pisa (1409), the Council of Constance (1414-1418) and the Council of Basel (1431-1449). The eventual victor in the conflict was the institution of the Papacy, confirmed by the condemnation of conciliarism at the Fifth Lateran Council, 1512-17. The final gesture however, the doctrine of Papal Infallibility, was not promulgated until the First Vatican Council of 1870.

Johann Eck

Dr. Johann Maier von Eck (November 13, 1486 - February 13, 1543) was a German theologian and defender of Catholicism during the Protestant Reformation. It was Eck who argued that the beliefs of Martin Luther and Jan Hus were similar.

Johann Eck was born Johann Maier at Eck (later Egg, near Memmingen, c. 70 km miles south of Augsburg) in Swabia, and derived his additional surname from his birthplace, which he himself, after 1505, always modified into Eckius or Eccius, i.e. "of Eck." His father, Michael Maier, was a peasant and bailiff, or Amtmann, of the village.

Hussite

The Hussites were a Christian movement following the teachings of Czech reformer Jan Hus (c. 1369-1415), who became one of the forerunners of the Protestant Reformation. This predominantly religious movement was propelled by social issues and strengthened Czech national awareness.

Chapter 3. REFORMATION AND RELIGIOUS WARFARE IN THE SIXTEENTH CENTURY

Chapter 3. REFORMATION AND RELIGIOUS WARFARE IN THE SIXTEENTH CENTURY

	After the Council of Constance lured Jan Hus in with a letter of indemnity, and then the state put him to death on 6 July 1415, the Hussites fought a series of wars (1420-1434) for their religious and political cause.
Johann	Johann, typically a male given name, is the Germanized form of the originally Hebrew language name "Yohanan" (meaning "God is merciful"). It is a form of the Germanic given name "Johannes", which comes from Johan. The English language form is John.
Justification	In Christian theology, justification is God's act of declaring or making a sinner righteous before God. The concept of justification occurs in many books of both the Old Testament and New Testament. The extent, means, and scope of justification are areas of significant debate.
Leipzig Debate	The Leipzig Debate was a theological disputation originally between Andreas Karlstadt and Johann Eck. Eck, a staunch defender of Roman Catholic doctrine, had challenged Karlstadt to a public debate concerning the doctrines of free will and grace. The Leipzig Debate took place at Pleissenburg Castle (now the location of the city hall) in Leipzig, and lasted from June to July 1519.
These	- In the English language, these is plural of This. - In Etruscan mythology, These is a version of the Greek Theseus.
Wittenberg	Wittenberg, officially Lutherstadt Wittenberg, is a town in Germany in the Bundesland Saxony-Anhalt, on the river Elbe. It has a population of about 50,000.

Chapter 3. REFORMATION AND RELIGIOUS WARFARE IN THE SIXTEENTH CENTURY

Chapter 3. REFORMATION AND RELIGIOUS WARFARE IN THE SIXTEENTH CENTURY

The importance of Wittenberg historically was due to its seat of the Elector of Saxony, a dignity held by the dukes of Saxe-Wittenberg and also to its close connection with Martin Luther and the dawn of the Protestant Reformation; several of its buildings are associated with the events of this time.

Faith

"Faith" was a #1 song, written and performed by George Michael, released as a single on Columbia Records, from his 1987 Faith album. According to Billboard magazine, it was the top-selling single of the year in the United States in 1988.

Track listing

7": UK / Epic EMU 2

1. "Faith" 3:14
2. "Hand To Mouth" - 4:36

12": UK / Epic EMU T2

1. "Faith" - 3:14
2. "Faith" (Instrumental) - 3:08
3. "Hand to Mouth" - 4:36

Chapter 3. REFORMATION AND RELIGIOUS WARFARE IN THE SIXTEENTH CENTURY

Chapter 3. REFORMATION AND RELIGIOUS WARFARE IN THE SIXTEENTH CENTURY

U.S. CD single

1. "Faith" - 3:16
2. "Faith" (dance remix radio edit) - 4:54
3. "Faith" (album version) - 3:16
4. "Hand to Mouth" - 5:49

Mixes

1. Album version - 3:16
2. 7" version - 3:14
3. Instrumental - 3:08
4. Dance remix radio edit - 5:22

History

Having disbanded Wham! the previous year, there was a keen expectation for Michael's solo career and "Faith" would go on to become one of his most popular and enduring songs, as well as being the most simplistic in its production.

German	German is a South Slavic mythological being, recorded in the folklore of eastern Serbia and northern Bulgaria. He is a male spirit associated with bringing rain and hail. His influence on these precipitations can be positive, resulting with the amount of rain beneficial for agriculture, or negative, with a drought, downpours, or hail.
Lutheranism	Lutheranism is a major branch of Western Christianity that identifies with the theology of Martin Luther, a German reformer. Luther's efforts to reform the theology and practice of the church launched the Protestant Reformation. Beginning with the 95 Theses, Luther's writings disseminated internationally, spreading the ideas of the Reformation beyond the ability of governmental and churchly authorities to control it.
The New Church	The New Church is the name for a New religious movement developed from the writings of the Swedish scientist and theologian Emanuel Swedenborg (1688-1772). Swedenborg claimed to have received a new revelation from Jesus Christ through continuous heavenly visions which he experienced over a period of at least twenty-five years. In his writings, he predicted that the Lord would establish a "New Church" following the Church of traditional Christianity, which worships God in one person, Jesus Christ.

Chapter 3. REFORMATION AND RELIGIOUS WARFARE IN THE SIXTEENTH CENTURY

Chapter 3. REFORMATION AND RELIGIOUS WARFARE IN THE SIXTEENTH CENTURY

Huguenot	The Huguenots were members of the Protestant Reformed Church of France from the sixteenth to the seventeenth centuries. Since the seventeenth century, Huguenots have been commonly designated "French Protestants," the title being suggested by their German co-religionists or "Calvinists." Protestants in France were inspired by the writings of John Calvin in the 1530s and the name Huguenots was already in use by the 1560s. By the end of the 17th century, roughly 200,000 Huguenots had been driven from France during a series of religious persecutions.
Evangelicalism	Evangelicalism is a Protestant Christian movement which began in Great Britain in the 1730s. Its key commitments are: - The need for personal conversion - Actively expressing and sharing the gospel - A high regard for biblical authority, especially biblical inerrancy - An emphasis on teachings that proclaim the death and resurrection of Jesus. David Bebbington has termed these four distinctive aspects conversionism, activism, biblicism, and crucicentrism, noting, "Together they form a quadrilateral of priorities that is the basis of Evangelicalism." Usage The term evangelical has its etymological roots in the Greek word for "gospel" or "good news": ευαγγελιον (evangelion), from eu- "good" and angelion "message." In that sense, to be evangelical would mean to be a believer in the gospel, that is the message of Jesus Christ. By the English Middle Ages the term had been expanded to include not only the message, but also the New Testament which contained the message, as well as more specifically the four books of the Bible in which the life, death and resurrection of Jesus are portrayed.
Lazarus	Lazarus is a name found in two separate contexts in the New Testament. Lazarus of Bethany is the subject of a miracle recounted only in the Gospel of John, in which Jesus restores Lazarus to life after four days dead. Another Lazarus appears as a character in Jesus' parable of Lazarus and Dives, or Lazarus and the Rich Man, recorded in the Gospel of Luke.

Chapter 3. REFORMATION AND RELIGIOUS WARFARE IN THE SIXTEENTH CENTURY

Chapter 3. REFORMATION AND RELIGIOUS WARFARE IN THE SIXTEENTH CENTURY

Pontiff	A pontiff was, in Roman antiquity, a member of the principal college of priests (Collegium Pontificum). The term "pontiff" was later applied to any high or chief priest and, in ecclesiastical usage, to a bishop and more particularly to the Bishop of Rome, the Pope or "Roman Pontiff".
	Etymology
	The English term derives through Old French pontif from Latin pontifex, a word commonly held to come from the Latin root words pons (bridge) + facere (to do, to make), and so to have the literal meaning of "bridge-builder".
Testaments	Testaments is a collective term, used exclusively within Christianity, to describe both the Old Testament and the New Testament, of The Bible. The Church of Jesus Christ of Latter-day Saints uses this term to include the Book of Mormon as another volume of scripture which specifically testifies of Jesus Christ's divinity.
	Judaism uses only the term Hebrew Bible (for part of the "Old Testament" alone) because it does not accept the "New Testament" as scripture.
Africa	Africa is the world's second-largest and second most-populous continent, after Asia. At about 30.2 million km² (11.7 million sq mi) including adjacent islands, it covers 6% of the Earth's total surface area and 20.4% of the total land area. With 1.0 billion people in 61 territories, it accounts for about 14.72% of the world's human population.
Baptism	In Mormonism, baptism is recognized as the first of several ordinances (rituals) of the gospel.
	Overview
	Much of the theology of Mormon baptism was established during the early Latter Day Saint movement founded by Joseph Smith, Jr. According to this theology, baptism must be by submersion for the remission of sins (meaning that through baptism, past sins are forgiven), and occurs after one has shown faith and repentance.

Chapter 3. REFORMATION AND RELIGIOUS WARFARE IN THE SIXTEENTH CENTURY

Chapter 3. REFORMATION AND RELIGIOUS WARFARE IN THE SIXTEENTH CENTURY

Catholic	The word catholic comes from the Greek phrase καθ?λου (kath'holou), meaning "on the whole," "according to the whole" or "in general", and is a combination of the Greek words κατ? meaning "about" and ?λος meaning "whole". The word in English can mean either "including a wide variety of things; all-embracing" or "of the Roman Catholic faith." as "relating to the historic doctrine and practice of the Western Church." It was first used to describe the Christian Church in the early 2nd century to emphasize its universal scope. In the context of Christian ecclesiology, it has a rich history and several usages.
Germany	The Germany Pavilion is part of the World Showcase within Epcot at the Walt Disney World Resort. History The original design of the pavilion called for a boat ride along the Rhine river. It was to have focused on German folklore, in a similar manner to the Mexico and Norway rides.
House of Habsburg	The House of Habsburg, also found as Hapsburg, and also known as House of Austria was one of the most important aristocratic royal houses of Europe and is best known for being an origin of all of the formally elected Holy Roman Emperors between 1438 and 1740, as well as rulers of the Austrian Empire and Spanish Empire and several other countries. Originally from Switzerland, the dynasty first reigned in Austria, which they ruled for over six centuries. A series of dynastic marriages enabled the family to vastly expand its domains, to include Burgundy, Spain, Bohemia, Hungary, and other territories into the inheritance.
Protestantism	Protestantism is one of the three major divisions (Catholicism, Orthodoxy, and Protestantism) within Christianity. It is a movement that began in northern Europe in the early 16th century as a reaction against medieval Roman Catholic doctrines and practices.

Chapter 3. REFORMATION AND RELIGIOUS WARFARE IN THE SIXTEENTH CENTURY

Chapter 3. REFORMATION AND RELIGIOUS WARFARE IN THE SIXTEENTH CENTURY

	The doctrines of the various Protestant denominations and non-denominations vary, but most non-denominational doctrines include justification by grace through faith and not through works, known as Sola Fide, the priesthood of all believers, and the Bible as the ultimate authority in matters of faith and order, known as Sola Scriptura, which is Latin for 'by scripture alone'.
Transubstantiation	In Roman Catholic theology, transubstantiation means the change of the substance of host bread and sacramental wine into the substance of the Body and Blood (respectively) of Jesus in the Eucharist, while all that is accessible to the senses (accidents) remains as before.
	Some Greek Orthodox Church confessions of faith use the term "transubstantiation" (metousiosis), but most Orthodox Christian traditions play down the term itself, and the notions of "substance" and "accidents", while adhering to the holy mystery that bread and wine become the body and blood of Christ during Divine Liturgy. Other terms such as "trans-elementation" (μεταστοιχε?ωσις metastoicheiosis) and "re-ordination" (μεταρρ?θμισις metarrhythmisis) are more common among the Orthodox.
Francis	Francis is a French and English first name and a surname of Latin origin.
	Francis is a name that has many derivatives in most European languages. The female version of the name in English is Frances, and (less commonly) Francine.
Holy Roman Empire	The Holy Roman Empire (Holy Roman Empire; German: Heiliges Römisches Reich (HRR), Latin: Imperium Romanum Sacrum (IRS), Italian: Sacro Romano Impero (SRI)) was a realm that existed for about a millennium in Central Europe, ruled by a Holy Roman Emperor. Its character changed during the Middle Ages and the Early Modern period, when the power of the emperor gradually weakened in favour of the princes. In its last centuries, its character became quite close to a union of territories.

Chapter 3. REFORMATION AND RELIGIOUS WARFARE IN THE SIXTEENTH CENTURY

Chapter 3. REFORMATION AND RELIGIOUS WARFARE IN THE SIXTEENTH CENTURY

Peace of Augsburg	The Peace of Augsburg was a treaty between Charles V and the forces of the Schmalkaldic League, an alliance of Lutheran princes, on September 25, 1555, at the imperial city of Augsburg, now in present-day Bavaria, Germany.
	It officially ended the religious struggle between the two groups and made the legal division of Christendom permanent within the Holy Roman Empire. The Peace established the principle Cuius regio, eius religio, which allowed German princes to select either Lutheranism or Catholicism within the domains they controlled, ultimately reaffirming the independence they had over their states.
Diet of Augsburg	The Diet of Augsburg were the meetings of the Reichstag of the Holy Roman Empire in the German city of Augsburg. There were many such sessions, but the three meetings during the Reformation and the ensuing religious wars between the Catholic emperor Charles V and the Protestant Schmalkaldic League in the early 16th century are especially noteworthy.
	The session of 1530 attempted to calm rising tensions over Protestantism.
Hungary	Hungary officially the Republic of Hungary, is a landlocked country in Central Europe. It is situated in the Pannonian Basin and it is bordered by Slovakia to the north, Ukraine and Romania to the east, Serbia and Croatia to the south, Slovenia to the southwest and Austria to the west. The capital and largest city is Budapest.
Rhode	In Greek mythology, Rhode also known as Rhodos was the sea nymph or goddess of the island of Rhodes.

Chapter 3. REFORMATION AND RELIGIOUS WARFARE IN THE SIXTEENTH CENTURY

Chapter 3. REFORMATION AND RELIGIOUS WARFARE IN THE SIXTEENTH CENTURY

	Though she does not appear among the lists of nereids in Iliad XVIII or Bibliotheke 1.2.7, such an ancient island nymph in other contexts might gain any of various Olympian parentages: she was thought of as a daughter of Poseidon with any of several primordial sea-goddesses-- with whom she might be identified herself-- notably Halia or Amphitrite. Pindar even urges his hearers to "Praise the sea maid, daughter of Aphrodite, bride of Helios, this isle of Rhodes." "All three names-- Halia, Aphrodite, Amphitrite, and furthermore also Kapheira-- must have been applied to one and the same great goddess", Karl Kerenyi observes.
Schmalkaldic League	The Schmalkaldic League was a defensive alliance of Lutheran princes within the Holy Roman Empire during the mid-16th century. Although originally started for religious motives soon after the start of the Protestant Reformation, its members eventually intended for the League to replace the Holy Roman Empire as their source of political allegiance. While it was not the first alliance of its kind, unlike previous formations, such as the League of Torgau, the Schmalkaldic League had a substantial military to defend its political and religious interests.
National church	In Roman Catholicism, the term national church can refer to the church claiming pastoral oversight over a specific country , but more often to either a parish catering to immigrants from another nation, or to a church building in Rome dedicated to a specific country. Such national churches may hold church services and other activities in that nation's language, and/or following that nation's liturgies, which may be slightly different from the liturgy approved by the local episcopal conference.
Puritan	The Puritans were a significant grouping of English Protestants in the 16th and 17th centuries. Puritanism in this sense was founded by some Marian exiles from the clergy shortly after the accession of Elizabeth I of England in 1559, as an activist movement within the Church of England. The designation "Puritan" is often incorrectly used, notably based on the assumption that hedonism and puritanism are antonyms: historically, the word was used to characterize the Protestant group as extremists similar to the Cathari of France, and according to Thomas Fuller in his Church History dated back to 1564. Archbishop Matthew Parker of that time used it and "precisian" with the sense of stickler.
Anabaptist	Anabaptists (Greek ανα (again, twice) +βαπτιζω (baptize), thus "re-baptizers") are Christians of the Radical Reformation of 16th-century Europe, and their direct descendents, particularly the Amish, Brethren, Hutterites, and Mennonites.

Chapter 3. REFORMATION AND RELIGIOUS WARFARE IN THE SIXTEENTH CENTURY

Chapter 3. REFORMATION AND RELIGIOUS WARFARE IN THE SIXTEENTH CENTURY

	Anabaptists rejected conventional Christian practices such as wearing wedding rings, taking oaths, and participating in civil government. They adhered to a literal interpretation of the Sermon on the Mount and Believer's baptism.
Bubonic plague	Bubonic plague is a zoonotic disease, circulating mainly among small rodents and their fleas, and is one of three types of infections caused by Yersinia pestis (formerly known as Pasteurella pestis), which belongs to the family Enterobacteriaceae. Without treatment, the bubonic plague kills about two out of three infected humans within 4 days. The term bubonic plague is derived from the Greek word bubo, meaning "swollen gland".
Colloquy	A religious colloquy is a meeting to settle differences of doctrine or dogma, also called a colloquium (meeting, discussion), as in the historical Colloquy at Poissy, and like the legal colloquy, most often with a certain degree of judging involved. Religious colloquys are relatively common as a means to avoid calling full synods and avoiding out and out breaches leading to schisms. Colloquy may also be considered, the conversation of prayer with God.
Marburg Colloquy	The Marburg Colloquy was a meeting at Marburg Castle, Marburg, Hesse, Germany which attempted to solve a dispute between Martin Luther and Huldrych Zwingli over the Real Presence of Christ in the Lord's Supper. It took place between 1 October and 4 October 1529. The leading Protestant reformers of the time attended at the behest of Philipp I of Hessen. Philipp's primary motivation for this conference was political; he wished to unite the Protestant states in political alliance, and to this end, religious harmony was an important constituent.
Radical Reformation	The Radical Reformation was a 16th century response to what was believed to be both the corruption in the Roman Catholic Church and the expanding Magisterial Protestant movement led by Martin Luther and many others. Beginning in Germany and Switzerland, the Radical Reformation birthed many radical Protestant groups throughout Europe. The term covers both radical reformers like Thomas Müntzer, Andreas Karlstadt, groups like the Zwickau prophets and anabaptist groups like the Hutterites and the Mennonites.

Chapter 3. REFORMATION AND RELIGIOUS WARFARE IN THE SIXTEENTH CENTURY

Chapter 3. REFORMATION AND RELIGIOUS WARFARE IN THE SIXTEENTH CENTURY

Amish	The Amish , sometimes referred to as Amish Mennonites, are a group of Christian church fellowships that form a subgroup of the Mennonite churches. The Amish are known for simple living, plain dress, and reluctance to adopt many conveniences of modern technology. The history of the Amish church began with a schism in Switzerland within a group of Swiss and Alsatian Anabaptists in 1693 led by Jakob Ammann.
Anne Boleyn	Anne Boleyn was Queen of England from 1533 to 1536 as the second wife of Henry VIII of England and the 1st Marquess of Pembroke in her own right for herself and her descendants. Henry's marriage to Anne, and her subsequent execution, made her a key figure in the political and religious upheaval that was the start of the English Reformation. A commoner, Anne was the daughter of Thomas Boleyn, 1st Earl of Wiltshire and his wife, Lady Elizabeth Howard, and was educated in the Netherlands and France, largely as a maid of honour to Claude of France. She returned to England in early 1522, in order to marry her Irish cousin James Butler, 9th Earl of Ormond; however, the marriage plans ended in failure and she secured a post at court as maid of honour to Henry VIII's queen consort, Catherine of Aragon.
Brethren	Brethren is a name adopted by several Protestant Christian bodies which do not necessarily share historical roots. As classified in The Pilgrim Church by EH Broadbent, the earliest primitive churches to Paulician Brethren, to Bogomil Brethren, to Anabaptist and to Moravian Brethren were historical Brethren Movement. Anabaptist groups These groups grew out of the Anabaptist movement at the time of the Protestant Reformation (16th century).
Catherine of Aragon	Catherine of Aragon also known as Katherine or Katharine, was Queen of England as the first wife of King Henry VIII of England and Princess of Wales as the wife to Arthur, Prince of Wales. In 1507, she also held the position of Ambassador for the Spanish Court in England when her father found himself without one, becoming the first female ambassador in European history. For six months, she served as regent of England while Henry VIII was in France.

Chapter 3. REFORMATION AND RELIGIOUS WARFARE IN THE SIXTEENTH CENTURY

Chapter 3. REFORMATION AND RELIGIOUS WARFARE IN THE SIXTEENTH CENTURY

Catholic Church	The Catholic Church, is the world's largest Christian church. Headed by the Pope, it sees its mission as spreading the gospel of Christ, administering its sacraments and exercising charity.
	The Catholic Church is one of the oldest religious institutions in the world and has played a prominent role in the history of Western civilisation.
Jerusalem	Jerusalem is the title of a book written by Moses Mendelssohn, which was first published in 1783 - the same year, when the Prussian officer Christian Wilhelm von Dohm published the second part of his Mémoire Concerning the amelioration of the civil status of the Jews. Moses Mendelssohn was one of the key figures of Jewish Enlightenment (Haskalah) and his philosophical treatise, dealing with social contract and political theory (especially concerning the question of the separation between religion and state), can be regarded as his most important contribution to Haskalah. The book which was written in Prussia on the eve of the French Revolution, consisted of two parts and each one was paged separately.
Mennonite	The Mennonites are a group of Christian Anabaptist denominations named after the Frisian Menno Simons (1496-1561), who, through his writings, articulated and thereby formalized the teachings of earlier Swiss founders. The teachings of the Mennonites were founded on their belief in both the mission and ministry of Jesus Christ, which they held to with great conviction despite persecution by the various Roman Catholic and Protestant states. Rather than fight, the majority survived by fleeing to neighboring states where ruling families were tolerant of their radical belief in adult baptism.
Millenarianism	Millenarianism is the belief by a religious, social, or political group or movement in a coming major transformation of society, after which all things will be changed, based on a one-thousand-year cycle. The term spawns from the word "millennium", and is more generically used to refer to any belief centered around 1000 year intervals. Millenarianism is a concept/theme that exists in many cultures and religions.
New Jerusalem	In religion, New Jerusalem, Holy City, City of God, Celestial City and Heavenly Jerusalem in the Book of Revelation, as well as Jerusalem Above, Zion and shining city on a hill in other books of the Bible, is a city that is or will be the dwelling place of the Saints, interpreted as a physical reconstruction, spiritual restoration, or divine recreation of the city of Jerusalem. It is also interpreted by many Christian groups as referring to the Church.

Chapter 3. REFORMATION AND RELIGIOUS WARFARE IN THE SIXTEENTH CENTURY

Chapter 3. REFORMATION AND RELIGIOUS WARFARE IN THE SIXTEENTH CENTURY

	John of Patmos describes the New Jerusalem in the Book of Revelation in the Christian Bible, and so the New Jerusalem holds an important place in Christian eschatology and Christian mysticism, and has also influenced Christian philosophy and Christian theology.
Menno Simons	Menno Simons was an Anabaptist religious leader from the Friesland region of the Low Countries. Simons was a contemporary of the Protestant Reformers and his followers became known as Mennonites.
	Biography
	Early life
	Menno Simons was born in 1496 in Witmarsum, Friesland, Holy Roman Empire.
Swiss Brethren	The Swiss Brethren are a branch of Anabaptism that started in Zürich, spread to nearby cities and towns, and then was exported to neighboring countries. Today's Swiss Mennonite Conference can be traced to the Swiss Brethren.
	In 1525, Felix Manz, Conrad Grebel, George Blaurock and other radical evangelical reformers broke from Ulrich Zwingli and formed a new group because they felt reforms were not moving fast enough.
Thomas Wolsey	Thomas Wolsey was an English political figure and cardinal of the Roman Catholic Church. When Henry VIII became king of England in 1509, Wolsey became the King's almoner. Wolsey's affairs prospered and by 1514 he had become the controlling figure in virtually all matters of state and was extremely powerful within the Church.
State	The term state is used in various senses by Catholic theologians and spiritual writers.

Chapter 3. REFORMATION AND RELIGIOUS WARFARE IN THE SIXTEENTH CENTURY

Chapter 3. REFORMATION AND RELIGIOUS WARFARE IN THE SIXTEENTH CENTURY

	It may be taken to signify a profession or calling in life, as where St. Paul says, in I Corinthians 7:20: "Let every man abide in the same calling in which he was called". States are classified in the Catholic Church as the clerical state, the religious state, and the secular state; and among religious states, again, we have those of the contemplative, the active, and the mixed orders.
Anne of Cleves	Anne of Cleves aka Anne of Cleve (22 September 1515 - 16 July 1557) was a German noblewoman and the fourth wife of Henry VIII of England and as such she was Queen of England from 6 January 1540 to 9 July 1540. The marriage was never consummated, and she was not crowned queen consort. Following the annulment of their marriage, Anne was given a generous settlement by the King, and thereafter referred to as the King's Beloved Sister. She lived to see the coronation of Mary I of England, outlasting the rest of Henry's wives.
Book of Common Prayer	The Book of Common Prayer is the common title of a number of prayer books of the Church of England and of other Anglican churches, used throughout the Anglican Communion. The first book, published in 1549 (Church of England 1957), in the reign of Edward VI, was a product of the English Reformation following the break with Rome. Prayer books, unlike books of prayers, contain the words of structured (or liturgical) services of worship.
Church of England	The Church of England is the officially established Christian church in England and the Mother Church of the worldwide Anglican Communion. The Church of England separated from the Roman Catholic Church in 1534 with the Act of Supremacy and understands itself to be both Catholic and Reformed: - Catholic in that it views itself as a part of the universal church of Jesus Christ in unbroken continuity with the early apostolic church. This is expressed in its emphasis on the teachings of the early Church Fathers, as formalised in the Apostles', Nicene, and Athanasian creeds. - Reformed in that it has been shaped by the doctrinal principles of the 16th century Protestant Reformation, in particular in the Thirty-Nine Articles and the Book of Common Prayer. History Early history

Chapter 3. REFORMATION AND RELIGIOUS WARFARE IN THE SIXTEENTH CENTURY

Chapter 3. REFORMATION AND RELIGIOUS WARFARE IN THE SIXTEENTH CENTURY

	According to tradition, Christianity arrived in Britain in the first or 2nd century.
Thomas Cranmer	Thomas Cranmer was a leader of the English Reformation and Archbishop of Canterbury during the reigns of Henry VIII, Edward VI, and for a short time, Mary I. He helped build a favourable case for Henry's divorce from Catherine of Aragon which resulted in the separation of the English Church from union with the Holy See. Along with Thomas Cromwell, he supported the principle of Royal Supremacy, in which the king was considered sovereign over the Church within his realm.
Elizabeth	Elizabeth is a 1998 biographical film written by Michael Hirst, directed by Shekhar Kapur, and starring Cate Blanchett in the title role of Queen Elizabeth I of England, alongside Geoffrey Rush, Christopher Eccleston, Joseph Fiennes, Sir John Gielgud, Fanny Ardant and Richard Attenborough. Loosely based on the early years of Elizabeth's reign, in 2007, Blanchett reprised the role in the sequel, Elizabeth: The Golden Age, covering the later part of her reign. The film brought Australian actress Blanchett to international attention.
Heresy	Heresy is a controversial or novel change to a system of beliefs, especially a religion, that conflicts with established dogma. It is distinct from apostasy, which is the formal denunciation of one's religion, principles or cause, and blasphemy, which is irreverence toward religion. The founder or leader of a heretical movement is called a heresiarch, while individuals who espouse heresy or commit heresy, are known as heretics.
Catherine Parr	Catherine Parr was Queen consort of England and Ireland and the last of the six wives of King Henry VIII of England. She married Henry VIII on 12 July 1543. She was the fourth commoner Henry had taken as his consort, and outlived him. She was also the most-married English queen, as she had a total of four husbands. Catherine enjoyed a close relationship with Henry's three children and was personally involved in the education of Elizabeth and Edward, both of whom became English monarchs. She was influential in Henry's passing of the Third Succession Act in 1543 that restored both Lady Mary and Lady Elizabeth to the line of succession to the throne.

Chapter 3. REFORMATION AND RELIGIOUS WARFARE IN THE SIXTEENTH CENTURY

Chapter 3. REFORMATION AND RELIGIOUS WARFARE IN THE SIXTEENTH CENTURY

Calvinism	Calvinism is a theological system and an approach to the Christian life. The Reformed tradition was advanced by several theologians such as Martin Bucer, Heinrich Bullinger, Peter Martyr Vermigli, and Huldrych Zwingli, but this branch of Christianity bears the name of the French reformer John Calvin because of his prominent influence on it and because of his role in the confessional and ecclesiastical debates throughout the 16th century. Today, this term also refers to the doctrines and practices of the Reformed churches of which Calvin was an early leader.
Children	"Children" is a single by electronica composer Robert Miles from his album Dreamland. "Children" is Miles' most successful single, being certified Gold and Platinum in several countries and it reaching #1 in more than 12 countries. Miles created several remixes himself with an additional remix by Tilt.
The Fellowship	The Fellowship, is a U.S.-based religious and political organization founded in 1935 by Abraham Vereide. The stated purpose of the Fellowship is to provide a fellowship forum for decision makers to share in Bible studies, prayer meetings, worship experiences and to experience spiritual affirmation and support. The organization has been described as one of the most politically well-connected ministries in the United States.
Institutes of the Christian Religion	Institutes of the Christian Religion is John Calvin's seminal work on Protestant systematic theology. Highly influential in the Western world and still widely read by theological students today, it was published in Latin in 1536 and in his native French in 1541, with the definitive editions appearing in 1559 and in 1560. The book was written as an introductory textbook on the Protestant faith for those with some previous knowledge of theology and covered a broad range of theological topics from the doctrines of church and sacraments to justification by faith alone and Christian liberty.
Predestination	Predestination, in theology, is the doctrine that all events have been willed by God. John Calvin interpreted predestination to mean that God willed eternal damnation for some people and salvation for others. Explanations of predestination often seek to address the so-called "paradox of free will", that God's omniscience is incompatible with human free will.

Chapter 3. REFORMATION AND RELIGIOUS WARFARE IN THE SIXTEENTH CENTURY

Chapter 3. REFORMATION AND RELIGIOUS WARFARE IN THE SIXTEENTH CENTURY

Salvation	In religion, salvation is the concept that, as part of divine providence, a God, or gods, or power saves people from either or all of the following: 1. from biological death, by providing for them an eternal life or long-lasting afterlife (cf. afterlife). 2. from spiritual death, by providing divine law, illumination, and judgment. 3. Acceptance into heaven. The world's religions hold varying positions on the way to attain salvation and on what it means. The theological study of salvation is called soteriology.
Geneva	Geneva is a first name of Germanic origin, that means 'juniper tree'. It is usually used as a name for women.
John Knox	John Knox was a Scottish clergyman and a leader of the Protestant Reformation who is considered the founder of the Presbyterian denomination in Scotland. He was believed to have been educated at the University of St Andrews and worked as a notary-priest. Influenced by early church reformers such as George Wishart, he joined the movement to reform the Scottish church.
Netherlands	More than one name is used to refer to the Netherlands, both in English and in other languages. Some of these names refer to different, but overlapping geographical, linguistic and political areas of the country. This is a common source of confusion for outsiders.
Ordinance	Ordinance is a Protestant Christian term for baptism, communion and other religious rituals. Some Protestants, like the Mennonites, do not call them "sacraments" because they believe these rituals are outward expressions of faith, rather than impartations of God's grace. While a sacrament is seen as something in and of itself sacred, an ordinance is a practice that merely demonstrates the participants' faith.

Chapter 3. REFORMATION AND RELIGIOUS WARFARE IN THE SIXTEENTH CENTURY

Chapter 3. REFORMATION AND RELIGIOUS WARFARE IN THE SIXTEENTH CENTURY

Sacrament	A sacrament, as defined in Hexam's Concise Dictionary of Religion, is what Roman Catholics believe to be "a rite in which God is uniquely active." Augustine of Hippo defined a Christian sacrament as "a visible sign of an invisible reality." The Anglican Book of Common Prayer speaks of them as "an outward and visible sign of an inward and invisible Grace." Examples of sacraments are Baptism and the Eucharist." Therefore a sacrament is a religious symbol or often a rite which conveys divine grace, blessing, or sanctity upon the believer who participates in it, or a tangible symbol which represents an intangible reality. As defined above, an example would be baptism in water, representing (and conveying) the grace of the gift of the Holy Spirit, the Forgiveness of Sins, and membership into the Church. Anointing with holy anointing oil is another example which is often synonymous with receiving the Holy Spirit and salvation.
18th century	The 18th century lasted from 1701 to 1800 in the Gregorian calendar. However, Western historians have occasionally defined the 18th century otherwise for the purposes of their work. For example, the "short" 18th century may be defined as 1715-1789, denoting the period of time between the death of Louis XIV of France and the start of the French Revolution with an emphasis on directly interconnected events.
Rule of Saint Benedict	The Rule of Saint Benedict is a book of precepts written by St. Benedict of Nursia for monks living communally under the authority of an abbot. Since about the 7th century it has also been adopted by communities of women. During the 1500 years of its existence, it has become the leading guide in Western Christianity for monastic living in community.
Carmelites	The Order of the Brothers of Our Lady of Mount Carmel or Carmelites is a Catholic religious order perhaps founded in the 12th century on Mount Carmel, hence its name. However, historical records about its origin remain uncertain. Saint Bertold has traditionally been associated with the founding of the order, but few clear records of early Carmelite history have survived and this is likely to be a later extrapolation by hagiographers.
Francis of Assisi	Saint Francis of Assisi was a Catholic friar and preacher. He founded the Franciscan Order, assisted in founding the woman's Order of St. Clare, and the lay Third Order of Saint Francis. St. Francis is one of the most venerated religious figures in history.
Ignatius of Loyola	Ignatius of Loyola was a Spanish knight from a Basque noble family, hermit, priest since 1537, and theologian, who founded the Society of Jesus and was its first Superior General. Ignatius emerged as a religious leader during the Counter-Reformation. Loyola's devotion to the Church was characterized by unquestioning obedience to the Church's authority and hierarchy.

Chapter 3. REFORMATION AND RELIGIOUS WARFARE IN THE SIXTEENTH CENTURY

Chapter 3. REFORMATION AND RELIGIOUS WARFARE IN THE SIXTEENTH CENTURY

Papal bull	A Papal bull is a particular type of letters patent or charter issued by a pope. It is named after the bulla that was appended to the end in order to authenticate it.
	Papal bulls were originally issued by the pope for many kinds of communication of a public nature, but after the fifteenth century, only for the most formal or solemn of occasions.
Bull	The worship of the Sacred Bull throughout the ancient world is most familiar to the Western world in the biblical episode of the idol of the Golden Calf made by people left behind by Moses during visit to mountain peak and worshipped by the Hebrews in the wilderness of Sinai (Exodus). Marduk is the "bull of Utu". Shiva's steed is Nandi, the Bull.
Pope	The Pope (from Latin: papa; from Greek: π?ππας (pappas), a child's word for father) is the Bishop of Rome, a position that makes him the leader of the worldwide Catholic Church . The current office holder is Pope Benedict XVI, who was elected in a papal conclave on 19 April 2005.
	The office of the pope is known as the Papacy.
Matteo Ricci	Matteo Ricci, SJ was an Italian Jesuit priest, and one of the founding figures of the Jesuit China Mission, as it existed in the 17th-18th centuries. His current title is Servant of God.
	Early life
	Matteo Ricci was born in 1552 in Macerata, today a city in the Italian region of Marche and then part of the Papal States.
Roman Catholic	The term Roman Catholic is generally used on its own to refer to individuals, and in compound forms to refer to worship, parishes, festivals, etc. Its usage has varied, depending on circumstances. It is sometimes identified with one or other of the terms "Catholic", "Western Catholic", and "Roman-Rite Catholic".

Chapter 3. REFORMATION AND RELIGIOUS WARFARE IN THE SIXTEENTH CENTURY

Chapter 3. REFORMATION AND RELIGIOUS WARFARE IN THE SIXTEENTH CENTURY

French Wars of Religion	The French Wars of Religion is the name given to a period of civil infighting and military operations, primarily fought between French Catholics and Protestants (Huguenots). The conflict involved the factional disputes between the aristocratic houses of France, such as the House of Bourbon and House of Guise (Lorraine), and both sides received assistance from foreign sources.
	The exact number of wars and their respective dates are the subject of continued debate by historians; some assert that the Edict of Nantes in 1598 concludes the wars, although a resurgence of rebellious activity following this leads some to believe the Peace of Alais in 1629 is the actual conclusion.
Politique	Politique rulers cared more about citizens simply obeying the laws and not of what religion they were. In the political parlance of ancien régime France, a politique was a ruler who governed without letting his or her personal feelings get in the way of doing what was best for his country.
	The term was used during the sixteenth and seventeenth century Wars of Religion to describe moderates of both religious faiths (Huguenots and Catholics) who held that only the restoration of a strong monarchy could save France from total collapse.
Edict of Nantes	The Edict of Nantes, issued on April 13, 1598, by Henry IV of France, granted the Calvinist Protestants of France (also known as Huguenots) substantial rights in a nation still considered essentially Catholic. In the Edict Henry aimed primarily to promote civil unity. The Edict separated civil from religious unity, treated some Protestants for the first time as more than mere schismatics and heretics, and opened a path for secularism and tolerance.
World	WORLD Magazine is a biweekly Christian news magazine, published in the United States of America by God's World Publications, a non-profit 501(c)(3) organization based in Asheville, North Carolina. WORLD differs from most other news magazines in that its declared perspective is one of conservative evangelical Protestantism. Its mission statement is "To report, interpret, and illustrate the news in a timely, accurate, enjoyable, and arresting fashion from a perspective committed to the Bible as the inerrant Word of God."

Chapter 3. REFORMATION AND RELIGIOUS WARFARE IN THE SIXTEENTH CENTURY

Chapter 3. REFORMATION AND RELIGIOUS WARFARE IN THE SIXTEENTH CENTURY

Each issue features both U.S. and international news, cultural analysis, editorials and commentary, as well as book, music and movie reviews.

Flemish	In English usage, Flemish can refer to 1. Belgian Dutch , the national variety of the Dutch language as spoken in Belgium, be it standard (as used in schools, government and the media) or informal (as used in daily speech, "tussentaal "); Nevertheless, the use of the word Flemish to refer to the official language in Flanders is misleading. The only official language in Flanders is Dutch. 2. East Flemish, West Flemish and French Flemish are related southwestern dialects of Dutch. Etymology Flemish is derived from the name of the County of Flanders, from Middle Dutch vlamisch, vlemesch. Dutch in Flanders Dutch is the majority language in Belgium, being spoken natively by three-fifths of the population.
Luxembourg	Luxembourg, officially the Grand Duchy of Luxembourg, is a landlocked country in western Europe, bordered by Belgium, France, and Germany. Luxembourg has a population of over half a million people in an area of approximately 2,586 square kilometres (999 sq mi). A representative democracy with a constitutional monarch, it is ruled by a grand duke.
Pacification of Ghent	The Pacification of Ghent, signed on November 8, 1576, was an alliance of the provinces of the Habsburg Netherlands for the purpose of driving mutinying Spanish mercenary troops from the country, and at the same time a peace treaty with the rebelling provinces Holland and Zeeland.

Chapter 3. REFORMATION AND RELIGIOUS WARFARE IN THE SIXTEENTH CENTURY

Chapter 3. REFORMATION AND RELIGIOUS WARFARE IN THE SIXTEENTH CENTURY

	In 1567 king Philip II of Spain, the overlord of the Habsburg Netherlands, sent Fernando Álvarez de Toledo, 3rd Duke of Alba as governor general to the Netherlands with an army of Spanish mercenaries to restore order after the political upheavals of 1566 that culminated in the Iconoclastic fury of that year. He soon replaced the most important advisors of the former Regent Margaret of Parma by summarily executing them, such as the counts of Egmont and Hoorn, or by driving them into exile, such as William the Silent, the Prince of Orange.
Republic	Republic is a Hungarian rock band formed in Budapest in 1989. Their style is a unique mix of Western rock music and traditional Hungarian folk music. The band is popular in its native country and among Hungarian speaking minorities elsewhere. Members The two founding members are László Bódi and László Attila Nagy.
Geuzen	Geuzen was a name assumed by the confederacy of Calvinist Dutch nobles and other malcontents, who from 1566 opposed Spanish rule in the Netherlands. The most successful group of them operated at sea, and so were called Watergeuzen . In the Eighty Years' War, the Capture of Brielle by the Watergeuzen in 1572 provided the first foothold on land for the rebels, who would conquer the northern Netherlands and establish an independent Dutch Republic.
Union of Utrecht	The Union of Utrecht was a treaty signed on 23 January 1579 in Utrecht, the Netherlands, unifying the northern provinces of the Netherlands, until then under the control of Habsburg Spain. The Union of Utrecht is regarded as the foundation of the Republic of the Seven United Provinces, which was not recognized by the Spanish Empire until the Twelve Years' Truce in 1609.

Chapter 3. REFORMATION AND RELIGIOUS WARFARE IN THE SIXTEENTH CENTURY

Chapter 3. REFORMATION AND RELIGIOUS WARFARE IN THE SIXTEENTH CENTURY

Thirty-Nine Articles	The Thirty-Nine Articles of Religion were established in 1563 and are the historic defining statements of Anglican doctrine in relation to the controversies of the English Reformation; especially in the relation of Calvinist doctrine and Roman Catholic practices to the nascent Anglican doctrine of the evolving English Church. The name is commonly abbreviated as the Thirty-Nine Articles or the XXXIX Articles. The Church of England was searching out its doctrinal position in relation to the Roman Catholic Church and the continental Protestants.
Chinas	The Chinas are a people mentioned in ancient Indian literature from the first millennium BC, such as the Mahabharata, Laws of Manu, as well the Puranic literature. They are believed to have been Chinese. Etymology The name Cina is commonly believed to have been derived from either the Qin (Tsin or Chin) dynasty which rule in China from 221 BC or the earlier Qin state which later became the Qin dynasty.
Francis Drake	Francis Drake was an English antiquary and surgeon, best known as the author of an influential history of York, which he entitled Eboracum after the Roman name for the city. Early life Drake was born in Pontefract, where his father was vicar, and was baptised there on 22 January 1696. While still an adolescent, he was apprenticed to a York surgeon called Christopher Birbeck. Birbeck died in 1717, and, at the age of 21, Drake took over the practice.

Chapter 3. REFORMATION AND RELIGIOUS WARFARE IN THE SIXTEENTH CENTURY

Chapter 3. REFORMATION AND RELIGIOUS WARFARE IN THE SIXTEENTH CENTURY

Monism	Monism is any philosophical view which holds that there is unity in a given field of inquiry, where this is not to be expected. Thus, some philosophers may hold that the universe is really just one thing, despite its many appearances and diversities; or theology may support the view that there is one God, with many manifestations in different religions. Hinduism is considered to be the primary proponent of Monism.
Spanish Armada	The Spanish Armada was the Spanish fleet that sailed against England under the command of the Duke of Medina Sidonia in 1588, with the intention of overthrowing Elizabeth I of England to stop English involvement in the Spanish Netherlands and English privateering in the Atlantic. The fleet's mission was to sail to the Gravelines in Flanders and transport an army under the Duke of Parma across the Channel to England. The mission eventually failed due to early English attacks on the Armada, especially during the Battle of Gravelines, strategic errors by the Duke of Medina Sidonia, and bad weather.

Chapter 3. REFORMATION AND RELIGIOUS WARFARE IN THE SIXTEENTH CENTURY

Chapter 4. EUROPE AND THE WORLD: NEW ENCOUNTERS, 1500-1800

World	WORLD Magazine is a biweekly Christian news magazine, published in the United States of America by God's World Publications, a non-profit 501(c)(3) organization based in Asheville, North Carolina. WORLD differs from most other news magazines in that its declared perspective is one of conservative evangelical Protestantism. Its mission statement is "To report, interpret, and illustrate the news in a timely, accurate, enjoyable, and arresting fashion from a perspective committed to the Bible as the inerrant Word of God." Each issue features both U.S. and international news, cultural analysis, editorials and commentary, as well as book, music and movie reviews.
Exploration	Exploration is a simulation strategy game designed by Software 2000 in 1994.
Black Death	The Black Death was one of the most devastating pandemics in human history, peaking in Europe between 1348 and 1350. It is widely thought to have been an outbreak of plague caused by the bacterium Yersinia pestis, an argument supported by recent forensic research, although this view has been challenged by a number of scholars. Thought to have started in China, it travelled along the Silk Road and had reached the Crimea by 1346. From there, probably carried by Oriental rat fleas residing on the black rats that were regular passengers on merchant ships, it spread throughout the Mediterranean and Europe. The Black Death is estimated to have killed 30% - 60% of Europe's population, reducing the world's population from an estimated 450 million to between 350 and 375 million in 1400. This has been seen as having created a series of religious, social and economic upheavals, which had profound effects on the course of European history.
Catholic	The word catholic comes from the Greek phrase καθ?λου (kath'holou), meaning "on the whole," "according to the whole" or "in general", and is a combination of the Greek words κατ? meaning "about" and ?λος meaning "whole". The word in English can mean either "including a wide variety of things; all-embracing" or "of the Roman Catholic faith." as "relating to the historic doctrine and practice of the Western Church."

Chapter 4. EUROPE AND THE WORLD: NEW ENCOUNTERS, 1500-1800

Chapter 4. EUROPE AND THE WORLD: NEW ENCOUNTERS, 1500-1800

	It was first used to describe the Christian Church in the early 2nd century to emphasize its universal scope. In the context of Christian ecclesiology, it has a rich history and several usages.
Catholic Church	The Catholic Church, is the world's largest Christian church. Headed by the Pope, it sees its mission as spreading the gospel of Christ, administering its sacraments and exercising charity. The Catholic Church is one of the oldest religious institutions in the world and has played a prominent role in the history of Western civilisation.
Chinas	The Chinas are a people mentioned in ancient Indian literature from the first millennium BC, such as the Mahabharata, Laws of Manu, as well the Puranic literature. They are believed to have been Chinese. Etymology The name Cina is commonly believed to have been derived from either the Qin (Tsin or Chin) dynasty which rule in China from 221 BC or the earlier Qin state which later became the Qin dynasty.
Church	A church building is a building or structure whose primary purpose is to facilitate the meeting of a church. Originally, Jewish Christians met in synagogues, such as the Cenacle, and in one another's homes, known as house churches. As Christianity grew and became more accepted by governments, notably with the Edict of Milan, rooms and, eventually, entire buildings were set aside for the explicit purpose of Christian worship, such as the Church of the Holy Sepulchre.
John Mandeville	"Jehan de Mandeville", translated as "Sir John Mandeville", is the name claimed by the compiler of a singular book of supposed travels, written in Anglo-Norman French, and published between 1357 and 1371.

Chapter 4. EUROPE AND THE WORLD: NEW ENCOUNTERS, 1500-1800

By aid of translations into many other languages it acquired extraordinary popularity. Despite the extremely unreliable and often fantastical nature of the travels it describes, it was used as a work of reference -- Christopher Columbus, for example, was heavily influenced by both this work and Marco Polo's earlier Il Milione (Adams 53).

Prester John

The legends of Prester John were popular in Europe from the 12th through the 17th centuries, and told of a Christian patriarch and king said to rule over a Christian nation lost amidst the Muslims and pagans in the Orient. Written accounts of this kingdom are variegated collections of medieval popular fantasy. Prester John was reportedly a descendant of one of the Three Magi, said to be a generous ruler and a virtuous man, presiding over a realm full of riches and strange creatures, in which the Patriarch of the Saint Thomas Christians resided.

Republic

Republic is a Hungarian rock band formed in Budapest in 1989. Their style is a unique mix of Western rock music and traditional Hungarian folk music. The band is popular in its native country and among Hungarian speaking minorities elsewhere.

Members

The two founding members are László Bódi and Lászlo Attila Nagy.

Astrolabe

An astrolabe is a historical astronomical instrument used by astronomers, navigators, and astrologers. Its many uses include locating and predicting the positions of the Sun, Moon, planets, and stars; determining local time given local latitude and vice-versa; surveying; triangulation; and to cast horoscopes. They were used in Classical Antiquity and through the Islamic Golden Age and the European Middle Ages and Renaissance for all these purposes.

Claudius

Tiberius Claudius Caesar Augustus Germanicus (1 August 10 BC - 13 October AD 54), born Tiberius Claudius Drusus, then Tiberius Claudius Nero Germanicus until his accession, was Roman Emperor from 41 to 54 AD. A member of the Julio-Claudian dynasty, he was the son of Drusus and Antonia Minor. He was born at Lugdunum in Gaul and was the first emperor to be born outside Italy. Afflicted with a limp and slight deafness due to sickness at a young age, his family ostracized him and excluded him from public office until his consulship with his nephew Caligula in 37 AD. Claudius' infirmity probably saved him from the fate of many other nobles during the purges of Tiberius' and Caligula's reigns; potential enemies did not see him as a serious threat.

Chapter 4. EUROPE AND THE WORLD: NEW ENCOUNTERS, 1500-1800

Chapter 4. EUROPE AND THE WORLD: NEW ENCOUNTERS, 1500-1800

Conquistador	Conquistador is the term widely used to refer to the Spanish and Portuguese soldiers, explorers, and adventurers who brought much of the Americas under the control of Spain and Portugal in the 15th to 19th centuries following Europe's discovery of the New World by Christopher Columbus in 1492. The two perhaps most famous conquistadores were Hernán Cortés who conquered the Aztec Empire and Francisco Pizarro who led the conquest of the Incan Empire.
	The conquistadors in the Americas were more volunteer militia than an actual organized military. They had to supply their own materials, weapons and horses.
Henry	Henry is an English male given name and a surname, from the Old French Henry derived itself from the Germanic name Haimric, which was derived from the word elements haim, meaning "home" and ric, meaning "power, ruler". Harry, its English short form, was considered the "spoken form" of Henry in medieval England. Most English kings named Henry were called Harry.
Ptolemy	The name Ptolemy, which means warlike. There have been many people named Ptolemy or Ptolemaeus, the most famous of which are the Greek-Egyptian astronomer Claudius Ptolemaeus and the Macedonian founder and ruler of the Ptolemaic Kingdom in Egypt, Ptolemy I Soter. The following sections summarise the history of the name, some of the people named Ptolemy, and some of the other uses of this name.
State	The term state is used in various senses by Catholic theologians and spiritual writers.
	It may be taken to signify a profession or calling in life, as where St. Paul says, in I Corinthians 7:20: "Let every man abide in the same calling in which he was called". States are classified in the Catholic Church as the clerical state, the religious state, and the secular state; and among religious states, again, we have those of the contemplative, the active, and the mixed orders.
Africa	Africa is the world's second-largest and second most-populous continent, after Asia. At about 30.2 million km² (11.7 million sq mi) including adjacent islands, it covers 6% of the Earth's total surface area and 20.4% of the total land area. With 1.0 billion people in 61 territories, it accounts for about 14.72% of the world's human population.

Chapter 4. EUROPE AND THE WORLD: NEW ENCOUNTERS, 1500-1800

Chapter 4. EUROPE AND THE WORLD: NEW ENCOUNTERS, 1500-1800

Central Africa	Central Africa is a core region of the African continent which includes Burundi, the Central African Republic, Chad, the Democratic Republic of the Congo, and Rwanda.
	Middle Africa (as used by the United Nations when categorising geographic subregions) is an analogous term that includes Angola, Cameroon, the Central African Republic, Chad, the Republic of the Congo, the Democratic Republic of the Congo, Equatorial Guinea, Gabon, and São Tomé and Príncipe. All of the states in the UN subregion of Middle Africa, plus those otherwise commonly reckoned in central Africa comprise the Economic Community of Central African States (ECCAS).
Afonso de Albuquerque	Afonso de Albuquerque[p][n] was a Portuguese fidalgo, or nobleman, an admiral whose military and administrative activities as second governor of Portuguese India conquered and established the Portuguese colonial empire in the Indian Ocean. He is generally considered a world conquest military genius, given his successful strategy; he attempted to close all the Indian ocean naval passages to the Atlantic, Red Sea, Persian Gulf, and to the Pacific, transforming it into a Portuguese mare clausum established over the Turkish power and their Muslim and Hindu allies. He was responsible for building numerous fortresses to defend key strategic positions and establishing a net of diplomatic relations.
Lanka	Lanka is the name given in Hindu mythology to the island fortress capital of the legendary king Ravana in the great Hindu epics, the Ramayana and the Mahabharata. The fortress was situated on a plateau between three mountain peaks known as the Trikuta Mountains. The ancient capital city of Lanka is thought to have been burnt down by Lord Hanuman.
America	America is a Wild West-themed real-time strategy. It is set during the era after the American civil war. The player can choose to play Native Americans (Sioux tribe), Mexicans, Outlaws or Settlers.
Cuba	In ancient Roman religion, Cuba was a goddess of infants.
	Early Roman religion was concerned with the interlocking and complex interrelations between gods and humans. In this, the Romans maintained a large selection of divinities with unusually specific areas of authority.

Chapter 4. EUROPE AND THE WORLD: NEW ENCOUNTERS, 1500-1800

Chapter 4. EUROPE AND THE WORLD: NEW ENCOUNTERS, 1500-1800

England	"England" is a song written by Justin Hawkins from The Darkness(music) ' Chas Bayfield (lyrics) and released by him under the name British Whale and used as the unofficial World Cup single for the England National Team in 2006
The Bowman and The Spearman	The Bowman and The Spearman, are two bronze equestrian sculptures standing as gatekeepers at the intersection of Congress Drive and Michigan Avenue in Grant Park, Chicago, United States. The sculptures were made in Zagreb by Croatian sculptor Ivan Meštrovic and installed at the entrance of the parkway in 1928. The pair of sculptures was funded by the Benjamin Ferguson Fund. An unusual aspect of the sculptures is that the figures in both sculptures are missing their weapons, the bow and arrow and the spear.
Maria	The gens Maria was a plebeian family at Rome. Its most celebrated member was Gaius Marius, one of the greatest generals of antiquity, and seven times consul. Origin of the gens The nomen Marius appears to be derived from the Oscan praenomen Marius, in which case the family is probably of Sabine or Sabellic origin.

Chapter 4. EUROPE AND THE WORLD: NEW ENCOUNTERS, 1500-1800

Chapter 4. EUROPE AND THE WORLD: NEW ENCOUNTERS, 1500-1800

Nina

Nina is a feminine given name. It is a short form of names such as Antonina and Giannina. Nina may refer to:

People with the given name

- Nina , Spanish musical actress and singer
- Nina Agapova, Russian actress
- Nina Alexeyevna Lobkovskaya, Russian sniper
- Nina Alisova, Russian actress
- Nina Ananiashvili, Georgian Ballerina
- Nina Andreyeva, Soviet Communist Party Official
- Nina Anisimova (sportswoman), Russian athlete
- Nina Anisimova (dancer), Russian dancer and choreographer
- Nina Antonia, British music critic
- Nina Arsenault, Canadian sex worker
- Nina Arvesen, American actress
- Nina Åström, Finnish singer
- Nina Auerbach, American professor
- Nina Axelrod, American actress
- Nina Baden-Semper, British actress
- Nina Badric, Croatian singer
- Nina Bang, Danish Politician
- Nina Bari, Russian Mathematician
- Nina Barka , French-Ukrainian naïve artist
- Nina Barr Wheeler, American artist
- Nina Bates, Bosnian figure skater
- Nina Bawden, British author
- Nina Bendigkeit, German singer
- Nina Berberova, Russian author
- Nina Berman, American photographer
- Nina Björk, Swedish author
- Nina Blackwood, American Disk Jockey
- Nina Bocharova, Soviet gymnast
- Nina Bonner, Australian field hockey goalkeeper
- Nina Bott, German actress
- Nina Bouraoui, French author
- Nina Bracewell-Smith, British royal
- Nina Brosh, Israeli model
- Nina Burleigh, American journalist
- Nina Byers, American physicist
- Nina Byron, American silent film actress
- Nina Carter, English singer
- Nina Cassian (pen name of Renèe Annie Cassian), Romanian poet

Chapter 4. EUROPE AND THE WORLD: NEW ENCOUNTERS, 1500-1800

Chapter 4. EUROPE AND THE WORLD: NEW ENCOUNTERS, 1500-1800

Aztec	The Aztec people were certain ethnic groups of central Mexico, particularly those groups who spoke the Nahuatl language and who dominated large parts of Mesoamerica in the 14th, 15th and 16th centuries, a period referred to as the late post-classic period in Mesoamerican chronology.
	Aztec is the Nahuatl word for "people from Aztlan", a mythological place for the Nahuatl-speaking culture of the time, and later adopted as the word to define the Mexica people. Often the term "Aztec" refers exclusively to the Mexica people of Tenochtitlan (now the location of Mexico City), situated on an island in Lake Texcoco, who referred to themselves as Mexica Tenochca or Colhua-Mexica. Sometimes the term also includes the inhabitants of Tenochtitlan's two principal allied city-states, the Acolhuas of Texcoco and the Tepanecs of Tlacopan, who together with the Mexica formed the Aztec Triple Alliance which has also become known as the "Aztec Empire".
Aztec	The Aztec people were certain ethnic groups of central Mexico, particularly those groups who spoke the Nahuatl language and who dominated large parts of Mesoamerica in the 14th, 15th and 16th centuries, a period referred to as the late post-classic period in Mesoamerican chronology.
	Aztec is the Nahuatl word for "people from Aztlan", a mythological place for the Nahuatl-speaking culture of the time, and later adopted as the word to define the Mexica people. Often the term "Aztec" refers exclusively to the Mexica people of Tenochtitlan (now the location of Mexico City), situated on an island in Lake Texcoco, who referred to themselves as Mexica Tenochca or Colhua-Mexica. Sometimes the term also includes the inhabitants of Tenochtitlan's two principal allied city-states, the Acolhuas of Texcoco and the Tepanecs of Tlacopan, who together with the Mexica formed the Aztec Triple Alliance which has also become known as the "Aztec Empire".
Lake Texcoco	Lake Texcoco was a natural lake formation within the Valley of Mexico. The Aztecs built the city of Tenochtitlan on an island in the lake. The Spaniards built Mexico City over Tenochtitlan.

Chapter 4. EUROPE AND THE WORLD: NEW ENCOUNTERS, 1500-1800

Chapter 4. EUROPE AND THE WORLD: NEW ENCOUNTERS, 1500-1800

Tenochtitlan	Tenochtitlan was a Nahua altepetl (city-state) located on an island in Lake Texcoco, in the Valley of Mexico. Founded in 1325, it became the capital of the abounding Aztec Empire in the 15th century, until captured by the Spanish in 1521. When paired with Mexico the name is a reference to Mexica, the people of the surrounding Aztec heartland. It subsequently became a cabecera of the Viceroyalty of New Spain, and today the ruins of Tenochtitlan are located in the central part of Mexico City.
Quetzalcoatl	Quetzalcoatl is a Mesoamerican deity whose name comes from the Nahuatl language and has the meaning of "feathered-serpent".
	The worship of a feathered serpent deity is first documented in Teotihuacan in the Late Preclassic through the Early Classic period (400 BCE-600CE) of Mesoamerican chronology--"Teotihuacan arose as a new religious center in the Mexican Highland, around the time of Christ..."--whereafter it appears to have spread throughout Mesoamerica by the Late Classic (600-900 CE). In the Postclassic period (900 - 1519 CE) the worship of the feathered serpent deity was based in the primary Mexican religious center of Cholula.
Inca Empire	The Inca Empire, was the largest empire in pre-Columbian America. The administrative, political and military center of the empire was located in Cusco in modern-day Peru. The Inca civilization arose from the highlands of Peru sometime in the early 13th century. From 1438 to 1533, the Incas used a variety of methods, from conquest to peaceful assimilation, to incorporate a large portion of western South America, centered on the Andean mountain ranges, including large parts of modern Ecuador, Peru, western and south central Bolivia, northwest Argentina, north and north-central Chile, and southern Colombia into a state comparable to the historical empires of the Old World.
Pachacuti	Pachacuti Inca Yupanqui (or Pachacutec) was the ninth Sapa Inca (1438-1471/1472) of the Kingdom of Cusco, which he transformed into the empire Tawantinsuyu, or the Inca Empire. Most archaeologists now believe that the famous Inca site of Machu Picchu was built as an estate for Pachacuti.
	In Quechua, Pachakutiq means "He who shakes the Earth", and Yupanqui means "With honor".

Chapter 4. EUROPE AND THE WORLD: NEW ENCOUNTERS, 1500-1800

Chapter 4. EUROPE AND THE WORLD: NEW ENCOUNTERS, 1500-1800

Topa Inca Yupanqui	Topa Inca Yupanqui translated as "noble Inca accountant," was the tenth Sapa Inca (1471-93 CE) of the Inca Empire, and fifth of the Hanan dynasty. His father was Pachacuti, and his son was Huayna Capac. Topa Inca belonged to the Qhapaq panaca.

Description

His father appointed him to head the Inca army in 1463. He extended the realm northward along the Andes through modern Ecuador, and developed a special fondness for the city of Quito, which he rebuilt with architects from Cuzco. |
| Andes | The Andecavi (also Andicavi, and Andes in Julius Caesar's Bellum Gallicum), were a people of ancient and early medieval Armorica.

Geography

The territory of the Andecavi roughly corresponded with the diocese of Angers (Anjou) in the department Maine-et-Loire in present-day France. Although Caesar locates the Andes "near the Ocean," they held no coast and were located inland along the Loire river.

Role in Gallic Wars

In Book 3 of the Bellum Gallicum, Caesar says that the Andes provided winterquarters for Publius Crassus after his mission into Armorica, which brought several Gallic polities into relations with Rome. |
| Atahualpa | Atahualpa, Atahuallpa, Atabalipa, or Atawallpa (March 20, 1497 Caranqui, Ecuador - Cajamarca, July 26, 1533), was the last Sapa Inca or sovereign emperor of the Tahuantinsuyu, or the Inca Empire. Atahualpa was the offspring of Inca Huayna Capac and Ñusta Pacha, from the Dinasty Hanan Cuzco. The union was a politically expedient one, as the southern Ecuadorian Andes had been conquered by Inca Huayna Capac's father, Inca Túpac Inca Yupanqui some years earlier. |

Chapter 4. EUROPE AND THE WORLD: NEW ENCOUNTERS, 1500-1800

Chapter 4. EUROPE AND THE WORLD: NEW ENCOUNTERS, 1500-1800

Encomienda	The encomienda was a system that was employed mainly by the Spanish crown during the colonization of the Americas to regulate Native American labour. In the encomienda, the crown granted a person a specified number of natives for whom they were to take responsibility. The receiver of the grant was to protect the natives from warring tribes and to instruct them in the Spanish language and in the Catholic faith.
Encomienda	The encomienda was a system that was employed mainly by the Spanish crown during the colonization of the Americas to regulate Native American labour. In the encomienda, the crown granted a person a specified number of natives for whom they were to take responsibility. The receiver of the grant was to protect the natives from warring tribes and to instruct them in the Spanish language and in the Catholic faith
Friar	A friar is a member of one of the mendicant orders. Friars and monks Friars differ from monks in that they are called to live the evangelical counsels (vows of poverty, chastity and obedience) in service to a community, rather than through cloistered asceticism and devotion. Whereas monks live cloistered away from the world in a self-sufficient community, friars are supported by donations or other charitable support.
Inca	Inca is a 1992 computer game developed by Coktel Vision and published by Sierra On-Line. Gameplay

Chapter 4. EUROPE AND THE WORLD: NEW ENCOUNTERS, 1500-1800

Chapter 4. EUROPE AND THE WORLD: NEW ENCOUNTERS, 1500-1800

	Inca has been famous for combining many different genres to form a certain storyline. Although mostly a fighting space simulator, some levels were purely shooting, had maze exploration, and some included riddles that could be solved by combining inventory items.
Santo	Santo is a traditional New Mexican genre of religious sculpture. The word "santo" is also used to refer to individual works in this genre. Santos are carvings, either in wood or ivory, that depict saints, angels, or other religious figures.
The Bowman and The Spearman	The Bowman and The Spearman, are two bronze equestrian sculptures standing as gatekeepers at the intersection of Congress Drive and Michigan Avenue in Grant Park, Chicago, United States. The sculptures were made in Zagreb by Croatian sculptor Ivan Meštrovic and installed at the entrance of the parkway in 1928. The pair of sculptures was funded by the Benjamin Ferguson Fund.

An unusual aspect of the sculptures is that the figures in both sculptures are missing their weapons, the bow and arrow and the spear. |
| Inquisition | The term Inquisition can apply to any one of several institutions which fought against heretics (or other offenders against canon law) within the justice-system of the Roman Catholic Church. Although similar institutions existed within Calvinist and other Protestant churches, the term "Inquisition" is usually applied to that of the Catholic Church. It may also refer to:

- an ecclesiastical tribunal
- the institution of the Roman Catholic Church for combating heresy
- a number of historical expurgation movements against heresy (orchestrated by some groups/individuals within the Catholic Church or within a Catholic state)
- the trial of an individual accused of heresy.

Inquisition tribunals and institutions |

Chapter 4. EUROPE AND THE WORLD: NEW ENCOUNTERS, 1500-1800

Chapter 4. EUROPE AND THE WORLD: NEW ENCOUNTERS, 1500-1800

	Before the 12th century, the Roman Catholic Church already suppressed heresy, usually through a system of ecclesiastical proscription or imprisonment, but without using torture and seldom resorting to executions.
European colonization of the Americas	The start of the European colonization of the Americas is typically dated to 1492, although there was at least one earlier colonization effort. The first known Europeans to reach the Americas were the Vikings (Norse) during the 11th century, who established several colonies in Greenland and one short-lived settlement at L'Anse aux Meadows (51°N) in the area the Norse called Vinland, present day Newfoundland and to the south. Settlements in Greenland survived for several centuries, during which time the Greenland Norse and the Inuit people experienced mostly hostile contact. By the end of the 15th century, the Norse Greenland settlements had collapsed.
Boer	Boer is the Dutch and Afrikaans word for farmer, which came to denote the descendants of the Dutch-speaking settlers of the eastern Cape frontier in Southern Africa during the 18th century, as well as those who left the Cape Colony during the 19th century to settle in the Orange Free State, Transvaal (which are together known as the Boer Republics), and to a lesser extent Natal. Their primary motivations for leaving the Cape were to escape British rule and extract themselves from the constant border wars between the British imperial government and the native tribes on the eastern frontier. History Origin The Trekboere, as they were originally known, were mainly of Dutch origin and included Calvinists, Flemish and Frisian Calvinists, as well as French Huguenot and German and British protestants who first arrived in the Cape of Good Hope during the period of its administration (1652 - 1795) by the Dutch East India Company (Verenigde Oostindische Compagnie or VOC).
Brazil	Brazil, is a phantom island which features in many Irish myths. It was said to be cloaked in mist, except for one day each seven years, when it became visible but still could not be reached. It probably has similar roots to St. Brendan's Island.

Chapter 4. EUROPE AND THE WORLD: NEW ENCOUNTERS, 1500-1800

Chapter 4. EUROPE AND THE WORLD: NEW ENCOUNTERS, 1500-1800

Company	Company magazine is a monthly fashion, celebrity and lifestyle magazine published in the United Kingdom. It celebrated its 30th birthday in 2008 and in that time has had only six editors: Maggie Goodman, Gil Hudson, Mandi Norwood, Fiona Macintosh, Sam Baker, and the current editor Victoria White. The magazine is seen as the UK version of Seventeen Magazine but is more high fashion.
Middle Passage	The Middle Passage was the stage of the triangular trade in which millions of people from Africa were taken to the New World, as part of the Atlantic slave trade. Ships departed Europe for African markets with manufactured goods, which were traded for purchased or kidnapped Africans, who were transported across the Atlantic as slaves; the slaves were then sold or traded for raw materials, which would be transported back to Europe to complete the voyage. A single voyage on the Middle Passage was a large financial undertaking, and they were generally organized by companies or groups of investors rather than individuals.
Netherlands	More than one name is used to refer to the Netherlands, both in English and in other languages. Some of these names refer to different, but overlapping geographical, linguistic and political areas of the country. This is a common source of confusion for outsiders.
Atlantic slave trade	The Atlantic slave trade, refers to the trade in slaves that took place across the Atlantic ocean from the sixteenth through to the nineteenth centuries. The vast majority of slaves involved in the Atlantic trade were Africans from the central and western parts of the continent, who were sold by African slave dealers to European traders, who transported them to the colonies in North and South America. There, the slaves were made to labor on coffee, cocoa and cotton plantations, in gold and silver mines, in rice fields, the construction industry, timber, and shipping or in houses to work as servants. The shippers were, in order of scale, the Portuguese, the British, the French, the Spanish, the Dutch, and North Americans.
Paracelsus	Paracelsus was a Swiss Renaissance physician, botanist, alchemist, astrologer, and general occultist. "Paracelsus", meaning "equal to or greater than Celsus", refers to the Roman encyclopedist Aulus Cornelius Celsus from the 1st century, known for his tract on medicine. He is also credited for giving zinc its name, calling it zincum and is regarded as the first systematic botanist.

Chapter 4. EUROPE AND THE WORLD: NEW ENCOUNTERS, 1500-1800

Chapter 4. EUROPE AND THE WORLD: NEW ENCOUNTERS, 1500-1800

Citizenship	Citizenship is the state of being a citizen of a particular social, political, national, or human resource community. Citizenship status, under social contract theory, carries with it both rights and responsibilities. "Active citizenship" is the philosophy that citizens should work towards the betterment of their community through economic participation, public, volunteer work, and other such efforts to improve life for all citizens.
American Revolution	The American Revolution was the political upheaval during the last half of the 18th century in which thirteen colonies in North America joined together to break free from the British Empire, combining to become the United States of America. They first rejected the authority of the Parliament of Great Britain to govern them from overseas without representation, and then expelled all royal officials. By 1774 each colony had established a Provincial Congress, or an equivalent governmental institution, to form individual self-governing states. The British responded by sending combat troops to re-impose direct rule.
Asia	Asia, the wife of the Titan Iapetus, and mother of Atlas, Prometheus, Epimetheus and Menoetius. Hesiod gives the name as Clymene in his Theogony (359) but Apollodorus (1.8) gives instead the name Asia as does Lycophron (1411) It is possible that the name Asia became preferred over Hesiod's Clymene to avoid confusion with what must be a different Oceanid named Clymene who was mother of Phaethon by Helios in some accounts.
Human sacrifice	Human sacrifice is the act of killing one or more human beings as part of a religious ritual (ritual killing). Its typology closely parallels the various practices of ritual slaughter of animals (animal sacrifice) and of religious sacrifice in general. Human sacrifice has been practiced in various cultures throughout history.
Java	The Java is a dance developed in France in the early part of the 20th century. The origin of its name is uncertain, but it probably evolved from the mazurka. It was mainly performed in the bal-musette between 1910 and 1960 in France.
Western	Western is a Franco-Belgian one shot comic written by Jean Van Hamme, illustrated by Grzegorz Rosinski and published by Le Lombard in French and Cinebook in English. Story Volume

Chapter 4. EUROPE AND THE WORLD: NEW ENCOUNTERS, 1500-1800

Chapter 4. EUROPE AND THE WORLD: NEW ENCOUNTERS, 1500-1800

- Western - May 2001 ISBN 2-80361-662-9

Translations

Cinebook Ltd plans to publish Western in June 2011

Cambodia	"Cambodia" is the fourth single by British singer Kim Wilde. It was released at the end of 1981; a year in which Wilde had already scored three highly successful hit singles and a best-selling debut album.
	The single was another international success, topping the charts in France, Sweden and Switzerland and hitting the Top 10 in several other nations.
Akbar	Abu'l Fath Jalaluddin Muhammad Akbar also known as Shahanshah Akbar-e-Azam or Akbar the Great (15 October 1542 - 27 October 1605), was the third Mughal Emperor. He was of Timurid descent; the son of Emperor Humayun, and the grandson of the memorable Mughal Emperor Zaheeruddin Muhammad Babur, the ruler who founded the Mughal dynasty in India. At the end of his reign in 1605 the Mughal empire covered most of the northern and central India.
Black hole	A black hole is a region of space from which nothing, not even light, can escape. The theory of general relativity predicts that a sufficiently compact mass will deform spacetime to form a black hole. Around a black hole there is an undetectable surface called an event horizon that marks the point of no return.
Central Asia	Central Asia is a core region of the Asian continent from the Caspian Sea in the west, China in the east, Afghanistan in the south, and Russia in the north. It is also sometimes referred to as Middle Asia, and, colloquially, "the 'stans" (as the five countries generally considered to be within the region all have names ending with that suffix) and is within the scope of the wider Eurasian continent.
	Various definitions of its exact composition exist, and no one definition is universally accepted.

Chapter 4. EUROPE AND THE WORLD: NEW ENCOUNTERS, 1500-1800

Chapter 4. EUROPE AND THE WORLD: NEW ENCOUNTERS, 1500-1800

French India	French India is a general name for the former French possessions in India These included Pondichéry (now Puducherry), Karikal and Yanaon (now Yañam) on the Coromandel Coast, Mahé on the Malabar coast, and Chandannagar in Bengal. In addition there were lodges (loges) located at Machilipatnam, Kozhikode and Surat, but they were merely nominal remnants of French factories.
	The total area amounted to 526 km² (203 square miles), of which 293 km² (113 square miles) belonged to the territory of Pondichéry.
Genghis Khan	Genghis Khan, IPA: ; (probably May 31, 1162 - August 25, 1227), born Borjigin Temüjin pronunciation , was the founder, Khan (ruler) and Khagan (emperor) of the Mongol Empire, which became the largest contiguous empire in history after his death.
	He came to power by uniting many of the nomadic tribes of northeast Asia. After founding the Mongol Empire and being proclaimed "Genghis Khan", he started the Mongol invasions that would result in the conquest of most of Eurasia.
Heaven	Traditionally, Christianity has taught Heaven as a place of eternal life, and a kingdom to which all the elect will be admitted, rather than an abstract experience. In most forms of Christianity, belief in the afterlife is professed in the major Creeds, such as the Nicene Creed, which states: "We look for the resurrection of the dead, and the life of the world to come."

Chapter 4. EUROPE AND THE WORLD: NEW ENCOUNTERS, 1500-1800

Chapter 4. EUROPE AND THE WORLD: NEW ENCOUNTERS, 1500-1800

Some specific descriptions of this Kingdom as given in the canon of scripture include-- (this list is by no means comprehensive):

- Peaceful Conditions on a New Earth -- Is. 2:2-4, 9:7, 11:6-9, 27:13, 32:17-18, 33:20-21, 60:17-18, Ez. 34:25-28, 37:26, Zech 9:10, Matt. 5:3-5, Rev. 21
- Eternal Rule by a Messiah-King -- Ps. 72, Jer 31:33-34, Zech 2:10-11, 8:3, 14:9, Matt 16:27, Rev 21:3-4
  - an heir of David, Is. 9:6-7, 11:1-5
- Bodily perfection -- No hunger, thirst, death, or sickness; a pure language, etc. - Is. 1:25, 4:4, 33:24, 35:5-6, 49:10, 65:20-24, Jer. 31:12-13, Ez. 34:29, 36:29-30, Micah 4:6-7, Zeph. 3:9-19, Matt 13:43
- Ruined cities inhabited by people and flocks of sheep -- Is. 32:14, 61:4-5, Ez. 36:10,33-38, Amos 9:14

Early Christian writing

The earliest of the Apostolic Fathers Clement of Rome does not mention entry into heaven after death but instead expresses belief in resurrection after a period of "slumber" at the Second Coming.

Madra

Madra, Mada or Madraka is the name of an ancient region and its inhabitants, located in the north-west division of the ancient Indian sub-continent.

Uttaramadra division

Aitareya Brahmana makes first reference to the Madras as Uttaramadras i.e northern Madras and locates them in the trans-Himalayan region as neighbors to the Uttara Kurus. The Uttara Madras, like the Uttara Kurus, are stated to follow the republican constitution.

French Canada

French Canada, is a term to distinguish the French Canadian population of Canada from English Canada.

Chapter 4. EUROPE AND THE WORLD: NEW ENCOUNTERS, 1500-1800

Chapter 4. EUROPE AND THE WORLD: NEW ENCOUNTERS, 1500-1800

	Because it has represented different realities at different times, the term French Canada can be interpreted in different ways. Roughly chronologically they are:
	Canada, New France
	Canada, New France, was the historic homeland of the French Canadian people, the St. Lawrence River valley, in the time of New France.
Middle Ages	The Middle Ages is a historical period following the Iron Age, beginning in the 5th century and lasting to the 15th century, and preceded the Early Modern Era. In Europe, the period saw the large-scale European Migration and fall of the Western Roman Empire. In South Asia, the middle kingdoms of India were the classical period of the region.
Dahomey	Dahomey was a country in west Africa in what is now the Republic of Benin. The Kingdom of Dahomey was a powerful west African state that was founded in the seventeenth century and survived until 1894. From 1894 until 1960 Dahomey was a part of French West Africa. The independent Republic of Dahomey existed from 1960 to 1975. In 1975, the country was re-named "The People's Republic of Benin" after the Bight of Benin (not the unrelated historical Kingdom of Benin) since "Benin," unlike "Dahomey," was deemed politically neutral for all ethnic groups in the state.
	Economy and politics
	Dahomey's origins trace back to a group of Aja from the coastal kingdom of Allada who moved north and settled among the Fon people of the interior.
Franciscan	Most Franciscans are members of Roman Catholic religious orders founded by Saint Francis of Assisi. Besides Roman Catholic communities, there are also Old Catholic, Anglican, and ecumenical Franciscan communities.

Chapter 4. EUROPE AND THE WORLD: NEW ENCOUNTERS, 1500-1800

Chapter 4. EUROPE AND THE WORLD: NEW ENCOUNTERS, 1500-1800

	The most prominent group is the Order of Friars Minor, commonly called simply the "Franciscans." They seek to follow most directly the manner of life that Saint Francis led.
Mestizo	Mestizo is a term traditionally used in Latin America, the Philippines and Spain for people of mixed European and Native American heritage or descent. The term originated as a racial category in the Casta system that was in use during the Spanish empire's control of their American colonies; it was used to describe those who had one European-born parent and one who was member of an indigenous American population. In the Casta system mestizos had fewer rights than European born persons called "Peninsular", and "Criollos" who were persons born in the New World of two European-born parents, but more rights than "Indios" and "Negros".
Impact	Impact is a monthly magazine published in the United Kingdom. It covers the field of action entertainment: including Hong Kong action cinema, worldwide martial arts films, Hollywood productions, anime, comics, action films and East Asian cinema in general. Originally founded and edited by Bey Logan, it is presently edited by John Mosby, with Mike Leeder acting as Eastern Editor from the Hong Kong office, and Andrez Bergen as Tokyo Correspondent.
Matteo Ricci	Matteo Ricci, SJ was an Italian Jesuit priest, and one of the founding figures of the Jesuit China Mission, as it existed in the 17th-18th centuries. His current title is Servant of God. Early life Matteo Ricci was born in 1552 in Macerata, today a city in the Italian region of Marche and then part of the Papal States.
The Pentecostal Mission	The Pentecostal Mission or New Testament Church (NTC) formerly known as Ceylon Pentecostal Mission (CPM), is a pentecostal denomination which originated in Ceylon, now Sri Lanka. The international headquarters is now situated in Chennai, Tamil Nadu, India. It is one of the largest Pentecostal denominations.

Chapter 4. EUROPE AND THE WORLD: NEW ENCOUNTERS, 1500-1800

Chapter 4. EUROPE AND THE WORLD: NEW ENCOUNTERS, 1500-1800

Columbian Exchange	The Columbian Exchange was a dramatically widespread exchange of animals, plants, culture, human populations (including slaves), communicable diseases, and ideas between the Eastern and Western hemispheres (Old World and New World). It was one of the most significant events concerning ecology, agriculture, and culture in all of human history. Christopher Columbus' first voyage to the Americas in 1492 launched the era of large-scale contact between the Old and the New Worlds that resulted in this ecological revolution, hence the name "Columbian" Exchange.
Economy	In the Eastern Orthodox, the Greek Catholic Churches and in the teaching of the Church Fathers which undergirds the theology of those Churches, economy or oeconomy has several meanings. The basic meaning of the word is "handling" or "disposition" or "management" of a thing, usually assuming or implying good or prudent handling (as opposed to poor handling) of the matter at hand. In short, economia is discretionary deviation from the letter of the law in order to adhere to the spirit of the law and charity.
Napoleonic code	The Napoleonic Code -- or Code Napoléon (originally, the Code civil des Français) -- is the French civil code, established under Napoléon I in 1804. The code forbade privileges based on birth, allowed freedom of religion, and specified that government jobs go to the most qualified. It was drafted rapidly by a commission of four eminent jurists and entered into force on March 21, 1804. The Napoleonic Code was not the first legal code to be established in a European country with a civil legal system -- it was preceded by the Codex Maximilianeus bavaricus civilis (Bavaria, 1756), the Allgemeines Landrecht and the West Galician Code, (Galicia, then part of Austria, 1797). It was, however, the first modern legal code to be adopted with a pan-European scope and it strongly influenced the law of many of the countries formed during and after the Napoleonic Wars.
Scientific revolution	The Scientific Revolution was a period when new ideas in physics, astronomy, biology, human anatomy, chemistry, and other sciences led to a rejection of doctrines that had prevailed starting in Ancient Greece and continuing through the Middle Ages, and laid the foundation of modern science. According to most accounts, the scientific revolution began in Europe towards the end of the Renaissance era and continued through the late 18th century, the latter period known as The Enlightenment. It was sparked by the publication (1543) of two works that changed the course of science: Nicolaus Copernicus's De revolutionibus orbium coelestium (On the Revolutions of the Heavenly Spheres) and Andreas Vesalius's De humani corporis fabrica (On the Fabric of the Human body).

Chapter 4. EUROPE AND THE WORLD: NEW ENCOUNTERS, 1500-1800

Chapter 4. EUROPE AND THE WORLD: NEW ENCOUNTERS, 1500-1800

Antwerp	Antwerp is a city and municipality in Belgium and the capital of the Antwerp province in Flanders, one of Belgium's three regions. Antwerp's total population is 472,071 (as of 1 January 2008) and its total area is 204.51 km² (78.96 sq mi), giving a population density of 2,308 inhabitants per km². The metropolitan area, including the outer commuter zone, covers an area of 1,449 km² (559 sq mi) with a total of 1,190,769 inhabitants as of 1 January 2008. The nickname of inhabitants of Antwerp is Sinjoren, after the Spanish word señor, which means 'mister' or 'gent'.
Fugger	The Fugger family was a historically prominent group of European bankers, members of the fifteenth and sixteenth-century mercantile patriciate of Augsburg, international mercantile bankers, and venture capitalists like the Welser and the Höchstetter families. This banking family replaced the family known as the Medici who influenced all of Europe during the Renaissance. The Fuggers took over many of the Medici assets as well as their political power and influence.
Jacob	Jacob is a German/Italian/American movie from 1994, based on the novel Giacobbe by Francesco Maria Nappi, which is in turn based on the Bible story about Jacob. Plot Jacob defrauds his twin Brother Esau and hIollogas to flee. In Haran he gets to know his cousin Rachel, and falls in love with her.
Price revolution	Used generally to describe a series of economic events from the second half of the 15th century to the first half of the 17th, the price revolution refers most specifically to the relatively high rate of inflation that characterized the period across Western Europe, with prices on average rising perhaps sixfold over 150 years. It was once thought that this high inflation was caused by the large influx of gold and silver from the Spanish treasure fleet from the New World, especially the silver of Bolivia and Mexico which began to be mined in large quantities from 1545. According to this theory, too many people with too much money chased too few goods.

Chapter 4. EUROPE AND THE WORLD: NEW ENCOUNTERS, 1500-1800

Chapter 4. EUROPE AND THE WORLD: NEW ENCOUNTERS, 1500-1800

The start of the price rises actually predated the large-scale influx of bullion from across the Atlantic, reflecting in part a quintupling of silver production in central Europe in 1460-1530: though this output fell by two-thirds by the 1610s, it was significant in fueling the early stages of inflation that undermined a price regime in place since the previous upsurge in silver production in 1170-1320.

Chapter 5. STATE BUILDING AND THE SEARCH FOR ORDER IN THE SEVENTEENTH CENTURY

Court	The court of a monarch, or at some periods an important nobleman, is a term for the extended household and all those who regularly attended on the ruler or central figure. In the largest courts many thousands of individuals comprised the court, many officials or servants in the permanent employ of the ruler, and others attending in hope of political or financial gain, or merely for the society and entertainments offered. As well as being the centre of political life, courts were usually the drivers of fashion, and often where literary, musical and artistic trends first developed.
Elder	An Elder in the Methodist Church -- sometimes called a Presbyter or Minister -- is someone who has been ordained by a Bishop to the ministry of Word, Sacrament, Order, and Service. Their responsibilities are to preach and teach, preside at the celebration of the sacraments, administer the Church through pastoral guidance, and lead the congregations under their care in service ministry to the world. The Book of Discipline of the United Methodist Church states that The office of Elder, then, is what most people tend to think of as the pastoral, priestly, clergy office within the church.
Secularism	Secularism is the concept that government or other entities should exist separately from religion and/or religious beliefs. In one sense, secularism may assert the right to be free from religious rule and teachings, and the right to freedom from governmental imposition of religion upon the people within a state that is neutral on matters of belief. In another sense, it refers to the view that human activities and decisions, especially political ones, should be based on evidence and fact unbiased by religious influence.
Western	Western is a Franco-Belgian one shot comic written by Jean Van Hamme, illustrated by Grzegorz Rosinski and published by Le Lombard in French and Cinebook in English. Story Volume

Chapter 5. STATE BUILDING AND THE SEARCH FOR ORDER IN THE SEVENTEENTH CENTURY

Chapter 5. STATE BUILDING AND THE SEARCH FOR ORDER IN THE SEVENTEENTH CENTURY

- Western - May 2001 ISBN 2-80361-662-9

Translations

Cinebook Ltd plans to publish Western in June 2011

Central Europe	Central Europe is an area of the European continent lying between the variously defined areas of Eastern and Western Europe. The term is becoming widespread just like the interest in the region itself after the end of the Cold War, which, along with the Iron Curtain, had divided Europe politically into East and West, splitting Europe in half. Central European journals are published.
Black Death	The Black Death was one of the most devastating pandemics in human history, peaking in Europe between 1348 and 1350. It is widely thought to have been an outbreak of plague caused by the bacterium Yersinia pestis, an argument supported by recent forensic research, although this view has been challenged by a number of scholars. Thought to have started in China, it travelled along the Silk Road and had reached the Crimea by 1346. From there, probably carried by Oriental rat fleas residing on the black rats that were regular passengers on merchant ships, it spread throughout the Mediterranean and Europe. The Black Death is estimated to have killed 30% - 60% of Europe's population, reducing the world's population from an estimated 450 million to between 350 and 375 million in 1400. This has been seen as having created a series of religious, social and economic upheavals, which had profound effects on the course of European history.
Economy	In the Eastern Orthodox, the Greek Catholic Churches and in the teaching of the Church Fathers which undergirds the theology of those Churches, economy or oeconomy has several meanings. The basic meaning of the word is "handling" or "disposition" or "management" of a thing, usually assuming or implying good or prudent handling (as opposed to poor handling) of the matter at hand. In short, economia is discretionary deviation from the letter of the law in order to adhere to the spirit of the law and charity.

Chapter 5. STATE BUILDING AND THE SEARCH FOR ORDER IN THE SEVENTEENTH CENTURY

Chapter 5. STATE BUILDING AND THE SEARCH FOR ORDER IN THE SEVENTEENTH CENTURY

Little Ice Age	The Little Ice Age was a period of cooling that occurred after the Medieval Warm Period. While not a true ice age, the term was introduced into scientific literature by François E. Matthes in 1939. It is conventionally defined as a period extending from the 16th to the 19th centuries, though climatologists and historians working with local records no longer expect to agree on either the start or end dates of this period, which varied according to local conditions. NASA defines the term as a cold period between 1550 AD and 1850 AD and notes three particularly cold intervals: one beginning about 1650, another about 1770, and the last in 1850, each separated by intervals of slight warming.
Bohemian	A Bohemian is a resident of the former Kingdom of Bohemia, either in a narrow sense as the region of Bohemia proper or in a wider meaning as the whole country, now known as the Czech Republic. The word "Bohemian" used to denote the Czech people as well as the Czech language before the word "Czech" became prevalent in English. The word "Bohemian" was never used by the local Czech (Slavic) population.
Catholic	The word catholic comes from the Greek phrase καθ?λου (kath'holou), meaning "on the whole," "according to the whole" or "in general", and is a combination of the Greek words κατ? meaning "about" and ?λος meaning "whole". The word in English can mean either "including a wide variety of things; all-embracing" or "of the Roman Catholic faith." as "relating to the historic doctrine and practice of the Western Church."
	It was first used to describe the Christian Church in the early 2nd century to emphasize its universal scope. In the context of Christian ecclesiology, it has a rich history and several usages.
Catholic Church	The Catholic Church, is the world's largest Christian church. Headed by the Pope, it sees its mission as spreading the gospel of Christ, administering its sacraments and exercising charity.
	The Catholic Church is one of the oldest religious institutions in the world and has played a prominent role in the history of Western civilisation.

Chapter 5. STATE BUILDING AND THE SEARCH FOR ORDER IN THE SEVENTEENTH CENTURY

Chapter 5. STATE BUILDING AND THE SEARCH FOR ORDER IN THE SEVENTEENTH CENTURY

Catholic League	The Catholic League for Religious and Civil Rights, often shortened to The Catholic League, is an American Catholic anti-defamation and civil rights organization. Describing itself as "the nation's largest Catholic civil rights organization," the Catholic League states that it "defends the right of Catholics - lay and clergy alike - to participate in American public life without defamation or discrimination." The Catholic League states that it is "motivated by the letter and the spirit of the First Amendment ... to safeguard both the religious freedom rights and the free speech rights of Catholics whenever and wherever they are threatened." Founded in 1973 by the late Father Virgil C. Blum, S.J., the Catholic League is known for press release statements about what they view as anti-Catholic and anti-Christian themes in mass media. Its current president and main public face is William A. Donohue.
Church	A church building is a building or structure whose primary purpose is to facilitate the meeting of a church. Originally, Jewish Christians met in synagogues, such as the Cenacle, and in one another's homes, known as house churches. As Christianity grew and became more accepted by governments, notably with the Edict of Milan, rooms and, eventually, entire buildings were set aside for the explicit purpose of Christian worship, such as the Church of the Holy Sepulchre.
German	German is a South Slavic mythological being, recorded in the folklore of eastern Serbia and northern Bulgaria. He is a male spirit associated with bringing rain and hail. His influence on these precipitations can be positive, resulting with the amount of rain beneficial for agriculture, or negative, with a drought, downpours, or hail.
Peace of Augsburg	The Peace of Augsburg was a treaty between Charles V and the forces of the Schmalkaldic League, an alliance of Lutheran princes, on September 25, 1555, at the imperial city of Augsburg, now in present-day Bavaria, Germany. It officially ended the religious struggle between the two groups and made the legal division of Christendom permanent within the Holy Roman Empire. The Peace established the principle Cuius regio, eius religio, which allowed German princes to select either Lutheranism or Catholicism within the domains they controlled, ultimately reaffirming the independence they had over their states.

Chapter 5. STATE BUILDING AND THE SEARCH FOR ORDER IN THE SEVENTEENTH CENTURY

Chapter 5. STATE BUILDING AND THE SEARCH FOR ORDER IN THE SEVENTEENTH CENTURY

Reformation in Switzerland	The Protestant Reformation in Switzerland was promoted initially by Huldrych Zwingli, who gained the support of the magistrate (Mark Reust) and population of Zürich in the 1520s. It led to significant changes in civil life and state matters in Zürich and spread to several other cantons of the Old Swiss Confederacy. Seven cantons remained Roman Catholic, though, which led to inter-cantonal wars known as the Wars of Kappel.
State	The term state is used in various senses by Catholic theologians and spiritual writers. It may be taken to signify a profession or calling in life, as where St. Paul says, in I Corinthians 7:20: "Let every man abide in the same calling in which he was called". States are classified in the Catholic Church as the clerical state, the religious state, and the secular state; and among religious states, again, we have those of the contemplative, the active, and the mixed orders.
Baltic region	The terms Baltic region, Baltic Rim countries, and Baltic Rim refer to slightly different combinations of countries in the general area surrounding the Baltic Sea. Etymology The first to name it the Baltic Sea ("Mare Balticum") was eleventh century German chronicler Adam of Bremen. Denotation

Chapter 5. STATE BUILDING AND THE SEARCH FOR ORDER IN THE SEVENTEENTH CENTURY

Chapter 5. STATE BUILDING AND THE SEARCH FOR ORDER IN THE SEVENTEENTH CENTURY

Depending on the context the Baltic region might stand for:

- The countries that have shorelines along the Baltic Sea: Denmark, Estonia, Latvia, Finland, Germany, Lithuania, Poland, Russia, and Sweden.

- The group of countries presently referred to by the short-hand Baltic states: Estonia, Latvia, and Lithuania, sometimes in addition the Russian Kaliningrad exclave.

- Historic East Prussia and the historical lands of Livonia, Courland and Estonia.

- The former Baltic province of Imperial Russia: Today's Estonia, Latvia, Lithuania.

- The countries on the historical British trade route through the Baltic Sea, i.e. including the Scandinavian Peninsula (Sweden and Norway).

- The Council of the Baltic Sea States, comprised by the countries with shorelines along the Baltic Sea, in addition to Norway, Iceland and the rest of European Union.

- The islands of the Euroregion B7 Baltic Seven Islands, which includes the islands and archipelagos Åland (autonomous), Bornholm (Denmark), Gotland (Sweden), Hiiumaa (Estonia), Öland (Sweden), Rügen, and Saaremaa (Estonia).

- On historic Scandinavian and German maps, the Balticum sometimes includes only the historically or culturally German-dominated lands, or provinces, of Estonia, Livonia, Courland and Latgale (corresponding to modern Estonia and Latvia), as well as sometimes Pommerania and East Prussia, while the historically less-Germanized Lithuania is occasionally excluded.

Christian	A Christian is a person who adheres to Christianity, an Abrahamic, monotheistic religion based on the life and teachings of Jesus of Nazareth as recorded in the Canonical gospels and the letters of the New Testament. Central to the Christian faith is love or Agape. Christians also believe Jesus is the Messiah prophesied in the Hebrew Bible, the Son of God, and the savior of mankind from their sins.

Chapter 5. STATE BUILDING AND THE SEARCH FOR ORDER IN THE SEVENTEENTH CENTURY

Chapter 5. STATE BUILDING AND THE SEARCH FOR ORDER IN THE SEVENTEENTH CENTURY

Danish	Danish pastry is a sweet pastry which has become a specialty of Denmark and the neighbouring Scandinavian countries and is popular throughout the industrialized world, although the form it takes can differ significantly from country to country. They are referred to as facturas in some Spanish speaking countries. Danish pastry is, like the croissant, said to originate from Vienna and is called wienerbrød (Danish pronunciation: ['?i??n??b?œ??ð], lit.
Alsace	Alsace is the fourth-smallest of the 26 regions of France in land area (8,280 km²), and the smallest in metropolitan France. It is also the sixth-most densely populated region in France and third most densely populated region in metropolitan France, with ca. 220 inhabitants per km² (total population in 2006: 1,815,488; January 1, 2008 estimate: 1,836,000). Alsace is located on France's eastern border and on the west bank of the upper Rhine adjacent to Germany and Switzerland.
Germany	The Germany Pavilion is part of the World Showcase within Epcot at the Walt Disney World Resort. History The original design of the pavilion called for a boat ride along the Rhine river. It was to have focused on German folklore, in a similar manner to the Mexico and Norway rides.
NOMAD	NOMAD was founded in 2002 as an independent formation and registered as association in 2006. It targets to produce and experiment new patterns in the digital art sphere by using various lenses of other disciplines. The core of the formation consists of designers, engineers, architects, curators and writers. The infrastructure is based on technical and theoretical levels to provide collaborations with affiliations of artists.
Peace of Westphalia	The term Peace of Westphalia denotes a series of peace treaties signed between May and October of 1648 in Osnabrück and Münster. These treaties ended the Thirty Years' War (1618-1648) in the Holy Roman Empire, and the Eighty Years' War (1568-1648) between Spain and the Dutch Republic.

Chapter 5. STATE BUILDING AND THE SEARCH FOR ORDER IN THE SEVENTEENTH CENTURY

Chapter 5. STATE BUILDING AND THE SEARCH FOR ORDER IN THE SEVENTEENTH CENTURY

	The Peace of Westphalia treaties involved the Holy Roman Emperor, Ferdinand III of the House of Habsburg, the Kingdoms of Spain, France, Sweden, the Dutch Republic, the Princes of the Holy Roman Empire, and sovereigns of the Free imperial cities and can be denoted by two major events.
Treaty of the Pyrenees	The Treaty of the Pyrenees was signed to end the 1635 to 1659 war between France and Spain, a war that was initially a part of the wider Thirty Years' War. It was signed on Pheasant Island, a river island on the border between the two countries. The kings Louis XIV of France and Philip IV of Spain were represented by their chief ministers, Cardinal Mazarin and Don Luis de Haro, respectively.
Restitution	Restitution in moral theology signifies an act of commutative justice by which exact reparation as far as possible is made for an injury that has been done to another.
Rococo	Rococo also referred to as "Late Baroque" is an 18th century style which developed as Baroque artists gave up their symmetry and became increasingly ornate, florid, and playful. Rococo rooms were designed as total works of art with elegant and ornate furniture, small sculptures, ornamental mirrors, and tapestry complementing architecture, reliefs, and wall paintings. It was largely supplanted by the Neoclassic style.
Russians	The Russian people are an ethnic group of the East Slavic peoples, primarily living in Russia and neighboring countries. The English term Russians is used to refer to the citizens of Russia, regardless of their ethnicity; the demonym Russian is translated into Russian as rossiyanin, while the ethnic Russians are referred to as russkiye (sg. русский, russkiy).
Austria	Austria officially the Republic of Austria, is a landlocked country of roughly 8.3 million people in Central Europe. It is bordered by the Czech Republic and Germany to the north, Slovakia and Hungary to the east, Slovenia and Italy to the south, and Switzerland and Liechtenstein to the west. The territory of Austria covers 83,855 square kilometres (32,377 sq mi) and has a temperate and alpine climate.

Chapter 5. STATE BUILDING AND THE SEARCH FOR ORDER IN THE SEVENTEENTH CENTURY

Chapter 5. STATE BUILDING AND THE SEARCH FOR ORDER IN THE SEVENTEENTH CENTURY

Simplicissimus	Simplicissimus was a satirical German weekly magazine started by Albert Langen in April 1896 and published through 1967, with a hiatus from 1944-1954. It became a biweekly in 1964. It took its name from the protagonist of Grimmelshausen's 1668 novel Der Abenteuerliche Simplicissimus Teutsch. Combining brash and politically daring content, with a bright, immediate, and surprisingly modern graphic style, Simplicissimus published the work of writers such as Thomas Mann and Rainer Maria Rilke. Its most reliable targets for caricature were stiff Prussian military figures, and rigid German social and class distinctions as seen from the more relaxed, liberal atmosphere of Munich.
Bodin	Bodin is a former municipality in Nordland county, Norway. History Bodin was established as a municipality January 1, 1838 . Some smaller parts of the municipality were transferred to the town of Bodø January 1, 1901 and July 1, 1938. The majority of the municipality Kjerringøy, as well as a small part of Sørfold, were merged into Bodin January 1, 1964. Bodin ceased to exist as a separate entity when it was merged into Bodø city January 1, 1968. At that point Bodin had a population of 13 323, Bodø had 14 252.
Jean Bodin	Jean Bodin born in Angers, was a French jurist and political philosopher, member of the Parlement of Paris and professor of law in Toulouse. He is best known for his theory of sovereignty . Bodin lived during the Reformation, writing against the background of religious and civil conflict - particularly that, in his native France, between the (Calvinist) Huguenots and the state-supported Catholic Church.

Chapter 5. STATE BUILDING AND THE SEARCH FOR ORDER IN THE SEVENTEENTH CENTURY

Chapter 5. STATE BUILDING AND THE SEARCH FOR ORDER IN THE SEVENTEENTH CENTURY

Huguenot	The Huguenots were members of the Protestant Reformed Church of France from the sixteenth to the seventeenth centuries. Since the seventeenth century, Huguenots have been commonly designated "French Protestants," the title being suggested by their German co-religionists or "Calvinists." Protestants in France were inspired by the writings of John Calvin in the 1530s and the name Huguenots was already in use by the 1560s. By the end of the 17th century, roughly 200,000 Huguenots had been driven from France during a series of religious persecutions.
Humanism	Humanism is an approach in study, philosophy, or practice that focuses on human values and concerns. The term can mean several things, for example: 1. A cultural movement of the Italian Renaissance based on the study of classical works. 2. An approach to education that uses literary means or a focus on the humanities to inform students. 3. A variety of perspectives in philosophy and social science which affirm some notion of 'human nature' (by contrast with anti-humanism). 4. A secular ideology which espouses reason, ethics, and justice, whilst specifically rejecting supernatural and religious dogma as a basis of morality and decision-making. The last interpretation may be attributed to Secular Humanism as a specific humanistic life stance. Modern meanings of the word have therefore come to be associated with a rejection of appeals to the supernatural or to some higher authority.
Renaissance	The Renaissance is a cultural movement that spanned roughly the 14th to the 17th century, beginning in Florence in the Late Middle Ages and later spreading to the rest of Europe. The term is also used more loosely to refer to the historic era, but since the changes of the Renaissance were not uniform across Europe, this is a general use of the term. As a cultural movement, it encompassed a resurgence of learning based on classical sources, the development of linear perspective in painting, and gradual but widespread educational reform.

Chapter 5. STATE BUILDING AND THE SEARCH FOR ORDER IN THE SEVENTEENTH CENTURY

Chapter 5. STATE BUILDING AND THE SEARCH FOR ORDER IN THE SEVENTEENTH CENTURY

Scientific revolution	The Scientific Revolution was a period when new ideas in physics, astronomy, biology, human anatomy, chemistry, and other sciences led to a rejection of doctrines that had prevailed starting in Ancient Greece and continuing through the Middle Ages, and laid the foundation of modern science. According to most accounts, the scientific revolution began in Europe towards the end of the Renaissance era and continued through the late 18th century, the latter period known as The Enlightenment. It was sparked by the publication (1543) of two works that changed the course of science: Nicolaus Copernicus's De revolutionibus orbium coelestium (On the Revolutions of the Heavenly Spheres) and Andreas Vesalius's De humani corporis fabrica (On the Fabric of the Human body).
Classicism	Classicism, in the arts, refers generally to a high regard for classical antiquity, as setting standards for taste which the classicists seek to emulate. The art of classicism typically seeks to be formal and restrained: of the Discobolus Sir Kenneth Clark observed, "if we object to his restraint and compression we are simply objecting to the classicism of classic art. A violent emphasis or a sudden acceleration of rhythmic movement would have destroyed those qualities of balance and completeness through which it retained until the present century its position of authority in the restricted repertoire of visual images." Classicism, as Clark noted, implies a canon of widely accepted ideal forms, whether in the Western canon that he was examining in The Nude (1956), or the Chinese classics.
Columbian Exchange	The Columbian Exchange was a dramatically widespread exchange of animals, plants, culture, human populations (including slaves), communicable diseases, and ideas between the Eastern and Western hemispheres (Old World and New World). It was one of the most significant events concerning ecology, agriculture, and culture in all of human history. Christopher Columbus' first voyage to the Americas in 1492 launched the era of large-scale contact between the Old and the New Worlds that resulted in this ecological revolution, hence the name "Columbian" Exchange.
Fronde	The Fronde was a civil war in France, occurring in the midst of the Franco-Spanish War, which had begun in 1635. The word fronde means sling, which Parisian mobs used to smash the windows of supporters of Cardinal Mazarin.
	The Fronde was divided into two campaigns, the Fronde of the parlements and the Fronde of the nobles. The timing of the outbreak of the Fronde des parlements, directly after the Peace of Westphalia (1648) that ended the Thirty Years War, was significant.

Chapter 5. STATE BUILDING AND THE SEARCH FOR ORDER IN THE SEVENTEENTH CENTURY

Chapter 5. STATE BUILDING AND THE SEARCH FOR ORDER IN THE SEVENTEENTH CENTURY

Voltaire	François-Marie Arouet, better known by the pen name Voltaire, was a French Enlightenment writer, historian and philosopher famous for his wit and for his advocacy of civil liberties, including freedom of religion and free trade. Voltaire was known as a prolific writer and produced works in almost every literary form including plays, poetry, novels, essays, historical and scientific works, more than 20,000 letters and more than 2,000 books and pamphlets. He was an outspoken supporter of social reform, despite strict censorship laws and harsh penalties for those who broke them.
Edict of Fontainebleau	The Edict of Fontainebleau was an edict issued by Louis XIV of France, also known as the Revocation of the Edict of Nantes of 1598, which had granted to the Huguenots the right to practice their religion without persecution from the state. Though Protestants had lost their independence in places of refuge under Richelieu, they continued to live in comparative security and political contentment. From the outset, religious toleration in France had been a royal, rather than a popular policy.
Edict of Nantes	The Edict of Nantes, issued on April 13, 1598, by Henry IV of France, granted the Calvinist Protestants of France (also known as Huguenots) substantial rights in a nation still considered essentially Catholic. In the Edict Henry aimed primarily to promote civil unity. The Edict separated civil from religious unity, treated some Protestants for the first time as more than mere schismatics and heretics, and opened a path for secularism and tolerance.
Charlotte	Charlotte is a female given name, a female form of the male name Charles.

Chapter 5. STATE BUILDING AND THE SEARCH FOR ORDER IN THE SEVENTEENTH CENTURY

Chapter 5. STATE BUILDING AND THE SEARCH FOR ORDER IN THE SEVENTEENTH CENTURY

These women are usually identified as Charlotte with an appended title rather than a surname:

- Charlotte Stuart, Duchess of Albany
- Charlotte, Grand Duchess of Luxembourg
- Charlotte, Princess Royal, later Queen Charlotte of Württemberg
- Charlotte of Belgium, Empress of Mexico
- Charlotte of Cyprus, Jerusalem and Armenia, Queen
- Charlotte of Mecklenburg-Strelitz ("Queen Charlotte"), the queen consort of George III
- Charlotte of Savoy, wife of Louis XI of France
- Charlotte Amalie of Hesse-Cassel (or Hesse-Kassel), Queen of Denmark
- Princess Charlotte, Duchess of Valentinois, Princess of Monaco
- Princess Charlotte Augusta of Wales, only legitimate child of George IV of the United Kingdom
- Archduchess Charlotte of Austria
- Amber O'Neal, a professional wrestler, who has also performed under the ring name Charlotte

- Princess Charlotte several women with the name

Fictional characters

- Charlotte a character in Making Fiends
- Charlotte York Goldenblatt, a main character in Sex and the City played by actress Kristin Davis
- Charlotte Lewis, a secondary character in the now completed ABC show, Lost. She is portrayed by actress Rebecca Mader, whose character's name is derived from literary author C.S. Lewis
- Charlotte, the object of the title character's unrequited love in The Sorrows of Young Werther by Johann Wolfgang von Goethe
- Charlotte, a main character in Elective Affinities by Johann Wolfgang von Goethe
- Charlotte, the spider, from Charlotte's Web
- Charlotte Adams, a character in As The Bell Rings, portrayed by Demi Lovato
- Charlotte a character of the Samurai Shodown video game series by SNK
- Charlotte Charlie Duncan, a character in Good Luck Charlie, portrayed by Mia Talerico
- Charlotte E Yeager, a character from the Strike Witches anime
- Charlotte a character from the anime/manga Strike Witches.

Charlotte Brehaut, character from Garfeild's unknown 78th book.

Chapter 5. STATE BUILDING AND THE SEARCH FOR ORDER IN THE SEVENTEENTH CENTURY

Chapter 5. STATE BUILDING AND THE SEARCH FOR ORDER IN THE SEVENTEENTH CENTURY

Eucharist	The Eucharist, Sacrament of the Altar, the Blessed Sacrament, or The Lord's Supper, and other names, is a Christian sacrament or ordinance, generally considered to be a re-enactment of the Last Supper, the final meal that Jesus Christ shared with his disciples before his arrest and crucifixion, during which he gave them bread, saying, "This is my body", and wine, saying, "This is my blood".
	There are different interpretations of the significance of the Eucharist, but "there is more of a consensus among Christians about the meaning of the Eucharist than would appear from the confessional debates over the sacramental presence, the effects of the Eucharist, and the proper auspices under which it may be celebrated."
	The phrase "the Eucharist" may refer not only to the rite but also to the consecrated bread (leavened or unleavened) and wine or, unfermented grape juice (in some Protestant denominations) or water (in Mormonism), used in the rite, and, in this sense, communicants may speak of "receiving the Eucharist", as well as "celebrating the Eucharist".
	Names and their origin
	Eucharist, from Greek ε?χαριστ?α (eucharistia), means "thanksgiving".
House of Habsburg	The House of Habsburg, also found as Hapsburg, and also known as House of Austria was one of the most important aristocratic royal houses of Europe and is best known for being an origin of all of the formally elected Holy Roman Emperors between 1438 and 1740, as well as rulers of the Austrian Empire and Spanish Empire and several other countries. Originally from Switzerland, the dynasty first reigned in Austria, which they ruled for over six centuries. A series of dynastic marriages enabled the family to vastly expand its domains, to include Burgundy, Spain, Bohemia, Hungary, and other territories into the inheritance.
Netherlands	More than one name is used to refer to the Netherlands, both in English and in other languages. Some of these names refer to different, but overlapping geographical, linguistic and political areas of the country. This is a common source of confusion for outsiders.

Chapter 5. STATE BUILDING AND THE SEARCH FOR ORDER IN THE SEVENTEENTH CENTURY

Chapter 5. STATE BUILDING AND THE SEARCH FOR ORDER IN THE SEVENTEENTH CENTURY

Orthodoxy	The word orthodox, from Greek orthos ("right", "true", "straight") + doxa ("opinion" or "belief", related to dokein, "to think"), is generally used to mean the adherence to accepted norms, more specifically to creeds, especially in religion. The Orthodox Churches in Slavic-language countries use a word derived from Old Church Slavonic, Правосла́ви? (pravosláviye) to mean Orthodoxy. The term did not exist in the sense in which it is now used prior to the advent of the State church of the Roman Empire.
Southern Netherlands	Southern Netherlands were a part of the Low Countries controlled by Spain, Austria and annexed by France (1794-1815). This region comprised most of modern Belgium (except for three Lower-Rhenish territories: the Prince-Bishopric of Liège, the Imperial Abbey of Stavelot-Malmedy and the County of Bouillon) and Luxembourg (including the homonymous present Belgian province), and in addition some parts of the Netherlands (namely the Duchy of Limburg now split in a Dutch and Belgian part) as well as, until 1678, most of the present Nord-Pas-de-Calais region in northern France. Unlike French Burgundy and the republican Northern Netherlands, these allodial states kept access to the Burgundian Circle of the Holy Roman Empire until its end.
War of the Spanish Succession	The War of the Spanish Succession was fought among several European powers, principally the Spanish loyal to Archduke Charles, the Holy Roman Empire, Great Britain, the Dutch Republic, Portugal and the Duchy of Savoy against the Spanish loyal to Philip V, France and the Electorate of Bavaria over a possible unification of the Kingdoms of Spain and France under one Bourbon monarch. Such a unification would have drastically changed the European balance of power. The war was fought mostly in Europe but included Queen Anne's War in North America and it was marked by the military leadership of notable generals including the Duc de Villars, the Jacobite Duke of Berwick, the Duke of Marlborough and Prince Eugene of Savoy.
European colonization of the Americas	The start of the European colonization of the Americas is typically dated to 1492, although there was at least one earlier colonization effort. The first known Europeans to reach the Americas were the Vikings (Norse) during the 11th century, who established several colonies in Greenland and one short-lived settlement at L'Anse aux Meadows (51°N) in the area the Norse called Vinland, present day Newfoundland and to the south. Settlements in Greenland survived for several centuries, during which time the Greenland Norse and the Inuit people experienced mostly hostile contact. By the end of the 15th century, the Norse Greenland settlements had collapsed.

Chapter 5. STATE BUILDING AND THE SEARCH FOR ORDER IN THE SEVENTEENTH CENTURY

Chapter 5. STATE BUILDING AND THE SEARCH FOR ORDER IN THE SEVENTEENTH CENTURY

The Bowman and The Spearman	The Bowman and The Spearman, are two bronze equestrian sculptures standing as gatekeepers at the intersection of Congress Drive and Michigan Avenue in Grant Park, Chicago, United States. The sculptures were made in Zagreb by Croatian sculptor Ivan Meštrovic and installed at the entrance of the parkway in 1928. The pair of sculptures was funded by the Benjamin Ferguson Fund. An unusual aspect of the sculptures is that the figures in both sculptures are missing their weapons, the bow and arrow and the spear.
Milan	Milan is a common Slavic male name derived from the Slavic element mil, with meanings kind, loving, and gracious. Milan was originally a diminutive or nickname for those whose Slavic names began with "Mil-". It is used predominantly by Czechs and Serbs but also frequently in Macedonia, Croatia, Slovenia, and Bulgaria.
Old Testament	The Old Testament Hebrew Scriptures are the collection of books that forms the first of the two-part Christian Biblical canon. The contents of the Old Testament canon vary from church to church, with the Orthodox communion having 51 books: the shared books are those of the shortest canon, that of the major Protestant communions, with 39 books. All Old Testament canons are related to the Jewish Bible Canon (Tanakh), but with variations.
Treaty of Utrecht	The Treaty of Utrecht, which established the Peace of Utrecht, comprises a series of individual peace treaties, rather than a single document, signed by the belligerents in the War of Spanish Succession, in the Dutch city of Utrecht in March and April 1713. The treaties between several European states, including Spain, Great Britain, France, Portugal, Savoy, and the Dutch Republic, helped end the War of the Spanish Succession. The treaties were concluded between the representatives of Louis XIV of France and Philip V of Spain on the one hand, and representatives of Queen Anne of Great Britain, the Duke of Savoy, the King of Portugal and the United Provinces on the other.

Chapter 5. STATE BUILDING AND THE SEARCH FOR ORDER IN THE SEVENTEENTH CENTURY

Chapter 5. STATE BUILDING AND THE SEARCH FOR ORDER IN THE SEVENTEENTH CENTURY

	The treaty registered the defeat of French ambitions expressed in the wars of Louis XIV and preserved the European system based on the balance of power.
Scotia	Scotia was originally a Roman name for Ireland, inhabited by the people they called Scoti or Scotii. Use of the name shifted in the Middle Ages to designate the part of the island of Great Britain lying north of the Firth of Forth, the Kingdom of Alba. By the later Middle Ages it had become the fixed Latin term for what in English is called Scotland.
Testaments	Testaments is a collective term, used exclusively within Christianity, to describe both the Old Testament and the New Testament, of The Bible. The Church of Jesus Christ of Latter-day Saints uses this term to include the Book of Mormon as another volume of scripture which specifically testifies of Jesus Christ's divinity. Judaism uses only the term Hebrew Bible (for part of the "Old Testament" alone) because it does not accept the "New Testament" as scripture.
Company	Company magazine is a monthly fashion, celebrity and lifestyle magazine published in the United Kingdom. It celebrated its 30th birthday in 2008 and in that time has had only six editors: Maggie Goodman, Gil Hudson, Mandi Norwood, Fiona Macintosh, Sam Baker, and the current editor Victoria White. The magazine is seen as the UK version of Seventeen Magazine but is more high fashion.
Prussia	Prussia was a German kingdom and historic state originating out of the Duchy of Prussia and the Margraviate of Brandenburg. For centuries, the House of Hohenzollern ruled Prussia, successfully expanding its size by way of an unusually well-organized and effective army. Prussia shaped the history of Germany, with its capital in Berlin after 1451. After 1871, Prussia was increasingly merged into Germany, losing its distinctive identity.
Carniola	Carniola was a historical region that comprised parts of what is now Slovenia. As part of Austria-Hungary, the region was a crown land officially known as the Duchy of Carniola until 1918. In 1849, the region was subdivided into Upper Carniola, Lower Carniola, and Inner Carniola. Since the 14th century, its capital was Laibach (now Ljubljana).

Chapter 5. STATE BUILDING AND THE SEARCH FOR ORDER IN THE SEVENTEENTH CENTURY

Chapter 5. STATE BUILDING AND THE SEARCH FOR ORDER IN THE SEVENTEENTH CENTURY

Italy	The Italy Pavilion is a part of the World Showcase within Epcot at the Walt Disney World Resort.
	Layout
	The Italian Pavilion features a plaza surrounded by a collection of buildings evocative of Venetian, Florentine, and Roman architecture. Venetian architecture is represented by a re-creation of St Mark's Campanile (bell tower) and a replica of the Doge's Palace.
Mantua	A Mantua is an article of women's clothing worn in the late 17th century and 18th century. Originally a loose gown, the later mantua was an overgown or robe typically worn over stays, stomacher and a co-ordinating petticoat.
	Evolution of the mantua
	The earliest mantuas emerged in the late 17th century as a comfortable alternative to the boned bodices and separate skirts then widely worn.
Boyar	A boyar, Kievan Rus'ian, Bulgarian, Wallachian, and Moldavian aristocracies, second only to the ruling princes (in Bulgaria, tsars), from the 10th century through the 17th century. The rank has lived on as a surname in Russia and Finland, where it is spelled "Pajari".
	Etymology
	According to most sources the word is of Proto-Bulgarian origin.
Great Russia	Great Russia is a new Russian political party established in April 2007 by former Rodina leader and legislator Dmitry Rogozin in conjunction with the nationalist Movement Against Illegal Immigration, the Congress of Russian Communities and former members of the Rodina party which won 9% of the vote at the 2003 Russian Parliamentary elections. The current Chairman of the party is Andrei Saveliyev.

Chapter 5. STATE BUILDING AND THE SEARCH FOR ORDER IN THE SEVENTEENTH CENTURY

Chapter 5. STATE BUILDING AND THE SEARCH FOR ORDER IN THE SEVENTEENTH CENTURY

	The colours of the party are the orange and yellow of the Amur Tiger. According to Dmitry Rogozin, he came up with the idea of using the tiger as the party's logo upon learning that the animal's population had increased in 2006 for the first time in recorded history.
The Bowman and The Spearman	The Bowman and The Spearman, are two bronze equestrian sculptures standing as gatekeepers at the intersection of Congress Drive and Michigan Avenue in Grant Park, Chicago, United States. The sculptures were made in Zagreb by Croatian sculptor Ivan Meštrovic and installed at the entrance of the parkway in 1928. The pair of sculptures was funded by the Benjamin Ferguson Fund. An unusual aspect of the sculptures is that the figures in both sculptures are missing their weapons, the bow and arrow and the spear.
Inquisition	The term Inquisition can apply to any one of several institutions which fought against heretics (or other offenders against canon law) within the justice-system of the Roman Catholic Church. Although similar institutions existed within Calvinist and other Protestant churches, the term "Inquisition" is usually applied to that of the Catholic Church. It may also refer to: • an ecclesiastical tribunal • the institution of the Roman Catholic Church for combating heresy • a number of historical expurgation movements against heresy (orchestrated by some groups/individuals within the Catholic Church or within a Catholic state) • the trial of an individual accused of heresy. Inquisition tribunals and institutions Before the 12th century, the Roman Catholic Church already suppressed heresy, usually through a system of ecclesiastical proscription or imprisonment, but without using torture and seldom resorting to executions.

Chapter 5. STATE BUILDING AND THE SEARCH FOR ORDER IN THE SEVENTEENTH CENTURY

Chapter 5. STATE BUILDING AND THE SEARCH FOR ORDER IN THE SEVENTEENTH CENTURY

Martin Luther	Martin Luther was a German priest and professor of theology who initiated the Protestant Reformation. He strongly disputed the claim that freedom from God's punishment of sin could be purchased with money. He confronted indulgence salesman Johann Tetzel with his Ninety-Five Theses in 1517. His refusal to retract all of his writings at the demand of Pope Leo X in 1520 and the Holy Roman Emperor Charles V at the Diet of Worms in 1521 resulted in his excommunication by the pope and condemnation as an outlaw by the emperor.
Romanov	Romanov is a breed of domestic sheep originating from the Upper Volga region in Russia. These domestic sheep got the name Romanov from the town of the same name. In the 18th century, these sheep first got noticed.
House of Romanov	The House of Romanov was the second and last imperial dynasty to rule over Russia, reigning from 1613 until the February Revolution abolished the crown in 1917. The later history of the Imperial House is sometimes referred to informally as the House of Holstein-Gottorp-Romanov. The Duke of Holstein-Gottorp, who was himself a member of a cadet branch of the Oldenburgs, married into the Romanov family early in the 18th century; all Romanov Tsars from the middle of that century to the revolution of 1917 were descended from that marriage. Though officially known as the House of Romanov, these descendants of the Romanov and Oldenburg Houses are sometimes referred to as Holstein-Gottorp-Romanov. Origins The Romanovs share their origin with two dozen other Russian noble families. Their earliest common ancestor is one Andrei Kobyla, attested as a boyar in the service of Semyon I of Moscow.
Russian Orthodox Church	The Russian Orthodox Church; or the Moscow Patriarchate (Russian: Русская Православная Церковь (Russkaya Pravoslavnaya Tserkov), or Московский Патриархат (Moskovskiy Patriarkhat) (the latter designation being another official name), Поместная Российская Православная Церковь (Pomestnaya Rossiyskaya Pravoslavnaya Tserkov) before the re-institution in 1943, also known as the Orthodox Christian Church of Russia, is a body of Christians who constitute an autocephalous Eastern Orthodox Church under the jurisdiction of the Patriarch of Moscow, in communion with the other Eastern Orthodox Churches.

Chapter 5. STATE BUILDING AND THE SEARCH FOR ORDER IN THE SEVENTEENTH CENTURY

Chapter 5. STATE BUILDING AND THE SEARCH FOR ORDER IN THE SEVENTEENTH CENTURY

	The Russian Orthodox Church is often said to be the largest of the Eastern Orthodox churches in the world and second only to the Roman Catholic Church among Christian churches, numbering over 135 million members world wide and growing numerically since late 1980s. Up to 65% of ethnic Russians and a similar percentage of Belarusians and Ukrainians identify themselves as "Orthodox".
Duchy	A duchy is a territory, fief, or domain ruled by a duke or duchess. Some duchies were sovereign in areas that would become unified realms only during the Modern era . In contrast, others were subordinate districts of those kingdoms that unified either partially or completely during the Medieval era (such as England, France, and Spain).
Chinas	The Chinas are a people mentioned in ancient Indian literature from the first millennium BC, such as the Mahabharata, Laws of Manu, as well the Puranic literature. They are believed to have been Chinese. Etymology The name Cina is commonly believed to have been derived from either the Qin (Tsin or Chin) dynasty which rule in China from 221 BC or the earlier Qin state which later became the Qin dynasty.
Estonia	Estonias are open wheel racing cars manufactured in Estonia. The first model Estonia 1 was built in 1958. Altogether there are about 1300 cars. The brand was in western Europe as TARK, Tallinna Autode Remondi Katsetehas.

Chapter 5. STATE BUILDING AND THE SEARCH FOR ORDER IN THE SEVENTEENTH CENTURY

Chapter 5. STATE BUILDING AND THE SEARCH FOR ORDER IN THE SEVENTEENTH CENTURY

Great Northern War	The Great Northern War was a conflict in which a coalition led by Russia successfully contested Swedish supremacy in northern Central and Eastern Europe. The initial leaders of the anti-Swedish alliance were Peter I, Peter the Great, of Russia, Frederik IV of Denmark-Norway and August II, Augustus the Strong, of Saxe-Poland-Lithuania. Frederik IV and August II were forced out of the alliance in 1700 and 1706 respectively, but re-joined it in 1709. George I of Brunswick-Lüneburg (Hanover) joined the coalition in 1714 for Hanover, and in 1717 for Britain, and Frederick William I of Brandenburg-Prussia in 1715.
Livonia	Livonia is a historic region along the eastern shores of the Baltic Sea. It was once the land of the Finnic Livonians inhabiting the principal ancient Livonian County Metsepole with its center at Turaida. The most prominent ruler of ancient Livonia was Caupo of Turaida.
Procurator	A procurator was the title of various officials of the Roman Empire, posts mostly filled by equites (Roman knights, the second order of nobility). A procurator Augusti was the governor of the smaller imperial provinces (i.e. those provinces whose governor was appointed by the emperor, rather than elected by the Roman Senate). The same title was held by the chief financial officers of provinces, who assisted governors of the larger imperial provinces (known as a legatus Augusti pro praetore, always a senator, who ranked above a knight).
Westernization	Westernization, also occidentalization or occidentalisation , is a process whereby societies come under or adopt Western culture in such matters as industry, technology, law, politics, economics, lifestyle, diet, language, alphabet, religion, philosophy, and/or values. Westernization has been a pervasive and accelerating influence across the world in the last few centuries. It is usually a two-sided process, in which Western influences and interests themselves are joined by a wish of at least parts of the affected society to change towards a more Westernised society, in the hope of attaining Western life or some aspects of it.
Orthodox Christianity	The term Orthodox Christianity may refer to - Eastern Orthodoxy: the Ancient communion of Eastern Christian Churches, historically of eastern Europe and parts of Asia, that recognize the Council of Chalcedon and the other of the first seven Ecumenical Councils. - Oriental Orthodoxy: the Miaphysite Eastern Christian churches adhering to the first three Ecumenical Councils and the 449 Council of Ephesus, and rejecting the Council of Chalcedon and the later councils that Eastern Orthodoxy classifies as ecumenical.

Chapter 5. STATE BUILDING AND THE SEARCH FOR ORDER IN THE SEVENTEENTH CENTURY

Chapter 5. STATE BUILDING AND THE SEARCH FOR ORDER IN THE SEVENTEENTH CENTURY

Republic	Republic is a Hungarian rock band formed in Budapest in 1989. Their style is a unique mix of Western rock music and traditional Hungarian folk music. The band is popular in its native country and among Hungarian speaking minorities elsewhere. Members The two founding members are László Bódi and Lászlo Attila Nagy.
England	"England" is a song written by Justin Hawkins from The Darkness(music) ' Chas Bayfield (lyrics) and released by him under the name British Whale and used as the unofficial World Cup single for the England National Team in 2006
House	A house is a home, building or structure that is a dwelling or place for habitation by human beings. The term house includes many kinds of dwellings ranging from rudimentary huts of nomadic tribes to free standing individual structures. In some contexts, "house" may mean the same as dwelling, residence, home, abode, lodging, accommodation, or housing, among other meanings.
House of Medici	The House of Medici, banking family and later royal house that first began to gather prominence under Cosimo de' Medici in the Republic of Florence during the late 14th century. The family originated in the Mugello region of the Tuscan countryside, gradually rising until they were able to found the Medici Bank. The bank was the largest in Europe during the 15th century, seeing the Medici gain political power in Florence -- though officially they remained simply citizens, rather than monarchs.
American Revolution	The American Revolution was the political upheaval during the last half of the 18th century in which thirteen colonies in North America joined together to break free from the British Empire, combining to become the United States of America. They first rejected the authority of the Parliament of Great Britain to govern them from overseas without representation, and then expelled all royal officials. By 1774 each colony had established a Provincial Congress, or an equivalent governmental institution, to form individual self-governing states. The British responded by sending combat troops to re-impose direct rule.

Chapter 5. STATE BUILDING AND THE SEARCH FOR ORDER IN THE SEVENTEENTH CENTURY

Chapter 5. STATE BUILDING AND THE SEARCH FOR ORDER IN THE SEVENTEENTH CENTURY

Book of Common Prayer	The Book of Common Prayer is the common title of a number of prayer books of the Church of England and of other Anglican churches, used throughout the Anglican Communion. The first book, published in 1549 (Church of England 1957), in the reign of Edward VI, was a product of the English Reformation following the break with Rome. Prayer books, unlike books of prayers, contain the words of structured (or liturgical) services of worship.
Church of England	The Church of England is the officially established Christian church in England and the Mother Church of the worldwide Anglican Communion.
	The Church of England separated from the Roman Catholic Church in 1534 with the Act of Supremacy and understands itself to be both Catholic and Reformed:
	- Catholic in that it views itself as a part of the universal church of Jesus Christ in unbroken continuity with the early apostolic church. This is expressed in its emphasis on the teachings of the early Church Fathers, as formalised in the Apostles', Nicene, and Athanasian creeds.
	- Reformed in that it has been shaped by the doctrinal principles of the 16th century Protestant Reformation, in particular in the Thirty-Nine Articles and the Book of Common Prayer.
	History
	Early history
	According to tradition, Christianity arrived in Britain in the first or 2nd century.
Common	The Common is a part of the Christian liturgy that consists of texts common to an entire category of saints, such as Apostles or Martyrs. The term is used in contrast to the ordinary, which is that part of the liturgy that is reasonably constant, or at least selected without regard to date, and to the proper, which is the part of the liturgy that varies according to the date, either representing an observance within the Liturgical Year, or of a particular saint or significant event.

Chapter 5. STATE BUILDING AND THE SEARCH FOR ORDER IN THE SEVENTEENTH CENTURY

Chapter 5. STATE BUILDING AND THE SEARCH FOR ORDER IN THE SEVENTEENTH CENTURY

	Commons contain collects, psalms, readings from Scripture, prefaces, and other portions of services that are common to a category of saints.
Oliver Cromwell	Oliver Cromwell was an English military and political leader best known in England for his overthrow of the monarchy and temporarily turning England into a republican Commonwealth, and for his rule as Lord Protector of England, Scotland and Ireland.
	Oliver Cromwell was one of the commanders of the New Model Army which defeated the royalists in the English Civil War. After the execution of King Charles I in 1649, Oliver Cromwell dominated the short-lived Commonwealth of England, conquered Ireland and Scotland, and ruled as Lord Protector from 1653 until his death in 1658.
English Civil War	The English Civil War was a series of armed conflicts and political machinations between Parliamentarians (Roundheads) and Royalists (Cavaliers). The first (1642-46) and second (1648-49) civil wars pitted the supporters of King Charles I against the supporters of the Long Parliament, while the third war (1649-51) saw fighting between supporters of King Charles II and supporters of the Rump Parliament. The Civil War ended with the Parliamentary victory at the Battle of Worcester on 3 September 1651.
Henrietta Marie	The Henrietta Marie was a slave ship that carried captive Africans to the West Indies, where they were sold as slaves. The ship wrecked at the southern tip of Florida on its way home to England, and is one of only a few wrecks of slave ships that have been identified.
Independent	In English church history, Independents advocated local congregational control of religious and church matters, without any wider geographical hierarchy, either ecclesiastical or political. Independents reached particular prominence between 1642 and 1660, in the period of the English Civil War and of the Commonwealth and Protectorate, wherein the Parliamentary Army became the champion of Independent religious views against the Anglicanism or the Catholicism of Royalists and the Presbyterianism favoured by Parliament itself.
	The Independents advocated freedom of religion for non-Catholics and the complete separation of church and state.

Chapter 5. STATE BUILDING AND THE SEARCH FOR ORDER IN THE SEVENTEENTH CENTURY

Chapter 5. STATE BUILDING AND THE SEARCH FOR ORDER IN THE SEVENTEENTH CENTURY

Long Parliament	The Long Parliament was made on November 3 1640, following the Bishops' Wars. It received its name from the fact that through an Act of Parliament, it could only be dissolved with the agreement of the members, and those members did not agree to its dissolution until after the English Civil War and at the end of Interregnum in 1660. It sat from 1640 until 1648, when it was purged, by the New Model Army, of those who were not sympathetic to the Army's concerns. When this failed, General George Monck allowed the members barred in 1648 to retake their seats so that they could pass the necessary legislation to allow the Restoration and dissolve the Long Parliament.
New Model Army	The New Model Army of England was formed in 1645 by the Parliamentarians in the English Civil War, and was disbanded in 1660 after the Restoration. It differed from other armies in the series of civil wars referred to as the Wars of the Three Kingdoms in that it was intended as an army liable for service anywhere in the country (including in Scotland and Ireland), rather than being tied to a single area or garrison. Its soldiers became full-time professionals, rather than part-time militia.
Puritan	The Puritans were a significant grouping of English Protestants in the 16th and 17th centuries. Puritanism in this sense was founded by some Marian exiles from the clergy shortly after the accession of Elizabeth I of England in 1559, as an activist movement within the Church of England. The designation "Puritan" is often incorrectly used, notably based on the assumption that hedonism and puritanism are antonyms: historically, the word was used to characterize the Protestant group as extremists similar to the Cathari of France, and according to Thomas Fuller in his Church History dated back to 1564. Archbishop Matthew Parker of that time used it and "precisian" with the sense of stickler.
Levellers	The Levellers were a political movement during the English Civil Wars which emphasised popular sovereignty, extended suffrage, equality before the law, and religious tolerance, all of which were expressed in the manifesto "Agreement of the People". They came to prominence at the end of the First English Civil War and were most influential before the start of the Second Civil War. Leveller views and support were found in the populace of the City of London and in some regiments in the New Model Army.
Lord Protector	Lord Protector is a title used in British constitutional law for certain heads of state at different periods of history. It is also a particular title for the British Heads of State in respect to the established church.
Rump Parliament	The Rump Parliament is the name of the English Parliament after Colonel Pride purged the Long Parliament on 6 December 1648 of those members hostile to the Grandees' intention to try King Charles I for high treason.

Chapter 5. STATE BUILDING AND THE SEARCH FOR ORDER IN THE SEVENTEENTH CENTURY

Chapter 5. STATE BUILDING AND THE SEARCH FOR ORDER IN THE SEVENTEENTH CENTURY

	"Rump" normally means the hind end of an animal; its use meaning "remnant" was first recorded in the above context. Since 1649, the term "rump parliament" has been used to refer to any parliament left over from the actual legitimate parliament.
Histories	Histories is a book by Tacitus, written c. 100-110, which covers the Year of Four Emperors following the downfall of Nero, the rise of Vespasian, and the rule of the Flavian Dynasty (69-96) up to the death of Domitian. Subject matter In one of the first chapters of the Agricola Tacitus said that he wished to speak about the years of Domitian, of Nerva, and of Trajan. In the Historiae the project has been modified: in the introduction, Tacitus says that he will deal with the age of Nerva and Trajan at a later time.
Cavalier Parliament	The Cavalier Parliament of England lasted from 8 May 1661 until 24 January 1679. It was the longest English Parliament, enduring for nearly 18 years of the quarter century reign of Charles II of England. Like its predecessor, the Convention Parliament, it was overwhelmingly Royalist and is also known as the Pensioner Parliament for the many pensions it granted to adherents of the King. It restored the Anglican church as the official church of England.
Declaration of Indulgence	The Declaration of Indulgence was two proclamations made by James II of England and VII of Scotland in 1687. The Indulgence was first issued for Scotland on 12 February, and then for England on 4 April 1687. It was a first step at establishing freedom of religion in the British Isles. The Declaration granted broad religious freedom in England by suspending penal laws enforcing conformity to the Church of England and allowing persons to worship in their homes or chapels as they saw fit, and it ended the requirement of affirming religious oaths before gaining employment in government office.

Chapter 5. STATE BUILDING AND THE SEARCH FOR ORDER IN THE SEVENTEENTH CENTURY

Chapter 5. STATE BUILDING AND THE SEARCH FOR ORDER IN THE SEVENTEENTH CENTURY

	By use of the Royal suspending power the King lifted the religious penal laws and granted toleration to the various Christian denominations, Catholic and Protestant, within his kingdoms.
Indulgence	In Catholic theology, an indulgence is the full or partial remission of temporal punishment due for sins which have already been forgiven. The indulgence is granted by the Catholic Church after the sinner has confessed and received absolution. The belief is that indulgences draw on the Treasure House of Merit accumulated by Christ's superabundantly meritorious sacrifice on the cross and the virtues and penances of the saints.
Restoration	In the Latter Day Saint movement, the Restoration was a period in its early history during which a number of events occurred that were understood to be necessary to restore the early Christian church as demonstrated in the New Testament, and to prepare the earth for the Second Coming of Jesus Christ. In particular, Latter Day Saints believe that angels appeared to Joseph Smith, Jr. and others and bestowed various Priesthood authorities to them.
House of Stuart	The House of Stuart is a European royal house. Founded by Robert II of Scotland, the Stewarts first became monarchs of the Kingdom of Scotland during the late 14th century, and subsequently held the position of the Kings of Great Britain and Ireland. Their direct ancestors (from Brittany) had held the title High Steward of Scotland since the 12th century, after arriving by way of Norman England.
Lollardy	Lollardy was the political and religious movement of the Lollards from the mid-14th century to the English Reformation. The term Lollards refers to the followers of John Wycliffe, a prominent theologian who was dismissed from the University of Oxford in 1381 for criticism of the Church, especially his doctrine on the Eucharist. Its demands were primarily for reform of Western Christianity.
Leviathan	Leviathan, Forme and Power of a Common Wealth Ecclesiasticall and Civil, commonly called Leviathan, is a book written by Thomas Hobbes which was published in 1651. It is titled after the biblical Leviathan. The book concerns the structure of society and legitimate government, and is regarded as one of the earliest and most influential examples of social contract theory. The publisher was Andrew Crooke, partner in Andrew Crooke and William Cooke.
John Locke	John Locke, widely known as the Father of Liberalism, was an English philosopher and physician regarded as one of the most influential of Enlightenment thinkers. Considered one of the first of the British empiricists, following the tradition of Francis Bacon, he is equally important to social contract theory. His work had a great impact upon the development of epistemology and political philosophy.

Chapter 5. STATE BUILDING AND THE SEARCH FOR ORDER IN THE SEVENTEENTH CENTURY

Chapter 5. STATE BUILDING AND THE SEARCH FOR ORDER IN THE SEVENTEENTH CENTURY

Mannerism	Mannerism is a period of European art that emerged from the later years of the Italian High Renaissance around 1520. It lasted until about 1580 in Italy, when a more Baroque style began to replace it, but Northern Mannerism continued into the early 17th century throughout much of Europe. Stylistically, Mannerism encompasses a variety of approaches influenced by, and reacting to, the harmonious ideals and restrained naturalism associated with artists such as Leonardo da Vinci, Raphael, and early Michelangelo. Mannerism is notable for its intellectual sophistication as well as its artificial (as opposed to naturalistic) qualities.
Baroque	Baroque is an artistic style prevalent from the late 16th century to the early 18th century in Europe. The popularity and success of the Baroque style was encouraged by the Roman Catholic Church, which had decided at the time of the Council of Trent, in response to the Protestant Reformation, that the arts should communicate religious themes in direct and emotional involvement. The aristocracy also saw the dramatic style of Baroque architecture and art as a means of impressing visitors and expressing triumphant power and control.
Marseille	Marseille, known in antiquity as Massalia, is the second largest city in France, after Paris, with a population of 852,395 within its administrative limits on a land area of 240.62 km^2 (93 sq mi). The urban area of Marseille extends beyond the city limits with a population of over 1,420,000 on an area of 1,204 km^2 (465 sq mi). 1,530,000 or 1,601,095 people live in the Marseille metropolitan area, ranking it 2nd among French metro areas.
Peter and Paul	Peter and Paul is a 1981 film starring Anthony Hopkins as Paul of Tarsus and Robert Foxworth as Peter the Fisherman, David Gwillim as Mark and Jon Finch as Luke. It was directed by Robert Day. The film mostly shows the works of Paul, beginning with his being struck down and converted by the Lord Jesus on the road to Damascus.
Protestantism	Protestantism is one of the three major divisions (Catholicism, Orthodoxy, and Protestantism) within Christianity. It is a movement that began in northern Europe in the early 16th century as a reaction against medieval Roman Catholic doctrines and practices.

Chapter 5. STATE BUILDING AND THE SEARCH FOR ORDER IN THE SEVENTEENTH CENTURY

Chapter 5. STATE BUILDING AND THE SEARCH FOR ORDER IN THE SEVENTEENTH CENTURY

	The doctrines of the various Protestant denominations and non-denominations vary, but most non-denominational doctrines include justification by grace through faith and not through works, known as Sola Fide, the priesthood of all believers, and the Bible as the ultimate authority in matters of faith and order, known as Sola Scriptura, which is Latin for 'by scripture alone'.
Realism	Realism was a general movement in 19th-century theatre that developed a set of dramatic and theatrical conventions with the aim of bringing a greater fidelity to real life to texts and performances.
	Realism began earlier in the 19th century in Russia than elsewhere in Europe and took a more uncompromising form. Beginning with the plays of Ivan Turgenev (who used "domestic detail to reveal inner turmoil"), Aleksandr Ostrovsky, Aleksey Pisemsky (whose A Bitter Fate (1859) anticipated Naturalism), and Leo Tolstoy (whose The Power of Darkness (1886) is "one of the most effective of naturalistic plays"), a tradition of psychological realism in Russia culminated with the establishment of the Moscow Art Theatre by Constantin Stanislavski and Vladimir Nemirovich-Danchenko.
Rembrandt	Rembrandt Harmenszoon van Rijn was a Dutch painter and etcher. He is generally considered one of the greatest painters and printmakers in European art history and the most important in Dutch history. His contributions to art came in a period that historians call the Dutch Golden Age.
Rembrandt	Rembrandt Harmenszoon van Rijn was a Dutch painter and etcher. He is generally considered one of the greatest painters and printmakers in European art history and the most important in Dutch history. His contributions to art came in a period that historians call the Dutch Golden Age.
Elizabeth	Elizabeth is a 1998 biographical film written by Michael Hirst, directed by Shekhar Kapur, and starring Cate Blanchett in the title role of Queen Elizabeth I of England, alongside Geoffrey Rush, Christopher Eccleston, Joseph Fiennes, Sir John Gielgud, Fanny Ardant and Richard Attenborough. Loosely based on the early years of Elizabeth's reign, in 2007, Blanchett reprised the role in the sequel, Elizabeth: The Golden Age, covering the later part of her reign.

Chapter 5. STATE BUILDING AND THE SEARCH FOR ORDER IN THE SEVENTEENTH CENTURY

Chapter 5. STATE BUILDING AND THE SEARCH FOR ORDER IN THE SEVENTEENTH CENTURY

	The film brought Australian actress Blanchett to international attention.
Euripides	Euripides was the last of the three great tragedians of classical Athens (the other two being Aeschylus and Sophocles). Ancient scholars thought that Euripides had written ninety-five plays, although four of those were probably written by Critias. Eighteen or nineteen of Euripides' plays have survived complete.

Chapter 5. STATE BUILDING AND THE SEARCH FOR ORDER IN THE SEVENTEENTH CENTURY

Chapter 6. TOWARD A NEW HEAVEN AND A NEW EARTH

Scientific revolution	The Scientific Revolution was a period when new ideas in physics, astronomy, biology, human anatomy, chemistry, and other sciences led to a rejection of doctrines that had prevailed starting in Ancient Greece and continuing through the Middle Ages, and laid the foundation of modern science. According to most accounts, the scientific revolution began in Europe towards the end of the Renaissance era and continued through the late 18th century, the latter period known as The Enlightenment. It was sparked by the publication (1543) of two works that changed the course of science: Nicolaus Copernicus's De revolutionibus orbium coelestium (On the Revolutions of the Heavenly Spheres) and Andreas Vesalius's De humani corporis fabrica (On the Fabric of the Human body).
Secularism	Secularism is the concept that government or other entities should exist separately from religion and/or religious beliefs.
	In one sense, secularism may assert the right to be free from religious rule and teachings, and the right to freedom from governmental imposition of religion upon the people within a state that is neutral on matters of belief. In another sense, it refers to the view that human activities and decisions, especially political ones, should be based on evidence and fact unbiased by religious influence.
Claudius	Tiberius Claudius Caesar Augustus Germanicus (1 August 10 BC - 13 October AD 54), born Tiberius Claudius Drusus, then Tiberius Claudius Nero Germanicus until his accession, was Roman Emperor from 41 to 54 AD. A member of the Julio-Claudian dynasty, he was the son of Drusus and Antonia Minor. He was born at Lugdunum in Gaul and was the first emperor to be born outside Italy. Afflicted with a limp and slight deafness due to sickness at a young age, his family ostracized him and excluded him from public office until his consulship with his nephew Caligula in 37 AD. Claudius' infirmity probably saved him from the fate of many other nobles during the purges of Tiberius' and Caligula's reigns; potential enemies did not see him as a serious threat.
Galileo Galilei	Galileo Galilei was an Italian physicist, mathematician, astronomer and philosopher who played a major role in the Scientific Revolution. His achievements include improvements to the telescope and consequent astronomical observations, and support for Copernicanism. Galileo has been called the "father of modern observational astronomy", the "father of modern physics", the "father of science", and "the Father of Modern Science".

Chapter 6. TOWARD A NEW HEAVEN AND A NEW EARTH

Chapter 6. TOWARD A NEW HEAVEN AND A NEW EARTH

Galileo Galilei	Galileo Galilei was an Italian physicist, mathematician, astronomer and philosopher who played a major role in the Scientific Revolution. His achievements include improvements to the telescope and consequent astronomical observations, and support for Copernicanism. Galileo has been called the "father of modern observational astronomy", the "father of modern physics", the "father of science", and "the Father of Modern Science".
Martin Luther	Martin Luther was a German priest and professor of theology who initiated the Protestant Reformation. He strongly disputed the claim that freedom from God's punishment of sin could be purchased with money. He confronted indulgence salesman Johann Tetzel with his Ninety-Five Theses in 1517. His refusal to retract all of his writings at the demand of Pope Leo X in 1520 and the Holy Roman Emperor Charles V at the Diet of Worms in 1521 resulted in his excommunication by the pope and condemnation as an outlaw by the emperor.
Plato	Plato, was a Classical Greek philosopher, mathematician, student of Socrates, writer of philosophical dialogues, and founder of the Academy in Athens, the first institution of higher learning in the Western world. Along with his mentor, Socrates, and his student, Aristotle, Plato helped to lay the foundations of Western philosophy and science.
Ptolemy	The name Ptolemy, which means warlike. There have been many people named Ptolemy or Ptolemaeus, the most famous of which are the Greek-Egyptian astronomer Claudius Ptolemaeus and the Macedonian founder and ruler of the Ptolemaic Kingdom in Egypt, Ptolemy I Soter. The following sections summarise the history of the name, some of the people named Ptolemy, and some of the other uses of this name.
Alchemy	Alchemy is an ancient tradition, the primary objective of which was the creation of a fabled elixir, known as the Philosopher's Stone, capable of turning any base metal into gold or silver, the same also acting as a universal medicine said to indefinitely prolong youth and keep one from death. The alchemists themselves stressed that the operation was natural, being a microcosm of the world itself, and following the same principles of development that apply to plants, animals and minerals. Today it is widely believed that the alchemical processes were allegorical as metaphors for a spiritual discipline, akin to a technique for the obtainment of enlightenment.
Bible	The Bible is the various collections of sacred scripture of the various branches of Judaism and Christianity. The Bible, in its various editions, is the best-selling book in history.

Chapter 6. TOWARD A NEW HEAVEN AND A NEW EARTH

Chapter 6. TOWARD A NEW HEAVEN AND A NEW EARTH

	There is no single Bible, and both the individual books (Biblical canon), their contents and their order vary between denominations.
Catholic	The word catholic comes from the Greek phrase καθ?λου (kath'holou), meaning "on the whole," "according to the whole" or "in general", and is a combination of the Greek words κατ? meaning "about" and ?λος meaning "whole". The word in English can mean either "including a wide variety of things; all-embracing" or "of the Roman Catholic faith." as "relating to the historic doctrine and practice of the Western Church."
	It was first used to describe the Christian Church in the early 2nd century to emphasize its universal scope. In the context of Christian ecclesiology, it has a rich history and several usages.
Catholic Church	The Catholic Church, is the world's largest Christian church. Headed by the Pope, it sees its mission as spreading the gospel of Christ, administering its sacraments and exercising charity.
	The Catholic Church is one of the oldest religious institutions in the world and has played a prominent role in the history of Western civilisation.
Church	A church building is a building or structure whose primary purpose is to facilitate the meeting of a church. Originally, Jewish Christians met in synagogues, such as the Cenacle, and in one another's homes, known as house churches. As Christianity grew and became more accepted by governments, notably with the Edict of Milan, rooms and, eventually, entire buildings were set aside for the explicit purpose of Christian worship, such as the Church of the Holy Sepulchre.

Chapter 6. TOWARD A NEW HEAVEN AND A NEW EARTH

Chapter 6. TOWARD A NEW HEAVEN AND A NEW EARTH

Nicolau	Nicolau may refer to: - Nicolau - Nicolau Coelho, Portuguese explorer - Nicolau dos Reis Lobato, East-Timorese politician and national hero - Nicolau Tolentino de Almeida, the foremost Portuguese satirical poet of the 18th century - Presidente Nicolau Lobato International Airport, airport located in Dili - Estádio Nicolau Alayon, stadium located in São Paulo
Geocentric model	In astronomy, the geocentric model is the superseded theory, that the Earth is the center of the universe, and that all other objects orbit around it. This geocentric model served as the predominant cosmological system in many ancient civilizations such as ancient Greece. As such, most Ancient Greek philosophers assumed that the Sun, Moon, stars, and naked eye planets circled the Earth, including the noteworthy systems of Aristotle and Ptolemy.
Bodies	"Bodies" is the lead single from British singer-songwriter Robbie Williams's eighth studio album Reality Killed the Video Star and was released on October 12, 2009 by EMI. It received its premiere on The Chris Moyles Show on BBC Radio 1 after an interview with Williams on Friday September 4, 2009 at 8am. It is Williams' first single release as a solo artist since "She's Madonna" in March 2007. "Bodies" entered the UK singles chart at number 2, selling 89,000 copies in its first week and attaining his best first-week sales since "Rock DJ". Williams was beaten to number 1 by Alexandra Burke, whose single "Bad Boys" (featuring rapper Flo Rida) was released on the same day and sold 187,000 in the same week.
Messenger	Messenger of the fullness of the Gospel is a Mormon fundamentalist publication, originally printed in Birmingham, England starting in 1991, which was in print in that country until 2001, and continues as a web-based publication. It went under the original title of "Truth Seeker" magazine, until it was found that there was an existing periodical that shared that name. Although originally printed quarterly, it was printed bi-monthly when it moved to an American-produced edition in 2003.

Chapter 6. TOWARD A NEW HEAVEN AND A NEW EARTH

Chapter 6. TOWARD A NEW HEAVEN AND A NEW EARTH

Roman Catholic	The term Roman Catholic is generally used on its own to refer to individuals, and in compound forms to refer to worship, parishes, festivals, etc. Its usage has varied, depending on circumstances. It is sometimes identified with one or other of the terms "Catholic", "Western Catholic", and "Roman-Rite Catholic".
World	WORLD Magazine is a biweekly Christian news magazine, published in the United States of America by God's World Publications, a non-profit 501(c)(3) organization based in Asheville, North Carolina. WORLD differs from most other news magazines in that its declared perspective is one of conservative evangelical Protestantism. Its mission statement is "To report, interpret, and illustrate the news in a timely, accurate, enjoyable, and arresting fashion from a perspective committed to the Bible as the inerrant Word of God." Each issue features both U.S. and international news, cultural analysis, editorials and commentary, as well as book, music and movie reviews.
World-systems theory	The world-systems theory is a multidisciplinary, macro-scale approach to world history and social change. The world-systems theory stresses that world-systems (and not nation states) should be the basic unit of social analysis. World-system refers to the international division of labor, which divides the world into core countries, semi-periphery countries and the periphery countries.
Renaissance	The Renaissance is a cultural movement that spanned roughly the 14th to the 17th century, beginning in Florence in the Late Middle Ages and later spreading to the rest of Europe. The term is also used more loosely to refer to the historic era, but since the changes of the Renaissance were not uniform across Europe, this is a general use of the term. As a cultural movement, it encompassed a resurgence of learning based on classical sources, the development of linear perspective in painting, and gradual but widespread educational reform.
Heart	"Heart" is a song recorded by Pet Shop Boys which reached #1 on the UK Singles Chart for three weeks in April 1988 . This is also their last number 1 song to date. The song was included on the group's third studio album, Actually.

Chapter 6. TOWARD A NEW HEAVEN AND A NEW EARTH

Chapter 6. TOWARD A NEW HEAVEN AND A NEW EARTH

Paracelsus	Paracelsus was a Swiss Renaissance physician, botanist, alchemist, astrologer, and general occultist. "Paracelsus", meaning "equal to or greater than Celsus", refers to the Roman encyclopedist Aulus Cornelius Celsus from the 1st century, known for his tract on medicine. He is also credited for giving zinc its name, calling it zincum and is regarded as the first systematic botanist.
Andreas Vesalius	Andreas Vesalius was an anatomist, physician, and author of one of the most influential books on human anatomy, De humani corporis fabrica (On the Fabric of the Human Body). Vesalius is often referred to as the founder of modern human anatomy. Vesalius is the Latinized form of Andreas van Wesel.
Berlin	Berlin is the capital city of Germany and is one of the 16 states of Germany. It has a population of 3.4 million people, and is Germany's largest city. It is the second most populous city proper and the eighth most populous urban area in the European Union.
Maria	The gens Maria was a plebeian family at Rome. Its most celebrated member was Gaius Marius, one of the greatest generals of antiquity, and seven times consul. Origin of the gens The nomen Marius appears to be derived from the Oscan praenomen Marius, in which case the family is probably of Sabine or Sabellic origin.
Dualism	In philosophy of mind, dualism is a set of views about the relationship between mind and matter, which begins with the claim that mental phenomena are, in some respects, non-physical. Ideas on mind/body dualism are presented in Hebrew Scripture (as early as Genesis 2:7) where the Creator is said to have formed the first human a living, psycho-physical fusion of mind and body--a holisitic dualism. Mind/body dualism is also seen in the writings of Zarathushtra.

Chapter 6. TOWARD A NEW HEAVEN AND A NEW EARTH

Chapter 6. TOWARD A NEW HEAVEN AND A NEW EARTH

Working class	Working class is a term used in the social sciences and in ordinary conversation to describe those employed in lower tier jobs (as measured by skill, education and lower incomes), often extending to those in unemployment or otherwise possessing below-average incomes. Working classes are mainly found in industrialized economies and in urban areas of non-industrialized economies. As with many terms describing social class, working class is defined and used in many different ways.
Bacon	Bacon is a cured meat prepared from a pig. It is first cured using large quantities of salt, either in a brine or in a dry packing; the result is fresh bacon. Fresh bacon may then be further dried for weeks or months in cold air, boiled, or smoked.
Francis	Francis is a French and English first name and a surname of Latin origin. Francis is a name that has many derivatives in most European languages. The female version of the name in English is Frances, and (less commonly) Francine.
Common	The Common is a part of the Christian liturgy that consists of texts common to an entire category of saints, such as Apostles or Martyrs. The term is used in contrast to the ordinary, which is that part of the liturgy that is reasonably constant, or at least selected without regard to date, and to the proper, which is the part of the liturgy that varies according to the date, either representing an observance within the Liturgical Year, or of a particular saint or significant event. Commons contain collects, psalms, readings from Scripture, prefaces, and other portions of services that are common to a category of saints.
England	"England" is a song written by Justin Hawkins from The Darkness(music) ' Chas Bayfield (lyrics) and released by him under the name British Whale and used as the unofficial World Cup single for the England National Team in 2006

Chapter 6. TOWARD A NEW HEAVEN AND A NEW EARTH

Chapter 6. TOWARD A NEW HEAVEN AND A NEW EARTH

Orthodoxy	The word orthodox, from Greek orthos ("right", "true", "straight") + doxa ("opinion" or "belief", related to dokein, "to think"), is generally used to mean the adherence to accepted norms, more specifically to creeds, especially in religion. The Orthodox Churches in Slavic-language countries use a word derived from Old Church Slavonic, Правосла́ви? (pravosláviye) to mean Orthodoxy. The term did not exist in the sense in which it is now used prior to the advent of the State church of the Roman Empire.
Diggers	The Diggers were an English group of Protestant agrarian communists, begun by Gerrard Winstanley as True Levellers in 1649, who became known as Diggers due to their activities. Their original name came from their belief in economic equality based upon a specific passage in the Book of Acts. The Diggers tried (by "levelling" real property) to reform the existing social order with an agrarian lifestyle based on their ideas for the creation of small egalitarian rural communities.
The Bowman and The Spearman	The Bowman and The Spearman, are two bronze equestrian sculptures standing as gatekeepers at the intersection of Congress Drive and Michigan Avenue in Grant Park, Chicago, United States. The sculptures were made in Zagreb by Croatian sculptor Ivan Meštrovic and installed at the entrance of the parkway in 1928. The pair of sculptures was funded by the Benjamin Ferguson Fund. An unusual aspect of the sculptures is that the figures in both sculptures are missing their weapons, the bow and arrow and the spear.

Chapter 6. TOWARD A NEW HEAVEN AND A NEW EARTH

Chapter 6. TOWARD A NEW HEAVEN AND A NEW EARTH

Levellers	The Levellers were a political movement during the English Civil Wars which emphasised popular sovereignty, extended suffrage, equality before the law, and religious tolerance, all of which were expressed in the manifesto "Agreement of the People". They came to prominence at the end of the First English Civil War and were most influential before the start of the Second Civil War. Leveller views and support were found in the populace of the City of London and in some regiments in the New Model Army.
New Model Army	The New Model Army of England was formed in 1645 by the Parliamentarians in the English Civil War, and was disbanded in 1660 after the Restoration. It differed from other armies in the series of civil wars referred to as the Wars of the Three Kingdoms in that it was intended as an army liable for service anywhere in the country (including in Scotland and Ireland), rather than being tied to a single area or garrison. Its soldiers became full-time professionals, rather than part-time militia.
Puritan	The Puritans were a significant grouping of English Protestants in the 16th and 17th centuries. Puritanism in this sense was founded by some Marian exiles from the clergy shortly after the accession of Elizabeth I of England in 1559, as an activist movement within the Church of England. The designation "Puritan" is often incorrectly used, notably based on the assumption that hedonism and puritanism are antonyms: historically, the word was used to characterize the Protestant group as extremists similar to the Cathari of France, and according to Thomas Fuller in his Church History dated back to 1564. Archbishop Matthew Parker of that time used it and "precisian" with the sense of stickler.
Pantheism	Pantheism is the view that the Universe (Nature) and God are identical. Pantheists thus do not believe in a personal, anthropomorphic or creator god. As such, pantheism denotes the idea that "God" is best seen as a way of relating to the Universe.
Blaise Pascal	Blaise Pascal, was a French mathematician, physicist, inventor, writer and Catholic philosopher. He was a child prodigy who was educated by his father, a Tax Collector in Rouen. Pascal's earliest work was in the natural and applied sciences where he made important contributions to the study of fluids, and clarified the concepts of pressure and vacuum by generalizing the work of Evangelista Torricelli.

Chapter 6. TOWARD A NEW HEAVEN AND A NEW EARTH

Chapter 7. THE EIGHTEENTH CENTURY: AN AGE OF ENLIGHTENMENT

Classicism

Classicism, in the arts, refers generally to a high regard for classical antiquity, as setting standards for taste which the classicists seek to emulate. The art of classicism typically seeks to be formal and restrained: of the Discobolus Sir Kenneth Clark observed, "if we object to his restraint and compression we are simply objecting to the classicism of classic art. A violent emphasis or a sudden acceleration of rhythmic movement would have destroyed those qualities of balance and completeness through which it retained until the present century its position of authority in the restricted repertoire of visual images." Classicism, as Clark noted, implies a canon of widely accepted ideal forms, whether in the Western canon that he was examining in The Nude (1956), or the Chinese classics.

Immanuel

Immanuel, meaning 'God') and ???????? (?Immanu, meaning 'with us'); Standard Hebrew ? Immanu'el, Tiberian Hebrew ?Immanû'el). It is a theophoric name used in the Bible in Isaiah 7:14 and Isaiah 8:8. It appears once in the Christian New Testament: in Matthew's quotation of Isaiah 7:14.

Christian usage

Christian belief holds that Immanuel is Jesus, and the Messiah foretold in the other prophecies of Isaiah.

Plurality

In religion, the term plurality refers to a system of church government or ecclesiastical polity, wherein the local assembly's decisions are made by a committee, each typically called an elder; in contrast to the "singularity" of the bishop hierarchy system (Roman Catholic, Eastern Orthodox, and Anglican churches); or the pastor / president system of many Protestant churches.

The plurality system is commonly encouraged among Presbyterians, Jehovah's Witnesses, Church of Christ, Disciples of Christ, Plymouth Brethren, and some Apostolics.

Chapter 7. THE EIGHTEENTH CENTURY: AN AGE OF ENLIGHTENMENT

Chapter 7. THE EIGHTEENTH CENTURY: AN AGE OF ENLIGHTENMENT

World	WORLD Magazine is a biweekly Christian news magazine, published in the United States of America by God's World Publications, a non-profit 501(c)(3) organization based in Asheville, North Carolina. WORLD differs from most other news magazines in that its declared perspective is one of conservative evangelical Protestantism. Its mission statement is "To report, interpret, and illustrate the news in a timely, accurate, enjoyable, and arresting fashion from a perspective committed to the Bible as the inerrant Word of God."
	Each issue features both U.S. and international news, cultural analysis, editorials and commentary, as well as book, music and movie reviews.
Christian	A Christian is a person who adheres to Christianity, an Abrahamic, monotheistic religion based on the life and teachings of Jesus of Nazareth as recorded in the Canonical gospels and the letters of the New Testament.
	Central to the Christian faith is love or Agape. Christians also believe Jesus is the Messiah prophesied in the Hebrew Bible, the Son of God, and the savior of mankind from their sins.
James Cook	Captain James Cook FRS RN (7 November [O.S. 27 October] 1728 - 14 February 1779) was a British explorer, navigator and cartographer, ultimately rising to the rank of Captain in the Royal Navy. Cook made detailed maps of Newfoundland prior to making three voyages to the Pacific Ocean during which he achieved the first European contact with the eastern coastline of Australia and the Hawaiian Islands as well as the first recorded circumnavigation of New Zealand.
	Cook joined the British merchant navy as a teenager and joined the Royal Navy in 1755. He saw action in the Seven Years' War, and subsequently surveyed and mapped much of the entrance to the Saint Lawrence River during the siege of Quebec.

Chapter 7. THE EIGHTEENTH CENTURY: AN AGE OF ENLIGHTENMENT

Chapter 7. THE EIGHTEENTH CENTURY: AN AGE OF ENLIGHTENMENT

The Bowman and The Spearman	The Bowman and The Spearman, are two bronze equestrian sculptures standing as gatekeepers at the intersection of Congress Drive and Michigan Avenue in Grant Park, Chicago, United States. The sculptures were made in Zagreb by Croatian sculptor Ivan Meštrovic and installed at the entrance of the parkway in 1928. The pair of sculptures was funded by the Benjamin Ferguson Fund. An unusual aspect of the sculptures is that the figures in both sculptures are missing their weapons, the bow and arrow and the spear.
Cultural relativism	Cultural relativism is the principle that an individual human's beliefs and activities should be understood by others in terms of that individual's own culture. This principle was established as axiomatic in anthropological research by Franz Boas in the first few decades of the 20th century and later popularized by his students. Boas first articulated the idea in 1887: "...civilization is not something absolute, but ... is relative, and ... our ideas and conceptions are true only so far as our civilization goes." but did not actually coin the term "cultural relativism." The first use of the term recorded in the Oxford English Dictionary was by philosopher and social theorist Alain Locke in 1924 to describe Robert Lowie's "extreme cultural relativism", found in the latter's 1917 book Culture and Ethnology.
John Locke	John Locke, widely known as the Father of Liberalism, was an English philosopher and physician regarded as one of the most influential of Enlightenment thinkers. Considered one of the first of the British empiricists, following the tradition of Francis Bacon, he is equally important to social contract theory. His work had a great impact upon the development of epistemology and political philosophy.
Tabula rasa	Tabula rasa is the epistemological theory that individuals are born without built-in mental content and that their knowledge comes from experience and perception. Generally proponents of the tabula rasa thesis favour the "nurture" side of the nature versus nurture debate, when it comes to aspects of one's personality, social and emotional behaviour, and intelligence. The term in Latin equates to the English "blank slate" (or more accurately, "erased slate") (which refers to writing on a slate sheet in chalk) but comes from the Roman tabula or wax tablet, used for notes, which was blanked by heating the wax and then smoothing it to give a tabula rasa.

Chapter 7. THE EIGHTEENTH CENTURY: AN AGE OF ENLIGHTENMENT

Chapter 7. THE EIGHTEENTH CENTURY: AN AGE OF ENLIGHTENMENT

Montesquieu	Charles-Louis de Secondat, baron de La Brède et de Montesquieu, generally referred to as simply Montesquieu, was a French social commentator and political thinker who lived during the Enlightenment. He is famous for his articulation of the theory of separation of powers, taken for granted in modern discussions of government and implemented in many constitutions throughout the world. He was largely responsible for the popularization of the terms feudalism and Byzantine Empire.
Persian	A Persian is an oval-shaped, cinnamon-bun-like pastry with a sweet, pink icing made of either raspberries or strawberries. It originated in and remains particular to the city of Thunder Bay, Ontario, Canada.

History

Traditional lore is that the Persian was named for U.S. general John 'Blackjack' Pershing but the exact date of its inception and circumstances of its creation are no longer known, giving rise to competing claims and myths among people in the region. |
| Spirit | The English word spirit has many differing meanings and connotations, all of them relating to a non-corporeal substance contrasted with the material body. The spirit of a human being is thus the animating, sensitive or vital principle in that individual, similar to the soul taken to be the seat of the mental, intellectual and emotional powers. The notions of a person's "spirit" and "soul" often also overlap, as both contrast with body and both are imagined as surviving the bodily death in religion and occultism, and "spirit" can also have the sense of "ghost", i.e. manifestations of the spirit of a deceased person. |
| Baron | Baron is a title of nobility. The word baron comes from Old French baron, itself from Old High German and Latin (liber) baro meaning "(free) man, (free) warrior"; it merged with cognate Old English beorn meaning "nobleman".

Barons in the United Kingdom and the Commonwealth

In the British peer system, barons rank below viscounts, and form the lowest rank in the peerage. |

Chapter 7. THE EIGHTEENTH CENTURY: AN AGE OF ENLIGHTENMENT

Chapter 7. THE EIGHTEENTH CENTURY: AN AGE OF ENLIGHTENMENT

Adam	Adam is a prominent figure in Abrahamic religions. He is the first man created by God in Judaism, Christianity, and Islam. He appears originally in the Hebrew Bible in the Book of Genesis.
Alexander	Saint Alexander was a martyr and companion of St. Pothinus. Alexander was a physician in Vienne, Gaul, when he converted to Christianity. Arrested during the persecutions conducted under Emperor Marcus Aurelius.
Voltaire	François-Marie Arouet, better known by the pen name Voltaire, was a French Enlightenment writer, historian and philosopher famous for his wit and for his advocacy of civil liberties, including freedom of religion and free trade. Voltaire was known as a prolific writer and produced works in almost every literary form including plays, poetry, novels, essays, historical and scientific works, more than 20,000 letters and more than 2,000 books and pamphlets. He was an outspoken supporter of social reform, despite strict censorship laws and harsh penalties for those who broke them.
Central Europe	Central Europe is an area of the European continent lying between the variously defined areas of Eastern and Western Europe. The term is becoming widespread just like the interest in the region itself after the end of the Cold War, which, along with the Iron Curtain, had divided Europe politically into East and West, splitting Europe in half. Central European journals are published.
Denis	"Denis" a.k.a. "Denee Denee" is a song by American New Wave band Blondie. It featured on the band's second studio album, Plastic Letters (1977), and was the second UK single release by Blondie on Chrysalis records.
Denis Diderot	Denis Diderot was a French philosopher, art critic, and writer. He was a prominent figure during the Enlightenment and is best-known for serving as co-founder and chief editor of and contributor to the Encyclopédie. Diderot also contributed to literature, notably with Jacques le fataliste et son maître (Jacques the Fatalist and his Master), which emulated Laurence Sterne in challenging conventions regarding novels and their structure and content, while also examining philosophical ideas about free will.

Chapter 7. THE EIGHTEENTH CENTURY: AN AGE OF ENLIGHTENMENT

Chapter 7. THE EIGHTEENTH CENTURY: AN AGE OF ENLIGHTENMENT

Candide	Candide, ou l'Optimisme is a French satire written in 1759 by Voltaire, a philosopher of the Age of Enlightenment. The novella has been widely translated, with English versions titled Candide: or, All for the Best (1759); Candide: or, The Optimist (1762); and Candide: or, Optimism (1947). It begins with a young man, Candide, who is living a sheltered life in an Edenic paradise and being indoctrinated with Leibnizian optimism (or simply Optimism) by his mentor, Pangloss.
Ignatius of Loyola	Ignatius of Loyola was a Spanish knight from a Basque noble family, hermit, priest since 1537, and theologian, who founded the Society of Jesus and was its first Superior General. Ignatius emerged as a religious leader during the Counter-Reformation. Loyola's devotion to the Church was characterized by unquestioning obedience to the Church's authority and hierarchy.
David Hume	David Hume was a Scottish philosopher, historian, economist, and essayist, known especially for his philosophical empiricism and skepticism. He is regarded as one of the most important figures in the history of Western philosophy and the Scottish Enlightenment. Hume is often grouped with John Locke, George Berkeley, and a handful of others as a British Empiricist.
Scientific revolution	The Scientific Revolution was a period when new ideas in physics, astronomy, biology, human anatomy, chemistry, and other sciences led to a rejection of doctrines that had prevailed starting in Ancient Greece and continuing through the Middle Ages, and laid the foundation of modern science. According to most accounts, the scientific revolution began in Europe towards the end of the Renaissance era and continued through the late 18th century, the latter period known as The Enlightenment. It was sparked by the publication (1543) of two works that changed the course of science: Nicolaus Copernicus's De revolutionibus orbium coelestium (On the Revolutions of the Heavenly Spheres) and Andreas Vesalius's De humani corporis fabrica (On the Fabric of the Human body).
Adam Smith	Adam Smith was a Scottish social philosopher and a pioneer of political economics. One of the key figures of the Scottish Enlightenment, Smith is the author of The Theory of Moral Sentiments and An Inquiry into the Nature and Causes of the Wealth of Nations. The latter, usually abbreviated as The Wealth of Nations, is considered his magnum opus and the first modern work of economics.
Mankind	Mankind is an English medieval morality play, written c.1470. The play is a moral allegory about Mankind, a representative of the human race, and follows his fall into sin and his repentance. Its author is unknown; the manuscript is signed by a monk named Hyngham, but he was probably only the scribe since some of the textual oddities are believed to derive from his miscopying of parts of the text because he was not familiar with it.
	Date

Chapter 7. THE EIGHTEENTH CENTURY: AN AGE OF ENLIGHTENMENT

Chapter 7. THE EIGHTEENTH CENTURY: AN AGE OF ENLIGHTENMENT

	In his critical edition of the play published by the Early English Text Society in 1969, Eccles argues for a date between 1465 and 1470. Wickham, in his Dent edition of 1976, agrees, finally settling on 1470. Similarly, Lester, in his New Mermaids edition of 1981, offers between 1464 and 1471. Baker and, following his suggestion, Southern agree on a date of 1466.
Jean-Jacques Rousseau	Jean-Jacques Rousseau was a major Genevan philosopher, writer, and composer of 18th-century Romanticism. His political philosophy heavily influenced the French Revolution, as well as the American Revolution and the overall development of modern political, sociological and educational thought. His novel, Émile: or, On Education is a seminal treatise on the education of the whole person for citizenship.
Liberalism	Liberalism is the belief in the importance of liberty and equal rights. Liberals espouse a wide array of views depending on their understanding of these principles, but most liberals support such fundamental ideas as constitutions, liberal democracy, free and fair elections, human rights, capitalism, free trade, and the freedom of religion. These ideas are widely accepted, even by political groups that do not openly profess a liberal ideological orientation.
Romanticism	Romanticism was a complex artistic, literary and intellectual movement that originated in the second half of the 18th century in Europe, and gained strength in reaction to the Industrial Revolution. In part, it was a revolt against aristocratic social and political norms of the Age of Enlightenment and a reaction against the scientific rationalization of nature. It was embodied most strongly in the visual arts, music, and literature, but had a major impact on historiography, education and natural history.
Mary Astell	Mary Astell was an English feminist writer and rhetorician. Her advocacy of equal educational opportunities for women has earned her the title "the first English feminist." Life and career

Chapter 7. THE EIGHTEENTH CENTURY: AN AGE OF ENLIGHTENMENT

Chapter 7. THE EIGHTEENTH CENTURY: AN AGE OF ENLIGHTENMENT

	Few records of Mary Astell's life have survived. As biographer Ruth Perry explains, "as a woman she had little or no business in the world of commerce, politics, or law.
American Revolution	The American Revolution was the political upheaval during the last half of the 18th century in which thirteen colonies in North America joined together to break free from the British Empire, combining to become the United States of America. They first rejected the authority of the Parliament of Great Britain to govern them from overseas without representation, and then expelled all royal officials. By 1774 each colony had established a Provincial Congress, or an equivalent governmental institution, to form individual self-governing states. The British responded by sending combat troops to re-impose direct rule.
Napoleonic code	The Napoleonic Code -- or Code Napoléon (originally, the Code civil des Français) -- is the French civil code, established under Napoléon I in 1804. The code forbade privileges based on birth, allowed freedom of religion, and specified that government jobs go to the most qualified. It was drafted rapidly by a commission of four eminent jurists and entered into force on March 21, 1804. The Napoleonic Code was not the first legal code to be established in a European country with a civil legal system -- it was preceded by the Codex Maximilianeus bavaricus civilis (Bavaria, 1756), the Allgemeines Landrecht and the West Galician Code, (Galicia, then part of Austria, 1797). It was, however, the first modern legal code to be adopted with a pan-European scope and it strongly influenced the law of many of the countries formed during and after the Napoleonic Wars.
Edinburgh	Edinburgh is the capital city of Scotland, the second largest city in Scotland and the seventh-most populous in the United Kingdom. The City of Edinburgh Council is one of Scotland's 32 local government council areas. The council area includes urban Edinburgh and a 30-square-mile (78 km^2) rural area.
Salon	The Salon, beginning in 1725 was the official art exhibition of the Académie des Beaux-Arts in Paris, France. Between 1748-1890 it was the greatest annual or biannual art event in the Western world. From 1881 onward, it has been organized by the Société des Artistes Français.
Secret	The Secret is a prayer said in a low voice by the priest or bishop during religious services. Western Christianity

Chapter 7. THE EIGHTEENTH CENTURY: AN AGE OF ENLIGHTENMENT

Chapter 7. THE EIGHTEENTH CENTURY: AN AGE OF ENLIGHTENMENT

	In the Roman Rite the secreta is said by the celebrant at the end of the Offertory in the Mass. It is the original and for a long time was the only offertory prayer.
Horatii	According to Livy, the Horatii were male triplets from Rome. During a war between Rome and Alba Longa during the reign of Tullus Hostilius (approx. 672-642 B.C.), it was agreed that settlement of the war would depend on the outcome of a battle between the Horatii and the Curiatii. The Curiatii were male triplets from Alba Longa and of the same age as the Horatii.
Neoclassicism	Neoclassicism is the name given to quite distinct movements in the decorative and visual arts, literature, theatre, music, and architecture that draw upon Western classical art and culture (usually that of Ancient Greece or Ancient Rome). These movements were dominant in northern Europe during the mid-18th to the end of the 19th century. Overview What any "neo-classicism" depends on most fundamentally is a consensus about a body of work that has achieved canonic status (illustration, below).
Netherlands	More than one name is used to refer to the Netherlands, both in English and in other languages. Some of these names refer to different, but overlapping geographical, linguistic and political areas of the country. This is a common source of confusion for outsiders.
Republic	Republic is a Hungarian rock band formed in Budapest in 1989. Their style is a unique mix of Western rock music and traditional Hungarian folk music. The band is popular in its native country and among Hungarian speaking minorities elsewhere. Members The two founding members are László Bódi and Lászlo Attila Nagy.

Chapter 7. THE EIGHTEENTH CENTURY: AN AGE OF ENLIGHTENMENT

Chapter 7. THE EIGHTEENTH CENTURY: AN AGE OF ENLIGHTENMENT

Rococo	Rococo also referred to as "Late Baroque" is an 18th century style which developed as Baroque artists gave up their symmetry and became increasingly ornate, florid, and playful. Rococo rooms were designed as total works of art with elegant and ornate furniture, small sculptures, ornamental mirrors, and tapestry complementing architecture, reliefs, and wall paintings. It was largely supplanted by the Neoclassic style.
Southern Netherlands	Southern Netherlands were a part of the Low Countries controlled by Spain, Austria and annexed by France (1794-1815). This region comprised most of modern Belgium (except for three Lower-Rhenish territories: the Prince-Bishopric of Liège, the Imperial Abbey of Stavelot-Malmedy and the County of Bouillon) and Luxembourg (including the homonymous present Belgian province), and in addition some parts of the Netherlands (namely the Duchy of Limburg now split in a Dutch and Belgian part) as well as, until 1678, most of the present Nord-Pas-de-Calais region in northern France. Unlike French Burgundy and the republican Northern Netherlands, these allodial states kept access to the Burgundian Circle of the Holy Roman Empire until its end.
Church	A church building is a building or structure whose primary purpose is to facilitate the meeting of a church. Originally, Jewish Christians met in synagogues, such as the Cenacle, and in one another's homes, known as house churches. As Christianity grew and became more accepted by governments, notably with the Edict of Milan, rooms and, eventually, entire buildings were set aside for the explicit purpose of Christian worship, such as the Church of the Holy Sepulchre.
Prince-Bishop	A Prince-Bishop is a bishop who is a territorial Prince of the Church on account of one or more secular principalities, usually pre-existent titles of nobility held concurrently with their inherent clerical office. Thus the principality ruled politically by a prince-bishop could wholly or largely overlap with his diocesan jurisdiction, but not necessarily; several lost their actual see (the city itself), which could obatin the status of free imperial city. If the see is an archbishopric, the correct term is prince-archbishop; the equivalent in the regular (monastic) clergy is prince-abbot.
Baroque	Baroque is an artistic style prevalent from the late 16th century to the early 18th century in Europe.

Chapter 7. THE EIGHTEENTH CENTURY: AN AGE OF ENLIGHTENMENT

Chapter 7. THE EIGHTEENTH CENTURY: AN AGE OF ENLIGHTENMENT

The popularity and success of the Baroque style was encouraged by the Roman Catholic Church, which had decided at the time of the Council of Trent, in response to the Protestant Reformation, that the arts should communicate religious themes in direct and emotional involvement. The aristocracy also saw the dramatic style of Baroque architecture and art as a means of impressing visitors and expressing triumphant power and control.

Johann

Johann, typically a male given name, is the Germanized form of the originally Hebrew language name "Yohanan" (meaning "God is merciful"). It is a form of the Germanic given name "Johannes", which comes from Johan. The English language form is John.

Fireworks

Fireworks is a British magazine about fireworks, aimed at enthusiasts and pyrotechnic professionals.

The magazine began life in February 1982 as a photocopied newsletter for firework enthusiasts. At the time, the number of British firework companies was in sharp decline and their tangible remains were being lost or destroyed.

Joseph

The Bible: Joseph is a German/Italian/American television movie from 1995, which tells the story of Joseph from the Old Testament.

Plot

The opening scene is at the slave market of Avaris. Potiphar, the chief steward of the Pharaoh, is looking to buy a slave.

Chapter 7. THE EIGHTEENTH CENTURY: AN AGE OF ENLIGHTENMENT

Chapter 7. THE EIGHTEENTH CENTURY: AN AGE OF ENLIGHTENMENT

Messiah	Messiah, Hebrew: ????????, Modern Mashia? Tiberian Mašîa? ("anointed"), is a term used in Judaism, Christianity and Islam for the redeemer figure expected in one form or another by each religion. More loosely, the term messiah denotes any redeemer figure and the adjective messianic is used in a broad sense to refer to beliefs or theories about an eschatological improvement of the state of humanity or the world. Messiah is used in the Hebrew Bible to describe priests and kings, who were traditionally anointed with holy anointing oil as described in Exodus 30:22-25. For example, Cyrus the Great, the king of Persia, though not a Hebrew, is referred to as "God's anointed" (messiah).
Edward Gibbon	Edward Gibbon was an English historian and Member of Parliament. His most important work, The History of the Decline and Fall of the Roman Empire, was published in six volumes between 1776 and 1788. The Decline and Fall is known for the quality and irony of its prose, its use of primary sources, and its open denigration of organized religion. Childhood Edward Gibbon was born in 1737, the son of Edward and Judith Gibbon at Lime Grove, in the town of Putney, Surrey.
Henry	Henry is an English male given name and a surname, from the Old French Henry derived itself from the Germanic name Haimric, which was derived from the word elements haim, meaning "home" and ric, meaning "power, ruler". Harry, its English short form, was considered the "spoken form" of Henry in medieval England. Most English kings named Henry were called Harry.
Histories	Histories is a book by Tacitus, written c. 100-110, which covers the Year of Four Emperors following the downfall of Nero, the rise of Vespasian, and the rule of the Flavian Dynasty (69-96) up to the death of Domitian. Subject matter In one of the first chapters of the Agricola Tacitus said that he wished to speak about the years of Domitian, of Nerva, and of Trajan. In the Historiae the project has been modified: in the introduction, Tacitus says that he will deal with the age of Nerva and Trajan at a later time.

Chapter 7. THE EIGHTEENTH CENTURY: AN AGE OF ENLIGHTENMENT

Chapter 7. THE EIGHTEENTH CENTURY: AN AGE OF ENLIGHTENMENT

Samuel Richardson	Samuel Richardson was an 18th-century English writer and printer. He is best known for his three epistolary novels: Pamela: Or, Virtue Rewarded (1740), Clarissa: Or the History of a Young Lady (1748) and The History of Sir Charles Grandison (1753). Richardson was an established printer and publisher for most of his life and printed almost 500 different works, with journals and magazines.
The Fellowship	The Fellowship, is a U.S.-based religious and political organization founded in 1935 by Abraham Vereide. The stated purpose of the Fellowship is to provide a fellowship forum for decision makers to share in Bible studies, prayer meetings, worship experiences and to experience spiritual affirmation and support. The organization has been described as one of the most politically well-connected ministries in the United States.
18th century	The 18th century lasted from 1701 to 1800 in the Gregorian calendar. However, Western historians have occasionally defined the 18th century otherwise for the purposes of their work. For example, the "short" 18th century may be defined as 1715-1789, denoting the period of time between the death of Louis XIV of France and the start of the French Revolution with an emphasis on directly interconnected events.
Joseph Addison	Joseph Addison was an English essayist, poet, playwright and politician. He was a man of letters, eldest son of Lancelot Addison. His name is usually remembered alongside that of his long-standing friend, Richard Steele, with whom he founded The Spectator magazine.
Lollardy	Lollardy was the political and religious movement of the Lollards from the mid-14th century to the English Reformation. The term Lollards refers to the followers of John Wycliffe, a prominent theologian who was dismissed from the University of Oxford in 1381 for criticism of the Church, especially his doctrine on the Eucharist. Its demands were primarily for reform of Western Christianity.

Chapter 7. THE EIGHTEENTH CENTURY: AN AGE OF ENLIGHTENMENT

Chapter 7. THE EIGHTEENTH CENTURY: AN AGE OF ENLIGHTENMENT

Austria	Austria officially the Republic of Austria, is a landlocked country of roughly 8.3 million people in Central Europe. It is bordered by the Czech Republic and Germany to the north, Slovakia and Hungary to the east, Slovenia and Italy to the south, and Switzerland and Liechtenstein to the west. The territory of Austria covers 83,855 square kilometres (32,377 sq mi) and has a temperate and alpine climate.
Cesare	Cesare, the Italian version of the given name Caesar, may refer to: - Giuseppe Cesare Abba (1838-1910), Italian patriot and writer - Cesare Battisti (disambiguation) - Cesare Borgia (1475-1507), Italian general and statesman - Joe Cesare Colombo, Italian industrial designer - Cesare Emiliani (1922-1995), Italian-American scientist - Cesare Negri, the late Renaissance dancing-master - Cesare Pavese (1908-1950), Italian poet and novelist - Cesare Bonizzi, Franciscan monk and heavy metal singer - Cesare, Marquis of Beccaria (1738-1794), an Italian philosopher and politician - Cesare, a manga series by Souryo Fuyumi
Reform	Reform is an evangelical organization within Anglicanism, active in the Church of England and the Church of Ireland. Reform describes itself as a "network of churches and individuals within the Church of England, committed to the reform of ourselves, our congregation and our world by the gospel". Several large Anglican churches in England are members of Reform, such as Jesmond Parish Church (in Newcastle upon Tyne), St Ebbe's, Oxford, and St Helen's Bishopsgate (located in the City of London).
Carnival	Carnival is a festive season which occurs immediately before Lent; the main events are usually during February. Carnival typically involves a public celebration or parade combining some elements of a circus, mask and public street party. People often dress up or masquerade during the celebrations, which mark an overturning of daily life

Chapter 7. THE EIGHTEENTH CENTURY: AN AGE OF ENLIGHTENMENT

Chapter 7. THE EIGHTEENTH CENTURY: AN AGE OF ENLIGHTENMENT

	Carnival is a festival traditionally held in Roman Catholic and, to a lesser extent, Eastern Orthodox societies.
England	"England" is a song written by Justin Hawkins from The Darkness(music) ' Chas Bayfield (lyrics) and released by him under the name British Whale and used as the unofficial World Cup single for the England National Team in 2006

Chapter 7. THE EIGHTEENTH CENTURY: AN AGE OF ENLIGHTENMENT

Chapter 7. THE EIGHTEENTH CENTURY: AN AGE OF ENLIGHTENMENT

Festival | A Festival is a type of observance in the Churches of the Anglican Communion, considered to be less significant than a Principal Feast or Principal Holy Day, but more significant than a Lesser Festival or Commemoration. In Common Worship each Festival is provided with a collect and an indication of liturgical colour.

Fixed Festivals

- 1 January: The Naming and Circumcision of Jesus
- 25 January: The Conversion of Paul
- 19 March: Joseph of Nazareth
- 23 April: George, Martyr, Patron of England
- 25 April: Mark the Evangelist
- 1 May: Philip and James, Apostles
- 14 May: Matthias the Apostle
- 31 May: The Visit of the Blessed Virgin Mary to Elizabeth
- 11 June: Barnabas the Apostle
- 24 June: The Birth of John the Baptist
- 29 June: Peter and Paul, Apostles
- 3 July: Thomas the Apostle
- 22 July: Mary Magdalene
- 25 July: James the Apostle
- 6 August: The Transfiguration of Our Lord
- 15 August: The Blessed Virgin Mary
- 24 August: Bartholomew the Apostle
- 14 September: Holy Cross Day
- 21 September: Matthew, Apostle and Evangelist
- 29 September: Michael and All Angels
- 18 October: Luke the Evangelist
- 28 October: Simon and Jude, Apostles
- 30 November: Andrew the Apostle
- 26 December: Stephen, Deacon, First Martyr
- 27 December: John, Apostle and Evangelist
- 28 December: The Holy Innocents

Moveable Festivals

- The Baptism of Christ - when the Epiphany is celebrated between 2 and 6 January, on the following Sunday; when the Epiphany is celebrated on 7 or 8 January, on the following Monday
- The Day of Thanksgiving for the Institution of Holy Communion (Corpus Christi) - Thursday after Trinity Sunday (observance optional)
- Christ the King - Sunday next before Advent

Chapter 7. THE EIGHTEENTH CENTURY: AN AGE OF ENLIGHTENMENT

Chapter 7. THE EIGHTEENTH CENTURY: AN AGE OF ENLIGHTENMENT

Protestantism

Protestantism is one of the three major divisions (Catholicism, Orthodoxy, and Protestantism) within Christianity. It is a movement that began in northern Europe in the early 16th century as a reaction against medieval Roman Catholic doctrines and practices.

The doctrines of the various Protestant denominations and non-denominations vary, but most non-denominational doctrines include justification by grace through faith and not through works, known as Sola Fide, the priesthood of all believers, and the Bible as the ultimate authority in matters of faith and order, known as Sola Scriptura, which is Latin for 'by scripture alone'.

Volksschule

A Volksschule was an 18th century system of state-supported primary schools established in the Habsburg Austrian Empire (in 1840) and Prussia (in 1717). Attendance was supposedly compulsory, but a 1781 census reveals that only one fourth of school-age children attended. At the time, this was one of the few examples of state-supported schooling.

Calvinism

Calvinism is a theological system and an approach to the Christian life. The Reformed tradition was advanced by several theologians such as Martin Bucer, Heinrich Bullinger, Peter Martyr Vermigli, and Huldrych Zwingli, but this branch of Christianity bears the name of the French reformer John Calvin because of his prominent influence on it and because of his role in the confessional and ecclesiastical debates throughout the 16th century. Today, this term also refers to the doctrines and practices of the Reformed churches of which Calvin was an early leader.

Catholic

The word catholic comes from the Greek phrase καθ?λου (kath'holou), meaning "on the whole," "according to the whole" or "in general", and is a combination of the Greek words κατ? meaning "about" and ?λος meaning "whole". The word in English can mean either "including a wide variety of things; all-embracing" or "of the Roman Catholic faith." as "relating to the historic doctrine and practice of the Western Church."

It was first used to describe the Christian Church in the early 2nd century to emphasize its universal scope. In the context of Christian ecclesiology, it has a rich history and several usages.

Chapter 7. THE EIGHTEENTH CENTURY: AN AGE OF ENLIGHTENMENT

Chapter 7. THE EIGHTEENTH CENTURY: AN AGE OF ENLIGHTENMENT

Catholic Church	The Catholic Church, is the world's largest Christian church. Headed by the Pope, it sees its mission as spreading the gospel of Christ, administering its sacraments and exercising charity.
	The Catholic Church is one of the oldest religious institutions in the world and has played a prominent role in the history of Western civilisation.
Church of England	The Church of England is the officially established Christian church in England and the Mother Church of the worldwide Anglican Communion.
	The Church of England separated from the Roman Catholic Church in 1534 with the Act of Supremacy and understands itself to be both Catholic and Reformed:
	<ul><li>Catholic in that it views itself as a part of the universal church of Jesus Christ in unbroken continuity with the early apostolic church. This is expressed in its emphasis on the teachings of the early Church Fathers, as formalised in the Apostles', Nicene, and Athanasian creeds.</li><li>Reformed in that it has been shaped by the doctrinal principles of the 16th century Protestant Reformation, in particular in the Thirty-Nine Articles and the Book of Common Prayer.</li></ul>
	History
	Early history
	According to tradition, Christianity arrived in Britain in the first or 2nd century.
Hannah	Hannah is an oratorio in three acts by Christopher Smart with a score composed by John Worgan. It was first performed in Haymarket theater 3 April 1764. It was supposed to have a second performance, but that performance was postponed and eventually cancelled over a lack of singers. A libretto was published for its run and a libretto with full score was published later that year.

Chapter 7. THE EIGHTEENTH CENTURY: AN AGE OF ENLIGHTENMENT

Chapter 7. THE EIGHTEENTH CENTURY: AN AGE OF ENLIGHTENMENT

Huguenot	The Huguenots were members of the Protestant Reformed Church of France from the sixteenth to the seventeenth centuries. Since the seventeenth century, Huguenots have been commonly designated "French Protestants," the title being suggested by their German co-religionists or "Calvinists." Protestants in France were inspired by the writings of John Calvin in the 1530s and the name Huguenots was already in use by the 1560s. By the end of the 17th century, roughly 200,000 Huguenots had been driven from France during a series of religious persecutions.
Lutheranism	Lutheranism is a major branch of Western Christianity that identifies with the theology of Martin Luther, a German reformer. Luther's efforts to reform the theology and practice of the church launched the Protestant Reformation. Beginning with the 95 Theses, Luther's writings disseminated internationally, spreading the ideas of the Reformation beyond the ability of governmental and churchly authorities to control it.
Conciliarism	Conciliarism, was a reform movement in the 14th, 15th and 16th century Roman Catholic Church which held that final authority in spiritual matters resided with the Roman Church as a corporation of Christians, embodied by a general church council, not with the pope. The movement emerged in response to the Avignon papacy; the popes were removed from Rome and subjected to pressures from the kings of France-- and the ensuing schism that inspired the summoning of the Council of Pisa (1409), the Council of Constance (1414-1418) and the Council of Basel (1431-1449). The eventual victor in the conflict was the institution of the Papacy, confirmed by the condemnation of conciliarism at the Fifth Lateran Council, 1512-17. The final gesture however, the doctrine of Papal Infallibility, was not promulgated until the First Vatican Council of 1870.
State	The term state is used in various senses by Catholic theologians and spiritual writers. It may be taken to signify a profession or calling in life, as where St. Paul says, in I Corinthians 7:20: "Let every man abide in the same calling in which he was called". States are classified in the Catholic Church as the clerical state, the religious state, and the secular state; and among religious states, again, we have those of the contemplative, the active, and the mixed orders.

Chapter 7. THE EIGHTEENTH CENTURY: AN AGE OF ENLIGHTENMENT

Chapter 7. THE EIGHTEENTH CENTURY: AN AGE OF ENLIGHTENMENT

Black Death	The Black Death was one of the most devastating pandemics in human history, peaking in Europe between 1348 and 1350. It is widely thought to have been an outbreak of plague caused by the bacterium Yersinia pestis, an argument supported by recent forensic research, although this view has been challenged by a number of scholars. Thought to have started in China, it travelled along the Silk Road and had reached the Crimea by 1346. From there, probably carried by Oriental rat fleas residing on the black rats that were regular passengers on merchant ships, it spread throughout the Mediterranean and Europe. The Black Death is estimated to have killed 30% - 60% of Europe's population, reducing the world's population from an estimated 450 million to between 350 and 375 million in 1400. This has been seen as having created a series of religious, social and economic upheavals, which had profound effects on the course of European history.
Orthodoxy	The word orthodox, from Greek orthos ("right", "true", "straight") + doxa ("opinion" or "belief", related to dokein, "to think"), is generally used to mean the adherence to accepted norms, more specifically to creeds, especially in religion. The Orthodox Churches in Slavic-language countries use a word derived from Old Church Slavonic, Правосла́ви? (pravosláviye) to mean Orthodoxy. The term did not exist in the sense in which it is now used prior to the advent of the State church of the Roman Empire.
Baptists	Baptists are a group of Christian denominations, churches, and individuals who subscribe to a theology of believer's baptism (as opposed to infant baptism), salvation through faith alone, Scripture alone as the rule of faith and practice, and the autonomy of the local church. They practice baptism by immersion (as opposed to affusion or sprinkling) and disavow authoritative creeds. Baptists recognize two ministerial offices, pastors and deacons.
Count	A count is a aristocratic nobleman in European countries; his wife is a countess. The word count came into English from the French comte, itself from Latin comes--in its accusative comitem-- meaning "companion", and later "companion of the emperor, delegate of the emperor". The adjective form of the word is "comital".

Chapter 7. THE EIGHTEENTH CENTURY: AN AGE OF ENLIGHTENMENT

Chapter 7. THE EIGHTEENTH CENTURY: AN AGE OF ENLIGHTENMENT

Pietism	Pietism was a movement within Lutheranism, lasting from the late 17th century to the mid-18th century and later. It proved to be very influential throughout Protestantism and Anabaptism, inspiring not only Anglican priest John Wesley to begin the Methodist movement, but also Alexander Mack to begin the Brethren movement. The Pietist movement combined the Lutheranism of the time with the Reformed emphasis on individual piety and living a vigorous Christian life.
Puritan	The Puritans were a significant grouping of English Protestants in the 16th and 17th centuries. Puritanism in this sense was founded by some Marian exiles from the clergy shortly after the accession of Elizabeth I of England in 1559, as an activist movement within the Church of England. The designation "Puritan" is often incorrectly used, notably based on the assumption that hedonism and puritanism are antonyms: historically, the word was used to characterize the Protestant group as extremists similar to the Cathari of France, and according to Thomas Fuller in his Church History dated back to 1564. Archbishop Matthew Parker of that time used it and "precisian" with the sense of stickler.
John Wesley	John Wesley was a Church of England cleric and Christian theologian. Wesley is largely credited, along with his brother Charles Wesley, as founding the Methodist movement which began when he took to open-air preaching in a similar manner to George Whitefield. In contrast to George Whitefield's Calvinism, Wesley embraced the Arminian doctrines that were dominant in the 18th-century Church of England.

Chapter 7. THE EIGHTEENTH CENTURY: AN AGE OF ENLIGHTENMENT

Chapter 8. THE EIGHTEENTH CENTURY: EUROPEAN STATES, INTERNATIONAL WARS, AND CHANGE

Johann	Johann, typically a male given name, is the Germanized form of the originally Hebrew language name "Yohanan" (meaning "God is merciful"). It is a form of the Germanic given name "Johannes", which comes from Johan. The English language form is John.
18th century	The 18th century lasted from 1701 to 1800 in the Gregorian calendar.
	However, Western historians have occasionally defined the 18th century otherwise for the purposes of their work. For example, the "short" 18th century may be defined as 1715-1789, denoting the period of time between the death of Louis XIV of France and the start of the French Revolution with an emphasis on directly interconnected events.
Joseph	The Bible: Joseph is a German/Italian/American television movie from 1995, which tells the story of Joseph from the Old Testament.
	Plot
	The opening scene is at the slave market of Avaris. Potiphar, the chief steward of the Pharaoh, is looking to buy a slave.
Renaissance	The Renaissance is a cultural movement that spanned roughly the 14th to the 17th century, beginning in Florence in the Late Middle Ages and later spreading to the rest of Europe. The term is also used more loosely to refer to the historic era, but since the changes of the Renaissance were not uniform across Europe, this is a general use of the term. As a cultural movement, it encompassed a resurgence of learning based on classical sources, the development of linear perspective in painting, and gradual but widespread educational reform.
State	The term state is used in various senses by Catholic theologians and spiritual writers.

Chapter 8. THE EIGHTEENTH CENTURY: EUROPEAN STATES, INTERNATIONAL WARS, AND CHANGE

Chapter 8. THE EIGHTEENTH CENTURY: EUROPEAN STATES, INTERNATIONAL WARS, AND CHANGE

	It may be taken to signify a profession or calling in life, as where St. Paul says, in I Corinthians 7:20: "Let every man abide in the same calling in which he was called". States are classified in the Catholic Church as the clerical state, the religious state, and the secular state; and among religious states, again, we have those of the contemplative, the active, and the mixed orders.
House of Stuart	The House of Stuart is a European royal house. Founded by Robert II of Scotland, the Stewarts first became monarchs of the Kingdom of Scotland during the late 14th century, and subsequently held the position of the Kings of Great Britain and Ireland. Their direct ancestors (from Brittany) had held the title High Steward of Scotland since the 12th century, after arriving by way of Norman England.
Central Europe	Central Europe is an area of the European continent lying between the variously defined areas of Eastern and Western Europe. The term is becoming widespread just like the interest in the region itself after the end of the Cold War, which, along with the Iron Curtain, had divided Europe politically into East and West, splitting Europe in half. Central European journals are published.
Black Death	The Black Death was one of the most devastating pandemics in human history, peaking in Europe between 1348 and 1350. It is widely thought to have been an outbreak of plague caused by the bacterium Yersinia pestis, an argument supported by recent forensic research, although this view has been challenged by a number of scholars. Thought to have started in China, it travelled along the Silk Road and had reached the Crimea by 1346. From there, probably carried by Oriental rat fleas residing on the black rats that were regular passengers on merchant ships, it spread throughout the Mediterranean and Europe. The Black Death is estimated to have killed 30% - 60% of Europe's population, reducing the world's population from an estimated 450 million to between 350 and 375 million in 1400. This has been seen as having created a series of religious, social and economic upheavals, which had profound effects on the course of European history.
Church	A church building is a building or structure whose primary purpose is to facilitate the meeting of a church. Originally, Jewish Christians met in synagogues, such as the Cenacle, and in one another's homes, known as house churches. As Christianity grew and became more accepted by governments, notably with the Edict of Milan, rooms and, eventually, entire buildings were set aside for the explicit purpose of Christian worship, such as the Church of the Holy Sepulchre.

Chapter 8. THE EIGHTEENTH CENTURY: EUROPEAN STATES, INTERNATIONAL WARS, AND CHANGE

Chapter 8. THE EIGHTEENTH CENTURY: EUROPEAN STATES, INTERNATIONAL WARS, AND CHANGE

Common	The Common is a part of the Christian liturgy that consists of texts common to an entire category of saints, such as Apostles or Martyrs. The term is used in contrast to the ordinary, which is that part of the liturgy that is reasonably constant, or at least selected without regard to date, and to the proper, which is the part of the liturgy that varies according to the date, either representing an observance within the Liturgical Year, or of a particular saint or significant event. Commons contain collects, psalms, readings from Scripture, prefaces, and other portions of services that are common to a category of saints.
Elder	An Elder in the Methodist Church -- sometimes called a Presbyter or Minister -- is someone who has been ordained by a Bishop to the ministry of Word, Sacrament, Order, and Service. Their responsibilities are to preach and teach, preside at the celebration of the sacraments, administer the Church through pastoral guidance, and lead the congregations under their care in service ministry to the world. The Book of Discipline of the United Methodist Church states that The office of Elder, then, is what most people tend to think of as the pastoral, priestly, clergy office within the church.
England	"England" is a song written by Justin Hawkins from The Darkness(music) ' Chas Bayfield (lyrics) and released by him under the name British Whale and used as the unofficial World Cup single for the England National Team in 2006
House	A house is a home, building or structure that is a dwelling or place for habitation by human beings. The term house includes many kinds of dwellings ranging from rudimentary huts of nomadic tribes to free standing individual structures. In some contexts, "house" may mean the same as dwelling, residence, home, abode, lodging, accommodation, or housing, among other meanings.

Chapter 8. THE EIGHTEENTH CENTURY: EUROPEAN STATES, INTERNATIONAL WARS, AND CHANGE

Chapter 8. THE EIGHTEENTH CENTURY: EUROPEAN STATES, INTERNATIONAL WARS, AND CHANGE

Lollardy	Lollardy was the political and religious movement of the Lollards from the mid-14th century to the English Reformation. The term Lollards refers to the followers of John Wycliffe, a prominent theologian who was dismissed from the University of Oxford in 1381 for criticism of the Church, especially his doctrine on the Eucharist. Its demands were primarily for reform of Western Christianity.
Marie Antoinette	Marie Antoinette was an Archduchess of Austria and the Queen of France and of Navarre. She was the fifteenth and penultimate child of Empress Maria Theresa of Austria and Emperor Francis I. In April 1770, on the day of her marriage to Louis-Auguste, Dauphin of France, she subsequently became Dauphine of France. Marie Antoinette assumed the title of Queen of France and of Navarre when her husband, Louis XVI of France, ascended the throne upon the death of Louis XV in May 1774. At the height of the French Revolution, Louis XVI was deposed and the monarchy abolished on 10 August 1792; the royal family was subsequently imprisoned at the Temple Prison. Nine months after her husband's execution, Marie Antoinette was herself tried, convicted of treason, and executed by guillotine on 16 October 1793.
European colonization of the Americas	The start of the European colonization of the Americas is typically dated to 1492, although there was at least one earlier colonization effort. The first known Europeans to reach the Americas were the Vikings (Norse) during the 11th century, who established several colonies in Greenland and one short-lived settlement at L'Anse aux Meadows (51°N) in the area the Norse called Vinland, present day Newfoundland and to the south. Settlements in Greenland survived for several centuries, during which time the Greenland Norse and the Inuit people experienced mostly hostile contact. By the end of the 15th century, the Norse Greenland settlements had collapsed.
Court	The court of a monarch, or at some periods an important nobleman, is a term for the extended household and all those who regularly attended on the ruler or central figure. In the largest courts many thousands of individuals comprised the court, many officials or servants in the permanent employ of the ruler, and others attending in hope of political or financial gain, or merely for the society and entertainments offered. As well as being the centre of political life, courts were usually the drivers of fashion, and often where literary, musical and artistic trends first developed.

Chapter 8. THE EIGHTEENTH CENTURY: EUROPEAN STATES, INTERNATIONAL WARS, AND CHANGE

Chapter 8. THE EIGHTEENTH CENTURY: EUROPEAN STATES, INTERNATIONAL WARS, AND CHANGE

Hanoverian	A Hanoverian is a warmblood horse originating in Germany, which is often seen in the Olympic Games and other competitive English riding styles, and have won gold medals in all three equestrian Olympic competitions. It is one of the oldest, most numerous, and most successful of the warmbloods. Originally a carriage horse, infusions of Thoroughbred blood lightened it to make it more agile and useful for competition.
Orthodoxy	The word orthodox, from Greek orthos ("right", "true", "straight") + doxa ("opinion" or "belief", related to dokein, "to think"), is generally used to mean the adherence to accepted norms, more specifically to creeds, especially in religion. The Orthodox Churches in Slavic-language countries use a word derived from Old Church Slavonic, Правосла́ви? (pravosláviye) to mean Orthodoxy. The term did not exist in the sense in which it is now used prior to the advent of the State church of the Roman Empire.
American Revolution	The American Revolution was the political upheaval during the last half of the 18th century in which thirteen colonies in North America joined together to break free from the British Empire, combining to become the United States of America. They first rejected the authority of the Parliament of Great Britain to govern them from overseas without representation, and then expelled all royal officials. By 1774 each colony had established a Provincial Congress, or an equivalent governmental institution, to form individual self-governing states. The British responded by sending combat troops to re-impose direct rule.
Austria	Austria officially the Republic of Austria, is a landlocked country of roughly 8.3 million people in Central Europe. It is bordered by the Czech Republic and Germany to the north, Slovakia and Hungary to the east, Slovenia and Italy to the south, and Switzerland and Liechtenstein to the west. The territory of Austria covers 83,855 square kilometres (32,377 sq mi) and has a temperate and alpine climate.
Catholic	The word catholic comes from the Greek phrase καθ?λου (kath'holou), meaning "on the whole," "according to the whole" or "in general", and is a combination of the Greek words κατ? meaning "about" and ?λος meaning "whole". The word in English can mean either "including a wide variety of things; all-embracing" or "of the Roman Catholic faith." as "relating to the historic doctrine and practice of the Western Church."

Chapter 8. THE EIGHTEENTH CENTURY: EUROPEAN STATES, INTERNATIONAL WARS, AND CHANGE

Chapter 8. THE EIGHTEENTH CENTURY: EUROPEAN STATES, INTERNATIONAL WARS, AND CHANGE

	It was first used to describe the Christian Church in the early 2nd century to emphasize its universal scope. In the context of Christian ecclesiology, it has a rich history and several usages.
Catholic Church	The Catholic Church, is the world's largest Christian church. Headed by the Pope, it sees its mission as spreading the gospel of Christ, administering its sacraments and exercising charity.
	The Catholic Church is one of the oldest religious institutions in the world and has played a prominent role in the history of Western civilisation.
Republic	Republic is a Hungarian rock band formed in Budapest in 1989. Their style is a unique mix of Western rock music and traditional Hungarian folk music. The band is popular in its native country and among Hungarian speaking minorities elsewhere.
	Members
	The two founding members are László Bódi and Lászlo Attila Nagy.
Prussia	Prussia was a German kingdom and historic state originating out of the Duchy of Prussia and the Margraviate of Brandenburg. For centuries, the House of Hohenzollern ruled Prussia, successfully expanding its size by way of an unusually well-organized and effective army. Prussia shaped the history of Germany, with its capital in Berlin after 1451. After 1871, Prussia was increasingly merged into Germany, losing its distinctive identity.
William the Conqueror	William the Conqueror was the first Norman King of England from Christmas 1066 until his death. He was also Duke of Normandy from 3 July 1035 until his death, under the name William II. Before his conquest of England, he was known as William the Bastard because of the illegitimacy of his birth.

Chapter 8. THE EIGHTEENTH CENTURY: EUROPEAN STATES, INTERNATIONAL WARS, AND CHANGE

Chapter 8. THE EIGHTEENTH CENTURY: EUROPEAN STATES, INTERNATIONAL WARS, AND CHANGE

	To press his claim to the English crown, William invaded England in 1066, leading an army of Normans, Bretons, Flemings, and Frenchmen (from Paris and Île-de-France) to victory over the English forces of King Harold Godwinson at the Battle of Hastings, and suppressed subsequent English revolts in what has become known as the Norman Conquest.
Maria	The gens Maria was a plebeian family at Rome. Its most celebrated member was Gaius Marius, one of the greatest generals of antiquity, and seven times consul. Origin of the gens The nomen Marius appears to be derived from the Oscan praenomen Marius, in which case the family is probably of Sabine or Sabellic origin.
Maria Theresa	Maria Theresa Walburga Amalia Christina (13 May 1717 - 29 November 1780) was the only female ruler of the Habsburg dominions and the last of the House of Habsburg. She was the sovereign of Austria, Hungary, Croatia, Bohemia, Mantua, Milan, Lodomeria and Galicia, the Austrian Netherlands and Parma. By marriage, she was Duchess of Lorraine, Grand Duchess of Tuscany and Holy Roman Empress.
Netherlands	More than one name is used to refer to the Netherlands, both in English and in other languages. Some of these names refer to different, but overlapping geographical, linguistic and political areas of the country. This is a common source of confusion for outsiders.
Reform	Reform is an evangelical organization within Anglicanism, active in the Church of England and the Church of Ireland. Reform describes itself as a "network of churches and individuals within the Church of England, committed to the reform of ourselves, our congregation and our world by the gospel". Several large Anglican churches in England are members of Reform, such as Jesmond Parish Church (in Newcastle upon Tyne), St Ebbe's, Oxford, and St Helen's Bishopsgate (located in the City of London).

Chapter 8. THE EIGHTEENTH CENTURY: EUROPEAN STATES, INTERNATIONAL WARS, AND CHANGE

Chapter 8. THE EIGHTEENTH CENTURY: EUROPEAN STATES, INTERNATIONAL WARS, AND CHANGE

Chinas	The Chinas are a people mentioned in ancient Indian literature from the first millennium BC, such as the Mahabharata, Laws of Manu, as well the Puranic literature. They are believed to have been Chinese.

Etymology

The name Cina is commonly believed to have been derived from either the Qin (Tsin or Chin) dynasty which rule in China from 221 BC or the earlier Qin state which later became the Qin dynasty. |
| Nakaz | Nakaz, of Catherine the Great was a statement of legal principles authored by Catherine II of Russia, and permeated with the ideas of the French Enlightenment. It was compiled as a guide for the All-Russian Legislative Commission convened in 1767 for the purpose of replacing the mid-17th-century Muscovite code of laws with a modern law code. Catherine believed that to strengthen law and institutions was above all else to strengthen the monarchy. |
| Baron | Baron is a title of nobility. The word baron comes from Old French baron, itself from Old High German and Latin (liber) baro meaning "(free) man, (free) warrior"; it merged with cognate Old English beorn meaning "nobleman".

Barons in the United Kingdom and the Commonwealth

In the British peer system, barons rank below viscounts, and form the lowest rank in the peerage. |
| Africa | Africa is the world's second-largest and second most-populous continent, after Asia. At about 30.2 million km² (11.7 million sq mi) including adjacent islands, it covers 6% of the Earth's total surface area and 20.4% of the total land area. With 1.0 billion people in 61 territories, it accounts for about 14.72% of the world's human population. |

Chapter 8. THE EIGHTEENTH CENTURY: EUROPEAN STATES, INTERNATIONAL WARS, AND CHANGE

Chapter 8. THE EIGHTEENTH CENTURY: EUROPEAN STATES, INTERNATIONAL WARS, AND CHANGE

Galicia	Galicia is an autonomous community in northwest Spain, with the status of a historic nationality. It is constituted under the Galician Statute of Autonomy of 1981. Its component provinces are A Coruña, Lugo, Ourense and Pontevedra. It is bordered by Portugal to the south, the Spanish regions of Castile and León and Asturias to the east, the Atlantic Ocean to the west, and the Bay of Biscay to the north.
Martin Luther	Martin Luther was a German priest and professor of theology who initiated the Protestant Reformation. He strongly disputed the claim that freedom from God's punishment of sin could be purchased with money. He confronted indulgence salesman Johann Tetzel with his Ninety-Five Theses in 1517. His refusal to retract all of his writings at the demand of Pope Leo X in 1520 and the Holy Roman Emperor Charles V at the Diet of Worms in 1521 resulted in his excommunication by the pope and condemnation as an outlaw by the emperor.
Russians	The Russian people are an ethnic group of the East Slavic peoples, primarily living in Russia and neighboring countries. The English term Russians is used to refer to the citizens of Russia, regardless of their ethnicity; the demonym Russian is translated into Russian as rossiyanin, while the ethnic Russians are referred to as russkiye (sg. русский, russkiy).
Volga	Volga is an automobile brand that originated in the Soviet Union to replace the venerated GAZ-M20 Pobeda in 1956. Modern in design, it became a symbol of higher status in the Soviet nomenklatura. Volga cars were also traditionally used as taxi cabs, road police interceptors, and ambulances (based on the estate versions). Four generations of Volga cars have been produced, each undergoing several updates during the production run. GAZ-M-21, GAZ-21

Chapter 8. THE EIGHTEENTH CENTURY: EUROPEAN STATES, INTERNATIONAL WARS, AND CHANGE

Chapter 8. THE EIGHTEENTH CENTURY: EUROPEAN STATES, INTERNATIONAL WARS, AND CHANGE

	The first Volga model was originally developed as a replacement for the very successful GAZ-M20 Pobeda mid-size car which was produced since 1946. However despite its design in form of chassis and body styling, the rapid evolution of the latter in the 1950s already caused Soviet designers in 1951 to put forward a project for its eventual replacement.
Calvinism	Calvinism is a theological system and an approach to the Christian life. The Reformed tradition was advanced by several theologians such as Martin Bucer, Heinrich Bullinger, Peter Martyr Vermigli, and Huldrych Zwingli, but this branch of Christianity bears the name of the French reformer John Calvin because of his prominent influence on it and because of his role in the confessional and ecclesiastical debates throughout the 16th century. Today, this term also refers to the doctrines and practices of the Reformed churches of which Calvin was an early leader.
Conciliarism	Conciliarism, was a reform movement in the 14th, 15th and 16th century Roman Catholic Church which held that final authority in spiritual matters resided with the Roman Church as a corporation of Christians, embodied by a general church council, not with the pope. The movement emerged in response to the Avignon papacy; the popes were removed from Rome and subjected to pressures from the kings of France-- and the ensuing schism that inspired the summoning of the Council of Pisa (1409), the Council of Constance (1414-1418) and the Council of Basel (1431-1449). The eventual victor in the conflict was the institution of the Papacy, confirmed by the condemnation of conciliarism at the Fifth Lateran Council, 1512-17. The final gesture however, the doctrine of Papal Infallibility, was not promulgated until the First Vatican Council of 1870.
Genoa	Genoa is a city and an important seaport in northern Italy, the capital of the Province of Genoa and of the region of Liguria. The city has a population of about 608,000 and the urban area has a population of about 900,000. Genoa's Metropolitan Area has a population of about 1,400,000. It is also called la Superba ("the Superb one") due to its glorious past. The city's rich art, music, gastronomy, architecture and history, made it 2004's EU Capital of Culture.

Chapter 8. THE EIGHTEENTH CENTURY: EUROPEAN STATES, INTERNATIONAL WARS, AND CHANGE

Chapter 8. THE EIGHTEENTH CENTURY: EUROPEAN STATES, INTERNATIONAL WARS, AND CHANGE

Humanism	Humanism is an approach in study, philosophy, or practice that focuses on human values and concerns. The term can mean several things, for example: 1. A cultural movement of the Italian Renaissance based on the study of classical works. 2. An approach to education that uses literary means or a focus on the humanities to inform students. 3. A variety of perspectives in philosophy and social science which affirm some notion of 'human nature' (by contrast with anti-humanism). 4. A secular ideology which espouses reason, ethics, and justice, whilst specifically rejecting supernatural and religious dogma as a basis of morality and decision-making. The last interpretation may be attributed to Secular Humanism as a specific humanistic life stance. Modern meanings of the word have therefore come to be associated with a rejection of appeals to the supernatural or to some higher authority.
Italy	The Italy Pavilion is a part of the World Showcase within Epcot at the Walt Disney World Resort. Layout The Italian Pavilion features a plaza surrounded by a collection of buildings evocative of Venetian, Florentine, and Roman architecture. Venetian architecture is represented by a re-creation of St Mark's Campanile (bell tower) and a replica of the Doge's Palace.
Scientific revolution	The Scientific Revolution was a period when new ideas in physics, astronomy, biology, human anatomy, chemistry, and other sciences led to a rejection of doctrines that had prevailed starting in Ancient Greece and continuing through the Middle Ages, and laid the foundation of modern science. According to most accounts, the scientific revolution began in Europe towards the end of the Renaissance era and continued through the late 18th century, the latter period known as The Enlightenment. It was sparked by the publication (1543) of two works that changed the course of science: Nicolaus Copernicus's De revolutionibus orbium coelestium (On the Revolutions of the Heavenly Spheres) and Andreas Vesalius's De humani corporis fabrica (On the Fabric of the Human body).

Chapter 8. THE EIGHTEENTH CENTURY: EUROPEAN STATES, INTERNATIONAL WARS, AND CHANGE

Chapter 8. THE EIGHTEENTH CENTURY: EUROPEAN STATES, INTERNATIONAL WARS, AND CHANGE

World	WORLD Magazine is a biweekly Christian news magazine, published in the United States of America by God's World Publications, a non-profit 501(c)(3) organization based in Asheville, North Carolina. WORLD differs from most other news magazines in that its declared perspective is one of conservative evangelical Protestantism. Its mission statement is "To report, interpret, and illustrate the news in a timely, accurate, enjoyable, and arresting fashion from a perspective committed to the Bible as the inerrant Word of God." Each issue features both U.S. and international news, cultural analysis, editorials and commentary, as well as book, music and movie reviews.
Duchy	A duchy is a territory, fief, or domain ruled by a duke or duchess. Some duchies were sovereign in areas that would become unified realms only during the Modern era. In contrast, others were subordinate districts of those kingdoms that unified either partially or completely during the Medieval era (such as England, France, and Spain).
Christian	A Christian is a person who adheres to Christianity, an Abrahamic, monotheistic religion based on the life and teachings of Jesus of Nazareth as recorded in the Canonical gospels and the letters of the New Testament. Central to the Christian faith is love or Agape. Christians also believe Jesus is the Messiah prophesied in the Hebrew Bible, the Son of God, and the savior of mankind from their sins.
Christian humanism	Christian humanism is the belief that human freedom and individualism are intrinsic (natural) parts of, or are at least compatible with, Christian doctrine and practice. It is a philosophical union of Christian and humanist principles. Origins

Chapter 8. THE EIGHTEENTH CENTURY: EUROPEAN STATES, INTERNATIONAL WARS, AND CHANGE

Chapter 8. THE EIGHTEENTH CENTURY: EUROPEAN STATES, INTERNATIONAL WARS, AND CHANGE

	Christian humanism may have begun as early as the 2nd century, with the writings of St. Justin Martyr, an early theologian-apologist of the early Christian Church.
War of the Austrian Succession	The War of the Austrian Succession - also known as King George's War in North America, and incorporating the War of Jenkins' Ear with Spain and two of the three Silesian wars - involved nearly all the powers of Europe, except for the Polish-Lithuanian Commonwealth, the Portuguese Empire and the Ottoman Empire. The war began under the pretext that Maria Theresa of Austria was ineligible to succeed to the Habsburg thrones of her father, Charles VI, because Salic law precluded royal inheritance by a woman, though in reality this was a convenient excuse put forward by Prussia and France to challenge Habsburg power. Austria was supported by Great Britain and the Dutch Republic, the traditional enemies of France, as well as the Kingdom of Sardinia and Saxony.
America	America is a Wild West-themed real-time strategy. It is set during the era after the American civil war. The player can choose to play Native Americans (Sioux tribe), Mexicans, Outlaws or Settlers.
Fortress of Louisbourg	The Fortress of Louisbourg is a national historic site and the location of a partial reconstruction of an 18th century French fortress at Louisbourg, Nova Scotia, a reminder of imperial battles for what would become Canada. The original fortress, constructed mainly between 1720 and 1740, was one of the most extensive (and expensive) European fortifications constructed in North America. It was supported by two smaller garrisons on Île Royale located at present-day St. Peter's and Englishtown. Fortress Louisbourg suffered key weaknesses, since its design was directed solely toward sea-based assaults, leaving the land-facing defenses relatively weak.
Madra	Madra, Mada or Madraka is the name of an ancient region and its inhabitants, located in the north-west division of the ancient Indian sub-continent. Uttaramadra division

Chapter 8. THE EIGHTEENTH CENTURY: EUROPEAN STATES, INTERNATIONAL WARS, AND CHANGE

Chapter 8. THE EIGHTEENTH CENTURY: EUROPEAN STATES, INTERNATIONAL WARS, AND CHANGE

	Aitareya Brahmana makes first reference to the Madras as Uttaramadras i.e northern Madras and locates them in the trans-Himalayan region as neighbors to the Uttara Kurus. The Uttara Madras, like the Uttara Kurus, are stated to follow the republican constitution.
British Empire	The British Empire comprised the dominions, colonies, protectorates, mandates, and other territories ruled or administered by the United Kingdom. It originated with the overseas colonies and trading posts established by England in the late 16th and early 17th centuries. At its height it was the largest empire in history and, for over a century, was the foremost global power.
Company	Company magazine is a monthly fashion, celebrity and lifestyle magazine published in the United Kingdom. It celebrated its 30th birthday in 2008 and in that time has had only six editors: Maggie Goodman, Gil Hudson, Mandi Norwood, Fiona Macintosh, Sam Baker, and the current editor Victoria White. The magazine is seen as the UK version of Seventeen Magazine but is more high fashion.
Elizabeth	Elizabeth is a 1998 biographical film written by Michael Hirst, directed by Shekhar Kapur, and starring Cate Blanchett in the title role of Queen Elizabeth I of England, alongside Geoffrey Rush, Christopher Eccleston, Joseph Fiennes, Sir John Gielgud, Fanny Ardant and Richard Attenborough. Loosely based on the early years of Elizabeth's reign, in 2007, Blanchett reprised the role in the sequel, Elizabeth: The Golden Age, covering the later part of her reign. The film brought Australian actress Blanchett to international attention.
The Bowman and The Spearman	The Bowman and The Spearman, are two bronze equestrian sculptures standing as gatekeepers at the intersection of Congress Drive and Michigan Avenue in Grant Park, Chicago, United States. The sculptures were made in Zagreb by Croatian sculptor Ivan Meštrovic and installed at the entrance of the parkway in 1928. The pair of sculptures was funded by the Benjamin Ferguson Fund. An unusual aspect of the sculptures is that the figures in both sculptures are missing their weapons, the bow and arrow and the spear.

Chapter 8. THE EIGHTEENTH CENTURY: EUROPEAN STATES, INTERNATIONAL WARS, AND CHANGE

Chapter 8. THE EIGHTEENTH CENTURY: EUROPEAN STATES, INTERNATIONAL WARS, AND CHANGE

The Bowman and The Spearman	The Bowman and The Spearman, are two bronze equestrian sculptures standing as gatekeepers at the intersection of Congress Drive and Michigan Avenue in Grant Park, Chicago, United States. The sculptures were made in Zagreb by Croatian sculptor Ivan Meštrovic and installed at the entrance of the parkway in 1928. The pair of sculptures was funded by the Benjamin Ferguson Fund. An unusual aspect of the sculptures is that the figures in both sculptures are missing their weapons, the bow and arrow and the spear.
Atlantic slave trade	The Atlantic slave trade, refers to the trade in slaves that took place across the Atlantic ocean from the sixteenth through to the nineteenth centuries. The vast majority of slaves involved in the Atlantic trade were Africans from the central and western parts of the continent, who were sold by African slave dealers to European traders, who transported them to the colonies in North and South America. There, the slaves were made to labor on coffee, cocoa and cotton plantations, in gold and silver mines, in rice fields, the construction industry, timber, and shipping or in houses to work as servants. The shippers were, in order of scale, the Portuguese, the British, the French, the Spanish, the Dutch, and North Americans.
Abraham	Abraham is a 1994 television movie based on the life of the Biblical patriarch Abraham. Plot Abram lives in Haran, a rich city. His wife Sarah is childless, and their only heir is Eliezer of Damascus.

Chapter 8. THE EIGHTEENTH CENTURY: EUROPEAN STATES, INTERNATIONAL WARS, AND CHANGE

CLAM 101

Chapter 8. THE EIGHTEENTH CENTURY: EUROPEAN STATES, INTERNATIONAL WARS, AND CHANGE

Columbian Exchange	The Columbian Exchange was a dramatically widespread exchange of animals, plants, culture, human populations (including slaves), communicable diseases, and ideas between the Eastern and Western hemispheres (Old World and New World). It was one of the most significant events concerning ecology, agriculture, and culture in all of human history. Christopher Columbus' first voyage to the Americas in 1492 launched the era of large-scale contact between the Old and the New Worlds that resulted in this ecological revolution, hence the name "Columbian" Exchange.
Economy	In the Eastern Orthodox, the Greek Catholic Churches and in the teaching of the Church Fathers which undergirds the theology of those Churches, economy or oeconomy has several meanings. The basic meaning of the word is "handling" or "disposition" or "management" of a thing, usually assuming or implying good or prudent handling (as opposed to poor handling) of the matter at hand. In short, economia is discretionary deviation from the letter of the law in order to adhere to the spirit of the law and charity.
Faith	"Faith" was a #1 song, written and performed by George Michael, released as a single on Columbia Records, from his 1987 Faith album. According to Billboard magazine, it was the top-selling single of the year in the United States in 1988. Track listing 7": UK / Epic EMU 2 1. "Faith" - 3:14 2. "Hand To Mouth" - 4:36 12": UK / Epic EMU T2 1. "Faith" - 3:14 2. "Faith" (Instrumental) - 3:08 3. "Hand to Mouth" - 4:36

Chapter 8. THE EIGHTEENTH CENTURY: EUROPEAN STATES, INTERNATIONAL WARS, AND CHANGE

Chapter 8. THE EIGHTEENTH CENTURY: EUROPEAN STATES, INTERNATIONAL WARS, AND CHANGE

U.S. CD single

1. "Faith" - 3:16
2. "Faith" (dance remix radio edit) - 4:54
3. "Faith" (album version) - 3:16
4. "Hand to Mouth" - 5:49

Mixes

1. Album version - 3:16
2. 7" version - 3:14
3. Instrumental - 3:08
4. Dance remix radio edit - 5:22

History

Having disbanded Wham! the previous year, there was a keen expectation for Michael's solo career and "Faith" would go on to become one of his most popular and enduring songs, as well as being the most simplistic in its production.

Children	"Children" is a single by electronica composer Robert Miles from his album Dreamland. "Children" is Miles' most successful single, being certified Gold and Platinum in several countries and it reaching #1 in more than 12 countries. Miles created several remixes himself with an additional remix by Tilt.
Jean-Jacques Rousseau	Jean-Jacques Rousseau was a major Genevan philosopher, writer, and composer of 18th-century Romanticism. His political philosophy heavily influenced the French Revolution, as well as the American Revolution and the overall development of modern political, sociological and educational thought. His novel, Émile: or, On Education is a seminal treatise on the education of the whole person for citizenship.

Chapter 8. THE EIGHTEENTH CENTURY: EUROPEAN STATES, INTERNATIONAL WARS, AND CHANGE

Chapter 8. THE EIGHTEENTH CENTURY: EUROPEAN STATES, INTERNATIONAL WARS, AND CHANGE

Arrangement	The American Federation of Musicians defines arranging as "the art of preparing and adapting an already written composition for presentation in other than its original form. An arrangement may include reharmonization, paraphrasing, and/or development of a composition, so that it fully represents the melodic, harmonic, and rhythmic structure" (Corozine 2002, p. 3). Orchestration differs in that it is only adapting music for an orchestra or musical ensemble while arranging "involves adding compositional techniques, such as new thematic material for introductions, transitions, or modulations, and endings...Arranging is the art of giving an existing melody musical variety" (ibid).
Bacon	Bacon is a cured meat prepared from a pig. It is first cured using large quantities of salt, either in a brine or in a dry packing; the result is fresh bacon. Fresh bacon may then be further dried for weeks or months in cold air, boiled, or smoked.
Primogeniture	Primogeniture is the right, by law or custom, of the firstborn to inherit the entire estate, to the exclusion of younger siblings (compare to ultimogeniture). Historically, the term implied male primogeniture, to the exclusion of females. According to the Norman tradition, the first-born son inherited the entirety of a parent's wealth, estate, title or office and then would be responsible for any further passing of the inheritance to his siblings.
The Fellowship	The Fellowship, is a U.S.-based religious and political organization founded in 1935 by Abraham Vereide. The stated purpose of the Fellowship is to provide a fellowship forum for decision makers to share in Bible studies, prayer meetings, worship experiences and to experience spiritual affirmation and support. The organization has been described as one of the most politically well-connected ministries in the United States.
Enclosure	Enclosure is the process which ends traditional rights such as mowing meadows for hay, or grazing livestock on common land. Once enclosed, these uses of the land become restricted to the owner, and it ceases to be common land. In England and Wales the term is also used for the process that ended the ancient system of arable farming in open fields.

Chapter 8. THE EIGHTEENTH CENTURY: EUROPEAN STATES, INTERNATIONAL WARS, AND CHANGE

Chapter 8. THE EIGHTEENTH CENTURY: EUROPEAN STATES, INTERNATIONAL WARS, AND CHANGE

Huguenot	The Huguenots were members of the Protestant Reformed Church of France from the sixteenth to the seventeenth centuries. Since the seventeenth century, Huguenots have been commonly designated "French Protestants," the title being suggested by their German co-religionists or "Calvinists." Protestants in France were inspired by the writings of John Calvin in the 1530s and the name Huguenots was already in use by the 1560s. By the end of the 17th century, roughly 200,000 Huguenots had been driven from France during a series of religious persecutions.
Putting-out system	The putting-out system was a means of subcontracting work. It was also known as the workshop system. In putting-out, work was contracted by a central agent to subcontractors who completed the work in their own facilities, usually their own homes. It was used in the English textile industry, in small farms, and lock making trades as late as the 19th century.
London	London is the capital of England and the United Kingdom, the largest metropolitan area in the United Kingdom and the largest urban zone in the European Union by most measures. London has been a major settlement for two millennia, its history going back to its founding by the Romans, who called it Londinium. London's ancient core, the City of London, largely retains its square-mile mediaeval boundaries.
Plantation economy	A plantation economy is an economy which is based on agricultural mass production, usually of a few staple products grown on large farms called plantations. Plantation economies rely on the export of cash crops as a source of income. Prominent plantation crops included cotton, rubber, sugar cane, tobacco, figs, rice, kapok, sisal and indigo.
Water frame	The water frame is the name given to the spinning frame, when water power is used to drive it. Both are credited to Richard Arkwright who patented the technology in 1768. It was based on an invention by Thomas Highs and the patent was later overturned. John Kay, a clock maker and mechanic who helped Highs build the spinning frame, sold the design to Arkwright (for what might be considered a derisory sum).
Montesquieu	Charles-Louis de Secondat, baron de La Brède et de Montesquieu, generally referred to as simply Montesquieu, was a French social commentator and political thinker who lived during the Enlightenment. He is famous for his articulation of the theory of separation of powers, taken for granted in modern discussions of government and implemented in many constitutions throughout the world. He was largely responsible for the popularization of the terms feudalism and Byzantine Empire.

Chapter 8. THE EIGHTEENTH CENTURY: EUROPEAN STATES, INTERNATIONAL WARS, AND CHANGE

Chapter 8. THE EIGHTEENTH CENTURY: EUROPEAN STATES, INTERNATIONAL WARS, AND CHANGE

Tithe	A tithe is a one-tenth part of something, paid as a (usually) voluntary contribution or as a levy or tax-like payment (technically not a tax as it is not paid to a level of government), usually to support a religious organization. Today, tithes (or tithing) are normally voluntary and paid in cash, cheques, or stocks, whereas historically tithes were required to be paid in kind, such as agricultural products (that grown of the land, or fruit of the tree). Several European countries operate a formal process linked to the tax system allowing some churches to assess tithes.
Conciliarism	Conciliarism, was a reform movement in the 14th, 15th and 16th century Roman Catholic Church which held that final authority in spiritual matters resided with the Roman Church as a corporation of Christians, embodied by a general church council, not with the pope. The movement emerged in response to the Avignon papacy; the popes were removed from Rome and subjected to pressures from the kings of France-- and the ensuing schism that inspired the summoning of the Council of Pisa (1409), the Council of Constance (1414-1418) and the Council of Basel (1431-1449). The eventual victor in the conflict was the institution of the Papacy, confirmed by the condemnation of conciliarism at the Fifth Lateran Council, 1512-17. The final gesture however, the doctrine of Papal Infallibility, was not promulgated until the First Vatican Council of 1870.
Andrea Palladio	Andrea Palladio was an Italian Renaissance architect active in the Republic of Venice. Palladio, influenced by Roman and Greek architecture, primarily by Vitruvius, is widely considered the most influential individual in the history of Western architecture. All of his buildings are located in northern Italy, but his teachings, summarized in the architectural treatise I Quattro Libri dell'Architettura (The Four Books of Architecture), gained him wide recognition.
Herculaneum	Herculaneum was an ancient Roman town destroyed by volcanic pyroclastic flows AD 79, located in the territory of the current commune of Ercolano, in the Italian region of Campania in the shadow of Mt. Vesuvius. It is most famous for having been lost, along with Pompeii, Stabiae and Oplontis, in the eruption of Mount Vesuvius beginning on August 24, AD 79, which buried them in superheated pyroclastic material that has solidified into volcanic tuff.
Charity	In Christian theology charity, means an unlimited loving-kindness toward all others.

Chapter 8. THE EIGHTEENTH CENTURY: EUROPEAN STATES, INTERNATIONAL WARS, AND CHANGE

The term should not be confused with the more restricted modern use of the word charity to mean benevolent giving.

Caritas: altruistic love

In Christian theology charity, or love (agape), is the greatest of the three theological virtues:

> Deus caritas est - "God is love".

Love, in this sense of an unlimited loving-kindness towards all others, is held to be the ultimate perfection of the human spirit, because it is said to both glorify and reflect the nature of God.

Chapter 8. THE EIGHTEENTH CENTURY: EUROPEAN STATES, INTERNATIONAL WARS, AND CHANGE

Chapter 9. A REVOLUTION IN POLITICS: THE ERA OF THE FRENCH REVOLUTION AND NAPOLEON

Bastille	The Bastille was a fortress-prison in Paris, known formally as Bastille Saint-Antoine--Number 232, Rue Saint-Antoine--best known today because of the storming of the Bastille on 14 July 1789, which along with the Tennis Court Oath is considered the beginning of the French Revolution. The event was commemorated one year later by the Fête de la Fédération. The French national holiday, celebrated annually on 14 July is officially the Fête Nationale, and officially commemorates the Fête de la Fédération, but it is commonly known in English as Bastille Day.
American Revolution	The American Revolution was the political upheaval during the last half of the 18th century in which thirteen colonies in North America joined together to break free from the British Empire, combining to become the United States of America. They first rejected the authority of the Parliament of Great Britain to govern them from overseas without representation, and then expelled all royal officials. By 1774 each colony had established a Provincial Congress, or an equivalent governmental institution, to form individual self-governing states. The British responded by sending combat troops to re-impose direct rule.
European colonization of the Americas	The start of the European colonization of the Americas is typically dated to 1492, although there was at least one earlier colonization effort. The first known Europeans to reach the Americas were the Vikings (Norse) during the 11th century, who established several colonies in Greenland and one short-lived settlement at L'Anse aux Meadows (51°N) in the area the Norse called Vinland, present day Newfoundland and to the south. Settlements in Greenland survived for several centuries, during which time the Greenland Norse and the Inuit people experienced mostly hostile contact. By the end of the 15th century, the Norse Greenland settlements had collapsed.
European Go Championship	The European Go Championship is the annual and main event of many organised by the European Go Federation for players of the board game Go. It consists of a 2-week open competition, one round per day, making a total of 10 rounds with a champion ultimately emerging - the player with the most (or best) wins. The congress has taken place in a different European city each year, since the first contest in 1983. During these two weeks, the best go players in Europe fight for the title of European Champion.
Continental Army	The American Continental Army was an army formed after the outbreak of the American Revolutionary War by the colonies that became the United States of America. Established by a resolution of the Continental Congress on June 14, 1775, it was created to coordinate the military efforts of the Thirteen Colonies in their revolt against the rule of Great Britain. The Continental Army was supplemented by local militias and other troops that remained under control of the individual states. General George Washington was the Commander-in-Chief of the army throughout the war.

Chapter 9. A REVOLUTION IN POLITICS: THE ERA OF THE FRENCH REVOLUTION AND NAPOLEON

Chapter 9. A REVOLUTION IN POLITICS: THE ERA OF THE FRENCH REVOLUTION AND NAPOLEON

Charles Cornwallis, 1st Marquess Cornwallis	Charles Cornwallis, 1st Marquess Cornwallis KG (31 December 1738 - 5 October 1805), styled Viscount Brome between 1753 and 1762 and known as The Earl Cornwallis between 1762 and 1792, was a British Army officer and colonial administrator. In the United States and the United Kingdom he is best remembered as one of the leading British generals in the American War of Independence. His surrender in 1781 to a combined American and French force at the Siege of Yorktown ended significant hostilities in North America. He also served as a civil and military governor in Ireland and India; in both places he brought about significant changes, including the Act of Union in Ireland and the Cornwallis Code, including the Permanent Settlement, in India.
Loyalist	In general, a loyalist is someone who maintains loyalty to an established government, political party, or sovereign, especially during war or revolutionary change such as the Republicans in the Spanish Civil War in the late 1930s. In modern English usage, the most common application is to loyalty to the British Crown, which is the focus of this article. Historical loyalism North America In North America, the term 'Loyalist' characterizes American colonists who rejected the American Revolution.
Second Continental Congress	The Second Continental Congress was a convention of delegates from the Thirteen Colonies that met beginning on May 10, 1775, in Philadelphia, Pennsylvania, soon after warfare in the American Revolutionary War had begun. It succeeded the First Continental Congress, which met briefly during 1774, also in Philadelphia. The second Congress managed the colonial war effort, and moved incrementally towards independence, adopting the United States Declaration of Independence on July 4, 1776. By raising armies, directing strategy, appointing diplomats, and making formal treaties, the Congress acted as the de facto national government of what became the United States.
England	"England" is a song written by Justin Hawkins from The Darkness(music) ' Chas Bayfield (lyrics) and released by him under the name British Whale and used as the unofficial World Cup single for the England National Team in 2006

Chapter 9. A REVOLUTION IN POLITICS: THE ERA OF THE FRENCH REVOLUTION AND NAPOLEON

Chapter 9. A REVOLUTION IN POLITICS: THE ERA OF THE FRENCH REVOLUTION AND NAPOLEON

Netherlands	More than one name is used to refer to the Netherlands, both in English and in other languages. Some of these names refer to different, but overlapping geographical, linguistic and political areas of the country. This is a common source of confusion for outsiders.
Rococo	Rococo also referred to as "Late Baroque" is an 18th century style which developed as Baroque artists gave up their symmetry and became increasingly ornate, florid, and playful. Rococo rooms were designed as total works of art with elegant and ornate furniture, small sculptures, ornamental mirrors, and tapestry complementing architecture, reliefs, and wall paintings. It was largely supplanted by the Neoclassic style.
State	The term state is used in various senses by Catholic theologians and spiritual writers.
	It may be taken to signify a profession or calling in life, as where St. Paul says, in I Corinthians 7:20: "Let every man abide in the same calling in which he was called". States are classified in the Catholic Church as the clerical state, the religious state, and the secular state; and among religious states, again, we have those of the contemplative, the active, and the mixed orders.
Adam	Adam is a prominent figure in Abrahamic religions. He is the first man created by God in Judaism, Christianity, and Islam. He appears originally in the Hebrew Bible in the Book of Genesis.
John Locke	John Locke, widely known as the Father of Liberalism, was an English philosopher and physician regarded as one of the most influential of Enlightenment thinkers. Considered one of the first of the British empiricists, following the tradition of Francis Bacon, he is equally important to social contract theory. His work had a great impact upon the development of epistemology and political philosophy.
Black Death	The Black Death was one of the most devastating pandemics in human history, peaking in Europe between 1348 and 1350. It is widely thought to have been an outbreak of plague caused by the bacterium Yersinia pestis, an argument supported by recent forensic research, although this view has been challenged by a number of scholars. Thought to have started in China, it travelled along the Silk Road and had reached the Crimea by 1346. From there, probably carried by Oriental rat fleas residing on the black rats that were regular passengers on merchant ships, it spread throughout the Mediterranean and Europe.

Chapter 9. A REVOLUTION IN POLITICS: THE ERA OF THE FRENCH REVOLUTION AND NAPOLEON

Chapter 9. A REVOLUTION IN POLITICS: THE ERA OF THE FRENCH REVOLUTION AND NAPOLEON

	The Black Death is estimated to have killed 30% - 60% of Europe's population, reducing the world's population from an estimated 450 million to between 350 and 375 million in 1400. This has been seen as having created a series of religious, social and economic upheavals, which had profound effects on the course of European history.
Citizenship	Citizenship is the state of being a citizen of a particular social, political, national, or human resource community. Citizenship status, under social contract theory, carries with it both rights and responsibilities. "Active citizenship" is the philosophy that citizens should work towards the betterment of their community through economic participation, public, volunteer work, and other such efforts to improve life for all citizens.
Declaration of the Rights of Man and of the Citizen	The Declaration of the Rights of Man and of the Citizen is a fundamental document of the French Revolution, defining the individual and collective rights of all the estates of the realm as universal. Influenced by the doctrine of natural right, the rights of man are universal: valid at all times and in every place, pertaining to human nature itself. Although it establishes fundamental rights for French citizens and "all the members of the social Body", it addresses neither the status of women nor slavery; despite that, it is a precursor document to international human rights instruments.
Martin Luther	Martin Luther was a German priest and professor of theology who initiated the Protestant Reformation. He strongly disputed the claim that freedom from God's punishment of sin could be purchased with money. He confronted indulgence salesman Johann Tetzel with his Ninety-Five Theses in 1517. His refusal to retract all of his writings at the demand of Pope Leo X in 1520 and the Holy Roman Emperor Charles V at the Diet of Worms in 1521 resulted in his excommunication by the pope and condemnation as an outlaw by the emperor.
Prussia	Prussia was a German kingdom and historic state originating out of the Duchy of Prussia and the Margraviate of Brandenburg. For centuries, the House of Hohenzollern ruled Prussia, successfully expanding its size by way of an unusually well-organized and effective army. Prussia shaped the history of Germany, with its capital in Berlin after 1451. After 1871, Prussia was increasingly merged into Germany, losing its distinctive identity.
Testaments	Testaments is a collective term, used exclusively within Christianity, to describe both the Old Testament and the New Testament, of The Bible. The Church of Jesus Christ of Latter-day Saints uses this term to include the Book of Mormon as another volume of scripture which specifically testifies of Jesus Christ's divinity.

Chapter 9. A REVOLUTION IN POLITICS: THE ERA OF THE FRENCH REVOLUTION AND NAPOLEON

Chapter 9. A REVOLUTION IN POLITICS: THE ERA OF THE FRENCH REVOLUTION AND NAPOLEON

	Judaism uses only the term Hebrew Bible (for part of the "Old Testament" alone) because it does not accept the "New Testament" as scripture.
Estates of the realm	The Estates of the realm were the broad social orders of the hierarchically conceived society, recognized in the Middle Ages and Early Modern period in Christian Europe; they are sometimes distinguished as the three estates: the clergy, the nobility, and commoners. "Medieval political speculation is imbued to the marrow with the idea of a structure of society based upon distinct orders," Johan Huizinga observes. The virtually synonymous terms estate and order designated a great variety of social realities, not at all limited to a class, Huizinga concluded, but applied to every social function, every trade, every recognizable grouping.
Christian	A Christian is a person who adheres to Christianity, an Abrahamic, monotheistic religion based on the life and teachings of Jesus of Nazareth as recorded in the Canonical gospels and the letters of the New Testament.
	Central to the Christian faith is love or Agape. Christians also believe Jesus is the Messiah prophesied in the Hebrew Bible, the Son of God, and the savior of mankind from their sins.
Christian humanism	Christian humanism is the belief that human freedom and individualism are intrinsic (natural) parts of, or are at least compatible with, Christian doctrine and practice. It is a philosophical union of Christian and humanist principles.
	Origins
	Christian humanism may have begun as early as the 2nd century, with the writings of St. Justin Martyr, an early theologian-apologist of the early Christian Church.

Chapter 9. A REVOLUTION IN POLITICS: THE ERA OF THE FRENCH REVOLUTION AND NAPOLEON

Chapter 9. A REVOLUTION IN POLITICS: THE ERA OF THE FRENCH REVOLUTION AND NAPOLEON

Classicism	Classicism, in the arts, refers generally to a high regard for classical antiquity, as setting standards for taste which the classicists seek to emulate. The art of classicism typically seeks to be formal and restrained: of the Discobolus Sir Kenneth Clark observed, "if we object to his restraint and compression we are simply objecting to the classicism of classic art. A violent emphasis or a sudden acceleration of rhythmic movement would have destroyed those qualities of balance and completeness through which it retained until the present century its position of authority in the restricted repertoire of visual images." Classicism, as Clark noted, implies a canon of widely accepted ideal forms, whether in the Western canon that he was examining in The Nude (1956), or the Chinese classics.
Middle class	The middle class is any class of people in the middle of a societal hierarchy. In Weberian socio-economic terms, the middle class is the broad group of people in contemporary society who fall socio-economically between the working class and upper class. The common measures of what constitutes middle class vary significantly between cultures.
Economy	In the Eastern Orthodox, the Greek Catholic Churches and in the teaching of the Church Fathers which undergirds the theology of those Churches, economy or oeconomy has several meanings. The basic meaning of the word is "handling" or "disposition" or "management" of a thing, usually assuming or implying good or prudent handling (as opposed to poor handling) of the matter at hand. In short, economia is discretionary deviation from the letter of the law in order to adhere to the spirit of the law and charity.
Humanism	Humanism is an approach in study, philosophy, or practice that focuses on human values and concerns. The term can mean several things, for example: 1. A cultural movement of the Italian Renaissance based on the study of classical works. 2. An approach to education that uses literary means or a focus on the humanities to inform students. 3. A variety of perspectives in philosophy and social science which affirm some notion of 'human nature' (by contrast with anti-humanism). 4. A secular ideology which espouses reason, ethics, and justice, whilst specifically rejecting supernatural and religious dogma as a basis of morality and decision-making.

Chapter 9. A REVOLUTION IN POLITICS: THE ERA OF THE FRENCH REVOLUTION AND NAPOLEON

Chapter 9. A REVOLUTION IN POLITICS: THE ERA OF THE FRENCH REVOLUTION AND NAPOLEON

	The last interpretation may be attributed to Secular Humanism as a specific humanistic life stance. Modern meanings of the word have therefore come to be associated with a rejection of appeals to the supernatural or to some higher authority.
Common	The Common is a part of the Christian liturgy that consists of texts common to an entire category of saints, such as Apostles or Martyrs. The term is used in contrast to the ordinary, which is that part of the liturgy that is reasonably constant, or at least selected without regard to date, and to the proper, which is the part of the liturgy that varies according to the date, either representing an observance within the Liturgical Year, or of a particular saint or significant event.
	Commons contain collects, psalms, readings from Scripture, prefaces, and other portions of services that are common to a category of saints.
Assignat	Assignat was the type of a monetary instrument used during the time of the French Revolution, and the French Revolutionary Wars.
	France
	Assignats were paper money issued by the National Assembly in France during the French Revolution. The assignats were issued after the confiscation of church properties in 1790 because the government was bankrupt.
Citizenship	Citizenship is the state of being a citizen of a particular social, political, national, or human resource community. Citizenship status, under social contract theory, carries with it both rights and responsibilities. "Active citizenship" is the philosophy that citizens should work towards the betterment of their community through economic participation, public, volunteer work, and other such efforts to improve life for all citizens.

Chapter 9. A REVOLUTION IN POLITICS: THE ERA OF THE FRENCH REVOLUTION AND NAPOLEON

Chapter 9. A REVOLUTION IN POLITICS: THE ERA OF THE FRENCH REVOLUTION AND NAPOLEON

Austria	Austria officially the Republic of Austria, is a landlocked country of roughly 8.3 million people in Central Europe. It is bordered by the Czech Republic and Germany to the north, Slovakia and Hungary to the east, Slovenia and Italy to the south, and Switzerland and Liechtenstein to the west. The territory of Austria covers 83,855 square kilometres (32,377 sq mi) and has a temperate and alpine climate.
Declaration of Pillnitz	The Declaration of Pillnitz on 27 August 1791, was a statement issued at the Castle of Pillnitz in Saxony (south of Dresden) by the Habsburg Holy Roman Emperor Leopold II and Frederick William II of Prussia.
	Calling on European powers to intervene if Louis XVI of France was threatened, this declaration was intended to serve as a warning to the French revolutionaries not to infringe further on the rights of Louis XVI and to allow his restoration to power. The statement helped begin the French Revolutionary Wars.
Paris Commune	The Paris Commune was a government that briefly ruled Paris from March 18 (more formally, from March 28) to May 28, 1871. It existed before the split between anarchists and Marxists had taken place, and it is hailed by both groups as the first assumption of power by the working class during the Industrial Revolution. Debates over the policies and outcome of the Commune contributed to the break between those two political groups.
	In a formal sense, the Paris Commune simply acted as the local authority, the city council, which exercised power in Paris for two months in the spring of 1871. However, the conditions in which it formed, its controversial decrees, and its violent end make its tenure one of the more important political episodes of the time.
Republic	Republic is a Hungarian rock band formed in Budapest in 1989. Their style is a unique mix of Western rock music and traditional Hungarian folk music. The band is popular in its native country and among Hungarian speaking minorities elsewhere.
	Members

Chapter 9. A REVOLUTION IN POLITICS: THE ERA OF THE FRENCH REVOLUTION AND NAPOLEON

Chapter 9. A REVOLUTION IN POLITICS: THE ERA OF THE FRENCH REVOLUTION AND NAPOLEON

	The two founding members are László Bódi and Laszlo Attila Nagy.
18th century	The 18th century lasted from 1701 to 1800 in the Gregorian calendar.
	However, Western historians have occasionally defined the 18th century otherwise for the purposes of their work. For example, the "short" 18th century may be defined as 1715-1789, denoting the period of time between the death of Louis XIV of France and the start of the French Revolution with an emphasis on directly interconnected events.
Marie Antoinette	Marie Antoinette was an Archduchess of Austria and the Queen of France and of Navarre. She was the fifteenth and penultimate child of Empress Maria Theresa of Austria and Emperor Francis I.
	In April 1770, on the day of her marriage to Louis-Auguste, Dauphin of France, she subsequently became Dauphine of France. Marie Antoinette assumed the title of Queen of France and of Navarre when her husband, Louis XVI of France, ascended the throne upon the death of Louis XV in May 1774. At the height of the French Revolution, Louis XVI was deposed and the monarchy abolished on 10 August 1792; the royal family was subsequently imprisoned at the Temple Prison. Nine months after her husband's execution, Marie Antoinette was herself tried, convicted of treason, and executed by guillotine on 16 October 1793.
Marseille	Marseille, known in antiquity as Massalia, is the second largest city in France, after Paris, with a population of 852,395 within its administrative limits on a land area of 240.62 km^2 (93 sq mi). The urban area of Marseille extends beyond the city limits with a population of over 1,420,000 on an area of 1,204 km^2 (465 sq mi). 1,530,000 or 1,601,095 people live in the Marseille metropolitan area, ranking it 2nd among French metro areas.

Chapter 9. A REVOLUTION IN POLITICS: THE ERA OF THE FRENCH REVOLUTION AND NAPOLEON

Chapter 9. A REVOLUTION IN POLITICS: THE ERA OF THE FRENCH REVOLUTION AND NAPOLEON

Children	"Children" is a single by electronica composer Robert Miles from his album Dreamland. "Children" is Miles' most successful single, being certified Gold and Platinum in several countries and it reaching #1 in more than 12 countries. Miles created several remixes himself with an additional remix by Tilt.
Republic of Virtue	The "Republic of Virtue" was a period in French history (1791-1794) where Maximilien Robespierre remained in power. Many proponents of the Republic of Virtue developed their notion of civic virtue from the writings of Jean-Jacques Rousseau. The "Republic of Virtue" was part of the de-Christianization of the French Revolution.
Cathedral	A cathedral (French cathédrale from Lat. cathedra, "seat" from the Greek kathedra (καθ?δρα), seat, bench, from kata "down" + hedra seat, base, chair) is a Christian church that contains the seat of a bishop. It is a religious building for worship, specifically of a denomination with an episcopal hierarchy, such as the Roman Catholic, Anglican, Orthodox, and some Lutheran and Methodist churches, which serves as a bishop's seat, and thus as the central church of a diocese, conference, or episcopate.
Temple	In the Latter Day Saint movement, a temple is a building dedicated to be a house of God and is reserved for special forms of worship. A temple differs from a church meetinghouse, which is used for weekly worship services. Temples have been a significant part of the Latter Day Saint movement since early in its inception.
America	America is a Wild West-themed real-time strategy. It is set during the era after the American civil war. The player can choose to play Native Americans (Sioux tribe), Mexicans, Outlaws or Settlers.
Frimaire	Frimaire was the third month in the French Republican Calendar. he French word frimas, which means frost.
	Frimaire was the third month of the autumn quarter (mois d'automne).
Middle Ages	The Middle Ages is a historical period following the Iron Age, beginning in the 5th century and lasting to the 15th century, and preceded the Early Modern Era. In Europe, the period saw the large-scale European Migration and fall of the Western Roman Empire. In South Asia, the middle kingdoms of India were the classical period of the region.

Chapter 9. A REVOLUTION IN POLITICS: THE ERA OF THE FRENCH REVOLUTION AND NAPOLEON

Chapter 9. A REVOLUTION IN POLITICS: THE ERA OF THE FRENCH REVOLUTION AND NAPOLEON

Elder	An Elder in the Methodist Church -- sometimes called a Presbyter or Minister -- is someone who has been ordained by a Bishop to the ministry of Word, Sacrament, Order, and Service. Their responsibilities are to preach and teach, preside at the celebration of the sacraments, administer the Church through pastoral guidance, and lead the congregations under their care in service ministry to the world. The Book of Discipline of the United Methodist Church states that The office of Elder, then, is what most people tend to think of as the pastoral, priestly, clergy office within the church.
Thermidorian Reaction	The Thermidorian Reaction was a revolt in the French Revolution against the excesses of the Reign of Terror. It was triggered by a vote of the Committee of Public Safety to execute Maximilien Robespierre, Antoine Louis Léon de Richebourg de Saint-Just and several other leading members of the Terror. This ended the most radical phase of the French Revolution.
Egypt	The Roman province of Egypt was established in 30 BC after Octavian (the future emperor Augustus) defeated his rival Mark Antony, deposed his lover Queen Cleopatra VII and annexed the Ptolemaic kingdom of Egypt to the Roman Empire. The province encompassed most of modern-day Egypt except for the Sinai Peninsula (which would later be conquered by Trajan). Aegyptus was bordered by the provinces of Creta et Cyrenaica to the West and Judaea to the East.
Italy	The Italy Pavilion is a part of the World Showcase within Epcot at the Walt Disney World Resort. Layout The Italian Pavilion features a plaza surrounded by a collection of buildings evocative of Venetian, Florentine, and Roman architecture. Venetian architecture is represented by a re-creation of St Mark's Campanile (bell tower) and a replica of the Doge's Palace.

Chapter 9. A REVOLUTION IN POLITICS: THE ERA OF THE FRENCH REVOLUTION AND NAPOLEON

Chapter 9. A REVOLUTION IN POLITICS: THE ERA OF THE FRENCH REVOLUTION AND NAPOLEON

Concordat	A concordat is an agreement between the Holy This often includes both recognition and privileges for the Catholic Church in a particular country. Privileges might include exemptions from certain legal matters and processes, and issues such as taxation as well as the right of a state to influence the selection of bishops within its territory.
	Although for a time after the Second Vatican Council, which ended in 1965, the term 'concordat' was dropped, it reappeared with the Polish Concordat of 1993 and the Portuguese Concordat of 2004. A different model of relations between the Vatican and various states is still evolving in the wake of the Second Vatican Council's Declaration on Religious Liberty, Dignitatis Humanae.
Pope Pius VII	Pope Pius VII, OSB (14 August 1742 - 20 August 1823), born Count Barnaba Niccolò Maria Luigi Chiaramonti, was Pope from 14 March 1800 to 20 August 1823.
	Following the death of Pius VI, virtually France's prisoner, at Valence in August 1799, the conclave met on 30 November 1799 in the Benedictine monastery of San Giorgio, Venice. There were three main candidates, two of whom proved to be unacceptable to the Habsburgs, whose candidate, Alessandro Mattei, could not secure sufficient votes. After several months of stalemate, Chiaramonti was elected as a compromise candidate, certainly not the choice of the die-hard opponents of the French Revolution. He was crowned Pope Pius VII at Venice on 21 March 1800 in a rather unusual ceremony, wearing a papier-mâché papal tiara, since the French had seized the original along with Pius VI, after which a barely sea-worthy Austrian ship, the "Bellona", with no cooking facilities, took 12 days to carry him to Pesaro, from where he proceeded to Rome.
Consul	Consul was the highest elected office of the Roman Republic and an appointive office under the Empire. The title was also used in other city states and also revived in modern states, notably in the First French Republic. The relating adjective is consular, from the Latin consularis (which has been used, substantiated, as a title in its own right).
Prefect	Prefect is a magisterial title of varying definition.

Chapter 9. A REVOLUTION IN POLITICS: THE ERA OF THE FRENCH REVOLUTION AND NAPOLEON

Chapter 9. A REVOLUTION IN POLITICS: THE ERA OF THE FRENCH REVOLUTION AND NAPOLEON

	A prefect's office, department, or area of control is called a prefecture, but in various post-Roman cases there is a prefect without a prefecture or vice versa. The words "prefect" and "prefecture" are also used, more or less conventionally, to render analogous words in other languages, especially Romance languages.
Confederation of the Rhine	The Confederation of the Rhine or Rhine Confederation was a confederation of client states of the First French Empire. It was formed initially from 16 German states by Napoleon after he defeated Austria's Francis II and Russia's Alexander I in the Battle of Austerlitz. The Treaty of Pressburg, in effect, led to the creation of the Confederation of the Rhine.
Continental System	The Continental System or Continental Blockade was the foreign policy of Napoleon I of France in his struggle against the United Kingdom of Great Britain and Ireland during the Napoleonic Wars. It was a large-scale embargo against British trade, inaugurated on November 21, 1806. This embargo ended in April 11, 1814 after Napoleon's first abdication. The United Kingdom was an important force in encouraging and financing alliances against Napoleonic France.
Duchy	A duchy is a territory, fief, or domain ruled by a duke or duchess. Some duchies were sovereign in areas that would become unified realms only during the Modern era. In contrast, others were subordinate districts of those kingdoms that unified either partially or completely during the Medieval era (such as England, France, and Spain).
Jerome	St. Jerome (formerly Saint Hierom) was an Illyrian Catholic priest and apologist. He was the son of Eusebius, of the city of Stridon, which was on the border of Dalmatia and Pannonia. He is best known for his translation of the Bible into Latin (the Vulgate), and his list of writings is extensive.

Chapter 9. A REVOLUTION IN POLITICS: THE ERA OF THE FRENCH REVOLUTION AND NAPOLEON

Chapter 9. A REVOLUTION IN POLITICS: THE ERA OF THE FRENCH REVOLUTION AND NAPOLEON

Johann Gottlieb Fichte	Johann Gottlieb Fichte was a German philosopher. He was one of the founding figures of the philosophical movement known as German idealism, a movement that developed from the theoretical and ethical writings of Immanuel Kant. Fichte is often perceived as a figure whose philosophy forms a bridge between the ideas of Kant and the German Idealist Georg Wilhelm Friedrich Hegel.
Johann Gottlieb Fichte	Johann Gottlieb Fichte was a German philosopher. He was one of the founding figures of the philosophical movement known as German idealism, a movement that developed from the theoretical and ethical writings of Immanuel Kant. Fichte is often perceived as a figure whose philosophy forms a bridge between the ideas of Kant and the German Idealist Georg Wilhelm Friedrich Hegel.
German	German is a South Slavic mythological being, recorded in the folklore of eastern Serbia and northern Bulgaria. He is a male spirit associated with bringing rain and hail. His influence on these precipitations can be positive, resulting with the amount of rain beneficial for agriculture, or negative, with a drought, downpours, or hail.
Johann	Johann, typically a male given name, is the Germanized form of the originally Hebrew language name "Yohanan" (meaning "God is merciful"). It is a form of the Germanic given name "Johannes", which comes from Johan. The English language form is John.
Johann Gottlieb	Johann Gottlieb was an Austrian chemist who first synthesized Propionic acid. Gottlieb was born in Brno, Bohemia in Austria (now Czech Republic). Since 1846 he was a professor at the University of Graz.
Lutheranism	Lutheranism is a major branch of Western Christianity that identifies with the theology of Martin Luther, a German reformer. Luther's efforts to reform the theology and practice of the church launched the Protestant Reformation. Beginning with the 95 Theses, Luther's writings disseminated internationally, spreading the ideas of the Reformation beyond the ability of governmental and churchly authorities to control it.
Battle of Borodino	The Battle of Borodino, fought on September 7, 1812, was the largest and bloodiest single-day action of the French invasion of Russia and all Napoleonic Wars, involving more than 250,000 troops and resulting in at least 70,000 casualties. The French Grande Armée under Emperor Napoleon I attacked the Imperial Russian Army of General Mikhail Kutuzov near the village of Borodino, west of the town of Mozhaysk, and eventually captured the main positions on the battlefield, but failed to destroy the Russian army. About a third of Napoleon's soldiers were killed or wounded; Russian losses, while heavier, could be replaced, since large forces of militia were already with the Russian Army and replacement depots which were close by had already been gathering and training troops.

Chapter 9. A REVOLUTION IN POLITICS: THE ERA OF THE FRENCH REVOLUTION AND NAPOLEON

Chapter 9. A REVOLUTION IN POLITICS: THE ERA OF THE FRENCH REVOLUTION AND NAPOLEON

Helena	Saint Helena, Helena Augusta or Helena of Constantinople (ca. 246/50 - 18 August 330) was the consort of Emperor Constantius, and the mother of Emperor Constantine I. She is traditionally credited with finding the relics of the True Cross, with which she is invariably represented in Christian iconography. Family life Helena's birthplace is not known with certainty. The sixth-century historian Procopius is the earliest authority for the statement that Helena was a native of Drepanum, in the province of Bithynia in Asia Minor.
Restoration	In the Latter Day Saint movement, the Restoration was a period in its early history during which a number of events occurred that were understood to be necessary to restore the early Christian church as demonstrated in the New Testament, and to prepare the earth for the Second Coming of Jesus Christ. In particular, Latter Day Saints believe that angels appeared to Joseph Smith, Jr. and others and bestowed various Priesthood authorities to them.
Protestantism	Protestantism is one of the three major divisions (Catholicism, Orthodoxy, and Protestantism) within Christianity. It is a movement that began in northern Europe in the early 16th century as a reaction against medieval Roman Catholic doctrines and practices. The doctrines of the various Protestant denominations and non-denominations vary, but most non-denominational doctrines include justification by grace through faith and not through works, known as Sola Fide, the priesthood of all believers, and the Bible as the ultimate authority in matters of faith and order, known as Sola Scriptura, which is Latin for 'by scripture alone'.
Catholic	The word catholic comes from the Greek phrase καθ?λου (kath'holou), meaning "on the whole," "according to the whole" or "in general", and is a combination of the Greek words κατ? meaning "about" and ?λος meaning "whole". The word in English can mean either "including a wide variety of things; all-embracing" or "of the Roman Catholic faith." as "relating to the historic doctrine and practice of the Western Church."

Chapter 9. A REVOLUTION IN POLITICS: THE ERA OF THE FRENCH REVOLUTION AND NAPOLEON

Chapter 9. A REVOLUTION IN POLITICS: THE ERA OF THE FRENCH REVOLUTION AND NAPOLEON

	It was first used to describe the Christian Church in the early 2nd century to emphasize its universal scope. In the context of Christian ecclesiology, it has a rich history and several usages.
Catholic Church	The Catholic Church, is the world's largest Christian church. Headed by the Pope, it sees its mission as spreading the gospel of Christ, administering its sacraments and exercising charity.
	The Catholic Church is one of the oldest religious institutions in the world and has played a prominent role in the history of Western civilisation.
Church	A church building is a building or structure whose primary purpose is to facilitate the meeting of a church. Originally, Jewish Christians met in synagogues, such as the Cenacle, and in one another's homes, known as house churches. As Christianity grew and became more accepted by governments, notably with the Edict of Milan, rooms and, eventually, entire buildings were set aside for the explicit purpose of Christian worship, such as the Church of the Holy Sepulchre.
War of the Austrian Succession	The War of the Austrian Succession - also known as King George's War in North America, and incorporating the War of Jenkins' Ear with Spain and two of the three Silesian wars - involved nearly all the powers of Europe, except for the Polish-Lithuanian Commonwealth, the Portuguese Empire and the Ottoman Empire. The war began under the pretext that Maria Theresa of Austria was ineligible to succeed to the Habsburg thrones of her father, Charles VI, because Salic law precluded royal inheritance by a woman, though in reality this was a convenient excuse put forward by Prussia and France to challenge Habsburg power. Austria was supported by Great Britain and the Dutch Republic, the traditional enemies of France, as well as the Kingdom of Sardinia and Saxony.

Chapter 9. A REVOLUTION IN POLITICS: THE ERA OF THE FRENCH REVOLUTION AND NAPOLEON

CPSIA information can be obtained at www.ICGtesting.com
Printed in the USA
BVOW031931260912

301443BV00001B/284/P

9 781614 906056